Equity in Health Services

Equity in Health Services: Empirical Analyses in Social Policy

Edited by

Ronald Andersen
Associate Professor
Center for Health Administration Studies
University of Chicago

Joanna Kravits
Director of Information Services
Massachusetts Hospital Association

Odin W. Anderson
Professor and Director
Center for Health Administration Studies
University of Chicago

Ballinger Publishing Company ● Cambridge, Mass.
A Subsidiary of J.B. Lippincott Company

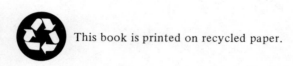
International Standard Book Number: 0–88410–104–5

Library of Congress Catalog Card Number: 75–22328

Printed in the United States of America

Library of Congress Cataloging in Publication Data

Main entry under title:

Equity in health services.

    Includes bibliographical references.
    1. Medical care—United States—Utilization. 2. Medical policy—
United States. I. Andersen, Ronald. II. Kravits, Joanna.
III. Anderson, Odin Waldemar, 1914– [DNLM: 1. Health services—
Utilization—United States. W84 AA1 E6]
RA410.7.E65   362.1'04'250973   75–22328
ISBN 0–88410–104–5

Contents

v

List of Tables

List of Figures

Foreword

This book has a number of dimensions. First, the data used were drawn from family interview surveys undertaken to study problems in the delivery of medical care which are current public issues. Second, while each survey in the series measures use, expenditures for and attitudes toward medical care and is reported separately, additional analysis in this volume compares findings from several of the surveys and relates them pertinently to current problems.

Finally, the authors are of the new generation of well educated social scientists studying health services. They use complex analytical tools acquired in the course of a long education culminating in a Ph.D. degree in their disciplines. All have been associated with the Center for Health Administration Studies at the University of Chicago which has made its contribution to understanding the health field. Their erudition, acquired in part working together in the Center, gave mutual stimulation as it did to the writer whose only seniority was in years and experience.

Health services research has had an understandable vogue in recent years. Problems in delivery of medical care and the pressures generated by public interest and criticism have been the incentives. However, the production of research results of value to policy makers has lagged in volume and in satisfying the anticipations of those providing funding. The conclusions derived from these surveys, first published some twenty years ago, are exceptions. From the first, they have clearly documented problems in need of attention. The surveys have progressed at approximately five year intervals, measuring changes and indeed improvements in the delivery of medical care.

Research on social policy requires objective and talented research personnel well grounded in a discipline and knowledgeable about the health field. They must be interested in health services research and trained in methodology which can be applied to important medical care delivery problems. Then there must be financial support. These resources came together at the University of Chicago.

The results from one major area of research are in some part reported in this volume. The authors are no longer all at the University of Chicago. On the contrary, as should be true, they are in a number of settings where their background facilitates an expansion in well mounted, pertinent health services research.

This volume relates research from these family interview projects to policy issues. Odin Anderson's chapter summarizes implications. The careful reader will find many other ideas expressed which help evaluate the current adequacy or inadequacy of medical care delivery in this country and point toward solutions to help judge need and possibility of corrections.

Comparison of findings from four similar surveys, data from a cooperative survey in Sweden and information available from other countries shows steady improvement in the distribution of medical care in the United States. Universal entitlement is the great untried change in organization and financing not yet demonstrated here. However, many current inequities relate to education, lifestyle and geography. Such inequities will not be greatly alleviated by national health insurance. Inevitably, universal entitlement will inflate demand which will generate the need for tighter controls on consumer and provider. Whether current inequities as documented in these chapters will be cured sufficiently by national entitlement is the public policy issue. There is some inevitable loss resulting from controls inherent in corrective legislation. Neither course insures total equity in the use of medical care.

Finally, the reader unless he is conversant and comfortable in complex data analysis must be prepared to accept the findings as expressed in each chapter without being able fully to follow their development. The authors have been careful to limit their findings to the results of analysis and to carefully outline their limitations. For the average reader, the complexity of the analysis is impressive, but may remain mysterious. While he may not fully understand, he can be assured that the writers have developed their findings with care.

The writer accepts the accuracy of the analysis and the derived conclusions. He is reminded of the comment by James Hague, an ex-newspaper man who for many years was editor of *Hospitals,* the journal of the American Hospital Association, attending one of the Symposiums on Hospital Affairs conducted annually at the University of Chicago. That Symposium presented a discussion of health services research and its application to hospital operations. As in this volume, conclusions often stemmed from complex analysis of data. During the discussion Hague commented, "I have not understood all the presentations, but my father would have been proud to know I was here." I am proud to know these authors.

George Bugbee

July 24, 1975

Preface

The ultimate test of health services research is whether the findings expand opportunities for improving the organization and delivery of medical care. For some research the policy implications are immediate while other research focuses on a more basic understanding of the health service universe and is, therefore, somewhat removed from direct policy implications. This study represents a first rate example of both of these perspectives.

Its major research commitment is to provide a better understanding of the factors that influence the distribution and utilization of health services. Its policy commitment is to provide a better understanding of the constraints that we face in achieving a major social objective—an equitable distribution of health services. To pursue this discussion the research team has drawn upon many disciplines. Each has provided a unique and significant perspective on examining and understanding the behavior of the health service delivery system—an understanding that is essential to the development of effective policy and to the achievement of social objectives. In many ways this study represents the spectrum of health service research. It is policy relevant, methodologically precise, interdisciplinary and directed at expanding knowledge in a way that serves the end of improving the system.

The National Center for Health Services Research has supported this research effort with an enthusiasm well justified by the results. The ultimate test, however, depends upon the degree to which the knowledge gained in this process is available to and utilized by the decision makers. The publication of this study should contribute to this end.

Gerald Rosenthal, Ph.D.
Director
National Center for Health Services
   Research
Rockville, Maryland
August, 1975

Acknowledgments

This work has been supported by the National Center for Health Services Research under Contracts HSM−110−70−392 and HRA−106−74−24. In addition to the authors whose work is represented here the book would not exist without extensive supportive work by myriad individuals with unique skills.

We particularly wish to acknowledge Daniel Walden, our project officer. George Yates, our overall systems analyst, provided technical expertise without which many of the crucial variables could not have been constructed. Research assistants Rachel Greeley, Elayne Howard, Joan Daley, Charles Brown and Alan Muenzer provided most of the backup support for the data, along with programmers Nelson Co and Kenneth Laitinen. Evelyn Friedman and Linda Randall typed much of the manuscript. Judith Kasper, in addition to contributing a chapter, has provided considerable editorial assistance.

There was one individual involved who will not have the pleasure of seeing his work come to fruition. This was Lloyd Ferguson, MD, our first medical consultant, who died before he was able to put many of his ideas about racial and income differences in medical care into print. However, much of the work in this book profited from his contributions.

Finally, we wish to note that the idea of this book was conceived while the authors were working together at the Center for Health Administration Studies, Graduate School of Business, University of Chicago, which was then under the direction of George Bugbee. While several of the authors and George Bugbee have since moved on to other positions, the supportive, interdisciplinary environment which stimulated the initial thinking for the volume has continued, thus facilitating the completion of this task.

The authors have agreed that all royalties from this publication will be contributed to the Fortieth Anniversary Advancement Fund for the Graduate Program in Hospital Administration, Center for Health Administration Studies.

Ronald Andersen
Joanna Kravits
Odin W. Anderson

Part I

Overview

Chapter One

Introduction*

Ronald Andersen

There appears to be general consensus in the United States that all people have a right to medical care regardless of their ability to pay for that care (Andersen et al. 1971:44–52). Despite this consensus, though, there continues to be major concern that cost barriers, maldistribution of facilities and personnel, and lack of knowledge contributing to an effective use of available health services limit access to medical care [1]. At the same time inflationary increases in the cost of health services, the growing proportion of the Gross National Product devoted to health services and lack of conclusive evidence that increasing use of health services improves the health status of the population has led to serious questioning of resource allocation to health and to efforts to contain cost increases in the health sector of the economy (Rice and Wilson, 1975).

Thus, the United States faces the dilemma of a growing consensus that all people should have relatively ready access to medical care on the one hand, and on the other, growing consternation at the cost of providing such access. Attempts to weigh these "costs" and "benefits" draw attention to a basic policy issue: What is equity in health care distribution and how can it be achieved?

The evident unanimity about people's rights to health care and the current state of the art in health services research suggest that empirical research concerning methods of implementing health service equity have policy relevance at this time.

As Anderson contends:

systematic data gathering and research do not appear until a public policy consensus emerges providing the framework for social and economic research bearing on policy. Such a framework quite unconsciously establishes the guidelines for the selection of data and research problems within

*The detailed critique of an earlier version of this chapter by Sandra Benham is gratefully acknowledged.

the feasibilities of time, resources and research methods. Social research relating to public policy is then largely instrumental, serving to analyze the context in which public policy decisions are made, to implement such decisions and to evaluate alternatives and their consequences in terms of the objectives sought. (1966:11)

Reviews of the development of health services research have noted the potential contribution of research to the equity issue. Flook and Sanazaro list "equity of access" along with moderation of costs and assurance of quality as the three major goals of a health care system. They go on to suggest:

health services research is being challenged to produce a body of knowledge which will provide sufficient predictability in health services to support major policy and operating decisions at various levels of the health services structure. (1973:1–2)

Aday and Eichhorn also note the potential but still largely unrealized contribution of health services research to the equity question:

The emergent national commitment to a more equitable distribution of health services, the evaluation of new methods of financing medical services, and the appearance of innovative modes of health care delivery have prompted a vigorous interest in the volume and patterns of health service utilization in the United States.

These demands have stimulated a flood of research on health services utilization in this and other countries within the last twenty years. However, the conclusions drawn from the literature are far from clear. (1972:1)

The aforementioned research problems are largely attributable to difficulties in measuring equity, but the problems involved in using health status indexes for policy purposes appear even greater. After pointing out the difficulties of measuring health status and assessing its determinants, Anderson continues:

since general health indices as guides to public policy are not found useful, the indicator of equity is suggested as serving that purpose. Given the pervasiveness of the faith that a modern health service somehow must have some relationship to longevity and better health, it follows that equal access to health services must become a civil right. The equitability of a given health service system appears quite easy to measure with modern data collection methods. From the standpoint of access and quantity of services used, social surveys can reveal how and where selected segments of the population enter the system and with what ailments. Measurements can also be made of those segments of the population who do not use the system. (1972:191)

This book, then, is an attempt to use social survey data and empirical analysis to measure health service equity. One way of judging the level of equity achieved is by examining the relative importance of various determinants of health service utilization. While judgments as to what is equitable may vary depending on the particular values of the judge, a general framework for judging health service equity using data collected from a national sample of the population is provided in this volume.

THE MODEL

The contents of the book are organized around the determinants of health service utilization originally specified in *A Behavioral Model of Families' Use of Health Services* (Andersen 1968). This model determined the information collected. It suggests that a person's decision to seek medical care and the volume of services received depends on: (1) the predisposition of the individual to use services (predisposing); (2) his ability to secure services (enabling); (3) his need for medical care (need). The process is diagrammed in Figure 1−1 and the major components of the model are discussed in the following paragraphs [2].

Predisposing Component
Some individuals have a propensity to use services more than other individuals. This propensity can be predicted by individual characteristics which exist prior to the onset of specific episodes of illness. Such characteristics include demographic, social structural and attitudinal-belief variables. Age and sex, for

Figure 1−1. The Behavioral Model of Health Services Use[a]

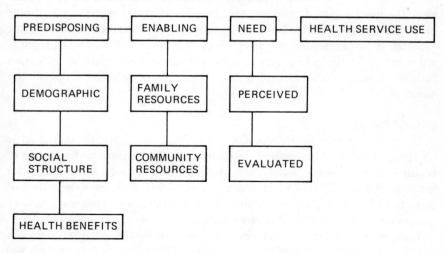

[a]Table 2−1 lists specific variables which operationalize these components of use.

example, among the demographic variables, are intimately related to health and illness. However, they are still considered to be predisposing conditions inasmuch as age per se is not considered a reason for seeking health care. Rather, people in different age groups have different types and amounts of illness and consequently different patterns of medical care.

The social structure variables reflect the location (status) of the individual in his society as measured by characteristics such as ethnicity, education and occupation of the family head. These characteristics suggest what the life style of the individual may be, and they point to the physical as well as social environment of the individual and associated behavior patterns which may be related to the use of health services.

Beliefs about medical care, physicians and disease may also influence health behavior. For example, people who strongly believe in the efficacy of treatment of their doctors might seek a physician sooner and use more services than those with less confidence in the results of treatment.

Enabling Component

Even though individuals may be predisposed to use health services, some means must be available for them to do so. We define as "enabling" those conditions which permit an individual to act on a value or satisfy a felt need regarding health service use. Enabling conditions include family resources such as income and level of health insurance coverage or other source of third party payment, and the existence, nature and accessibility of a regular source of health care.

Characteristics of the community or region can also affect the use of services. An example is the amount of health facilities and personnel within a community. The more plentiful these are, the lower the time and money costs of using health services are likely to be. Consequently, higher utilization rates would be expected in communities with lower costs. Region of residence and the rural-urban nature of the community of residence may also be linked to utilization because of local norms concerning medical practice or behavior of community members.

Need Component

Given the presence of predisposing and enabling conditions, the individual or his family must perceive illness or the probability of its occurrence for the use of health services to occur. Need, then, is the stimulus or most direct reason for health service use. Clinical evaluation is a part of this since, once the individual seeks formal medical care, the nature and extent of need for services are, in large part, determined by the medical care system.

Data on various measures of illness as perceived by the individual were collected: (1) number of disability days reported; (2) symptoms experienced; and (3) self-perceived general state of health as excellent, good, fair or poor.

Evaluated illness measures are clinical judgments of the nature and severity of illness the individual is experiencing. Ideally, such judgments would be made through direct observation of respondents by health professionals. Since this is often not feasible in social surveys, an alternative approach is to have panels of physicians rank the need for care associated with various conditions and symptoms reported by respondents.

THE DATA

All of the chapters in this volume use data from the national study of health services utilization conducted by the Center for Health Administration Studies and the National Opinion Research Center of the University of Chicago in 1971. The studies here expand analytically on the more descriptive presentation of a companion volume, "Two Decades of Health Services," which is based on the same 1971 survey plus three earlier national studies (Andersen et al., Ballinger Publishing Co., Cambridge, Mass. 1976) [3] . "Two Decades of Health Services" examines changes in health service utilization, expenditures and methods of payment over some 20 years, emphasizing in particular the period 1963–1970 during which Medicare and Medicaid were introduced.

For the 1971 survey 3,880 families comprising 11,822 individuals were interviewed in their homes in early 1971. One or more members of each family provided information regarding use of health services, the cost of these services, perceptions of illness and health beliefs [4] . Efforts were made to collect data on people's predisposing, enabling and need characteristics expected to be related to health service utilization.

The sample was designed so that the inner city poor, the aged and the residents of rural areas were overrepresented, in order to allow more detailed analyses of these groups. Weights were developed which correct for the oversampling of the above groups and allow estimates to be made for the total noninstitutionalized population of the United States. The weighted response rate was 82 percent.

In addition to data provided by the families interviewed, information was collected from physicians, clinics, hospitals, insuring organizations and employers concerning the families' medical care and health insurance for the survey year. This was used to verify the family information and to provide additional details.

PLAN OF THE VOLUME

All chapters in this edited volume are original works using data from the 1971 national study. The chapters are generally ordered according to major components of the behavioral model (predisposing, enabling and need) with each analyzing the effect of a variable or group of variables on health service distribution.

Authors from various disciplinary backgrounds have been asked to study those variables which appear most compatible with their training and interests. For the most part, economists have considered enabling variables while authors from other behavioral science and medical backgrounds have emphasized the predisposing and need variables. In all cases authors have been encouraged to consider the policy relevance of their work. They were further requested to undertake the difficult task of using whatever disciplinary tools and concepts seemed appropriate while at the same time writing up their results in a fashion which would prove understandable not only to their disciplinary colleagues but also to people from other disciplines and the broader health services community including policy makers, planners, administrators and practitioners. While various methods and statistics employed may prove unfamiliar to some readers, abstracts of each chapter and a summary chapter help to highlight key findings and implications.

The following chapter provides an overview analysis of health service determinants. Subsequent sections of the volume consider the major determinants in detail: II, Predisposing factors—age, race, education, beliefs and family size; III, Enabling factors—income, health insurance status and availability of health care resources such as physicians and hospitals; and IV, Need components—symptoms experienced, disability days experienced, severity of diagnoses for which a physician was seen and seriousness of dental care required. In addition, Section V addresses more basic issues which transcend specific determinants and examines broader issues related to utilization. These issues include whether medical care does, in fact, improve health status, the patterns of medical care use for those experiencing "major illness episodes" and methodological considerations which may influence the conclusions drawn about various population groups. Finally, Section VI provides a synthesis of the major issues raised in the preceding analyses.

NOTES TO CHAPTER ONE

1. For example, the recently passed national health planning act identifies all of these as major problems in health care delivery (PL 93–641, 1975: 2–3).

2. The most recent extensions of this approach are found in Andersen and Newman (1973) and Aday and Andersen (1975).

3. For preliminary results, see Andersen et al. (1972) and Andersen et al. (1973).

4. Details on the methodology of the study are provided in Andersen et al. (in press).

Chapter Two

Health Service Distribution and Equity*

Ronald Andersen

This chapter defines equity. It examines the relative importance of various determinants of health service use as a means to assess the degree of equity attained in the U.S. in distributing health services. A high degree of equity is assumed when need and the demographic factors are found to be the prime determinants of use. Less equity is suggested when social and economic factors are important. The results indicate that there is less equity: (1) for dental services than for hospital and physician services; and (2) for gaining entry into the medical care system than for subsequent numbers of services used. It is suggested that providing a regular source of care to minority groups is a health service policy that might reduce inequity in obtaining physician services. The large inequity observed in obtaining dental care for minorities, low income persons and rural farm residents may be reduced by financing mechanisms. Dental care inequity is, however, also related to more immutable factors such as low education and social class. This suggests difficulties in effecting social change.

An underlying premise of this volume is that decisionmaking about health services delivery will be aided by understanding the differential importance of various determinants of health service utilization. Such understanding depends on a theoretical framework and empirical analysis. To this end, this book offers a model of the determinants of health care utilization: what they are, how they are related and how they influence utilization. It also presents empirical estimates of the importance of various subsets of these determinants.

The present chapter is devoted to an overview of the subject. The first section suggests a means for defining equitable distribution of health care services and for judging the extent to which equity is achieved. It makes further analytic distinctions concerning the susceptability of various determinants of

*Detailed critiques of an earlier version of this chapter by Sandra Benham and Joel May are gratefully acknowledged.

health care utilization to policy control. The second section of the chapter describes the health care services which will be studied. The third section broadly investigates the relative influence of the various components of the model of utilization of physician, hospital and dentist services. The chapter's fourth section looks at the relative utilization of such services by aged, non-white, low income, inner city and rural population groups in the U.S. The final section summarizes the findings.

DEFINING EQUITABLE DISTRIBUTION OF SERVICES

It is suggested in the introductory chapter that an impetus for the kind of analyses found in this volume is the growing consensus that this country should have an "equitable distribution of services." Webster's defines equitable as that which is "fair to all concerned without prejudice, favor or rigor entailing undue hardship" (1967:769). Any operational definition of such a concept is likely to be tenuous and subject to criticism. The attempt must be made, however, if empirical studies are to follow.

"Equitable distribution" does not imply that everyone should receive the same amount of health services. Instead, I propose that an "equitable distribution" of health care services is one in which illness (as defined by the patient and his family or by health care professionals) is the major determinant of the distribution, in terms of the model shown in Figure 1−1. Perceived need and evaluated need are the major determinants of health services use in an equitable system. It follows that demographic variables should also be highly correlated with use in such a system, because of the well established relationships between health and age, sex and marital status. On the other hand, social structure, health beliefs, family resources and community resources should have less impact on utilization. Inequity is suggested, for example, if the distribution of services is determined by race, income or availability of facilities. Empirically, a distribution of health services may be defined as more equitable, the stronger the association between utilization, perceived and evaluated need and demographic variables on the one hand, and the weaker the association between utilization and social structure, health benefits, family resources and community resources on the other hand.

While this operational definition of "equitable distribution" will be accepted for the purposes of this chapter it should not be assumed that all authors of the following chapters would necessarily accept the same definition. Rather, a unifying purpose of the volume is to provide the reader with a framework and empirical evidence to assist him in making his own judgment concerning what is equity in health services and how it should be achieved.

When change is desired to achieve greater equity in distribution, the concept of "mutability" becomes important. Mutability refers to the extent to which a variable can be manipulated to attain some desired end. This is close to Coleman's distinction between policy variables, "those variables which can be or have been amenable to policy control," and situational variables, which "play a part in the causal structure which leads to outcome variables, and thus must be controlled in the analysis of the design, but are not subject to policy control" (Coleman 1972:5). Decision makers are generally interested in the more mutable variables, but the less mutable ones are also important because their strength suggests the probable success of changing a given situation and the limits within which the decision maker must work. In general, the enabling variables appear more mutable than the predisposing ones. For example, in the short run alterations appear easier to bring about in the insurance benefit structure than in the educational structure.

TYPES OF HEALTH SERVICE UTILIZATION

The health services examined in this chapter include hospital, physician and dental care. They were selected to include a range of discretionary and nondiscretionary services and also to represent both contact and volume measures.

Nondiscretionary services are those determined by prevailing norms for the society as a whole, by decisions of the provider of medical care and by the nature of the illness condition itself. Services which are used in response to individual and family choice are considered discretionary. Among types of medical services, discretion is assumed to be lowest for hospitalization, intermediate for physician services and highest for dental care (Andersen 1968: 17–19).

Measures of contact (e.g., whether an individual sees a physician or dentist at all or is admitted to a hospital during a given time period) and measures of volume (e.g., the number of times an individual sees a physician or dentist or days spent in a hospital during a given time period) are both included as units of analysis. Policy makers are interested in contact measures to assess who gets into the medical care system and, more importantly, who does not. Volume measures provide some indication of what happens to the patient in terms of amount of services received once he has gained entry to the system.

Analyses are done of both contact and volume measures for hospital, physician and dental utilization. The total sample from the 1970 study was used in the analyses of contact. Analysis of volume for each service is limited to persons who used the service during the calendar year 1970. All of the measures of health service utilization are described in the Appendix.

DETERMINANTS OF HEALTH
SERVICE UTILIZATION

This section has two objectives: (1) to show the simple relationship between each determinant of health service utilization (independent variable) and each type of health service use (dependent variable) and (2) to examine the effects of each independent variable on health service use taking into account the effects of the other independent variables. The study was designed so that independent variables representing all components of the behavioral model were available. These operational measures are described in the Appendix.

Table 2–1 indicates the relative impact of each independent variable on the various measures of utilization, not taking into account any of the other independent variables [1]. Tables 2–2 and 2–3 indicate the relative impact of each independent variable taking into account the effects of all the other independent variables. Table 2–2 presents automatic interaction detection (AID) analyses, while Table 2–3 shows multiple classification analyses (MCA) [2].

In the AID analyses, all the relevant variables are introduced. AID divides the sample through a series of dichotomous divisions into a mutually exclusive series of subgroups. It seeks to answer the question, "What single predictor will give a maximum improvement in ability to predict values of the dependent variable at any stage of the analysis?" (Sonquist and Morgan 1964:4). This program is particularly well suited to uncover interaction effects, i.e., combinations of categories of independent variables which are important in explaining utilization. Table 2–2 indicates the variables actually used in the AID analyses and the total percent variance (R^2) accounted for by the variables [3]. These estimates are additive, so the total R^2 is the sum of the contributions of all the independent variables.

MCA is a technique for examining the interrelationships between several predictor variables and a dependent variable within the context of an additive model [4] (Andrews et al. 1973:1). It is used in addition to AID because it appears to be more efficient in determining additive effects of the independent variables [5]. It also indicates the cumulative effect of independent variables on the dependent variable. Its weaknesses for present purposes are that it assumes the effects of all independent variables are additive (i.e., does not take into account interaction effects) and it works best with relatively few independent variables (Ibid., pp. 17–28). Table 2–3 shows the variables included in the MCA analyses. Beta squared (β^2) provides a measure of the ability of the predictor to explain variation in the dependent variable after adjusting for the effects of all other predictors (Ibid., p. 7). These β^2 s are not additive in that they may sum to either more or less than the total R^2. They do, however, indicate the relative importance of the predictors. The particular variables were selected on the basis of the magnitude of their contribution independent of the other variables, or because of their particular theoretical or policy relevance. Because of our special interest in certain subgroups of the population, age, income, residence and ethnicity were included in all MCA analyses (no more than 13 variables were included in any particular analysis).

Hospital Utilization

Tables 2–1 through 2–3 support other findings that illness is the major determinant of who enters a hospital (Aday and Eichhorn, 1972:27–28). Disability days (excluding days in the hospital) is the operational measure most closely associated with being admitted to a hospital. The predisposing and enabling components appear to play relatively minor roles. The AID analysis suggests that being separated or divorced and having comprehensive insurance coverage increases the probability of entering the hospital. MCA further suggests that long traveling time to a regular source of medical care increases the chances of hospitalization.

Illness measures were also the most important predictors of the number of days patients stay in the hospital once admitted. Amount of worry about health is the illness measure most closely associated with hospital days, but other components are also important. Age is the second best predictor (elderly people stay longer). Other demographic variables—social structure, beliefs, and the availability of facilities and personnel—also affect hospital days. The larger R^2 obtained from the AID as compared to the MCA analysis suggests some interactions among these variables in determining length of stay. In sum, it appears that while admission decisions are primarily made according to degree of illness, length of hospital stay depends on personal and environmental characteristics as well.

The findings for admissions suggest that hospital care is a low discretion service, since the demographic and need variables are of prime importance. However, the findings for number of days suggest that more discretion with respect to length of stay may be exercised than was originally supposed. Physicians' decisions about when to discharge patients may be influenced by such factors as: (1) conduciveness of the home environment to recuperation; (2) emotional and physical strain on the family in providing nursing services; (3) special requests of the patient or family for early or late discharge; (4) work load of the attending physicians; (5) availability of beds; and (6) availability of nursing home and extended care facilities. Further study is necessary to determine the relative impact of these factors on the number of days spent by patients in hospitals. It might be noted that community characteristics do appear to have more impact on volume of hospital days than on entry to the hospital.

According to the criteria suggested in this chapter, the distribution of hospital services in the U.S. in 1970 appeared reasonably equitable. The major determinants are the illness and demographic components. Furthermore, when social structural and enabling variables show any relationship to hospital use, the higher utilization is often associated with the group generally assumed to have the greatest need (e.g., lower income, education and social class) [6].

This judgment of equity should be tempered by two observations. First, much of the variance in hospital use is left unexplained; it is possible that the

Table 2–1. Percent of Variation in Utilization Explainable by Each Predictor by Type of Service

	Service					
	Hospital		Physician		Dental	
Type Predictor	1 Contact[a]	2 Volume	3 Contact	4 Volume	5 Contact	6 Volume
			percent			
Predisposing—demographic						
7[a] Age	1.2	9.8	1.1	3.9	4.3	0.6
8 Sex	0.5	0.2	0.7	0.4	0.1	0.2
9 Marital status	1.4	4.1	0.9	2.9	0.9	1.2
10 Family size	0.6	3.4	2.3	3.1	0.9	0.6
11 Birth order	0.8	2.2	1.0	3.1	1.0	0.5
12 Past hospitalization	1.8	1.7	1.9	2.7	0.6	0.7
13 Neighborhood tenure	0.5	1.4	0.4	0.1	0.3	0.2
Predisposing—social structure						
14 Education head	0.1	2.5	1.1	0.4	4.9	0.2
15 Social class head	0.1	0.6	0.6	0.4	4.4	0.2
16 Occupation head	0.1	1.1	0.6	0.5	2.6	0.3
17 Ethnicity	0.1	0.1	1.0	0.1	3.0	0.1
18 Religion	1.0	2.9	0.3	2.3	0.8	1.4
Predisposing—beliefs						
19 Value of health services	0.1	0.4	0.4	0.3	1.8	0.5
20 Value of MDs	0.1	0.3	0.2	0.1	0.4	*
21 Knowledge of disease	*	0.9	0.1	*	1.0	0.3
22 Response threshold	0.1	1.5	0.2	0.1	0.5	0.4
Enabling—family						
23 Family income	0.4	1.6	0.2	1.0	4.5	0.3
24 Insurance	0.1	1.8	0.9	0.3	—	—
25 Enrollment	0.1	2.2	0.1	0.3	—	—

26 MD office coverage	*	1.0	0.7	0.2	–	–
27 Dental coverage	–	–	–	–	0.5	*
28 Regular care	0.6	0.6	4.3	0.6	–	–
29 Group practice	0.2	0.4	2.4	0.4	0.8	1.0
30 Appointment time	0.3	0.6	1.2	0.4	–	–
31 Travel time	0.6	2.6	1.7	0.3	–	–
32 Waiting time	0.4	0.2	2.3	0.3	–	–
Community–enabling						
33 Residence	0.1	0.7	0.4	0.1	1.2	0.7
34 Region	0.1	0.9	0.3	0.4	0.8	1.5
35 MD ratio	0.1	0.8	0.6	0.1	0.4	1.9
36 Hospital bed ratio	0.2	0.5	0.1	0.3	0.6	0.4
Illness–perceived						
37 Disability days	8.8	7.5	7.6	8.9	2.0	0.2
38 Symptoms	2.4	1.5	5.5	6.0	0.7	0.6
39 Perceived health	2.3	7.0	2.3	6.7	1.1	0.3
40 Worry about health	7.0	10.9	7.6	7.7	0.4	0.4
41 Pain frequency	5.3	7.1	4.7	8.6	0.5	0.2
42 Dental symptoms	–	–	–	–	4.9	0.8
Illness–evaluated						
43 Diagnosis	–	2.4	–	13.3	–	–
44 Symptoms	3.0	1.3	5.4	6.3	–	–

– Indicates not included in analysis.
* Less than 0.05 percent.
aThe variable numbers in this and subsequent tables in Chapter Two identify the variables described in the Appendix.

Table 2–2.   Percent of Variation in Utilization Explained by Type of Predictor and Type of Service in AID Analyses[a]

Type Predictor	Service					
	Hospital		Physician		Dental	
	1 Contact	2 Volume	3 Contact	4 Volume	5 Contact	6 Volume
	percent					
Predisposing—demographic						
7 Age	—	7.6	—	—	2.1	—
8 Sex	—	1.0	—	—	—	—
9 Marital status	0.8	1.0	—	—	—	0.9
12 Past hospitalization	—	3.1	—	0.6	—	0.8
Predisposing—social structure						
14 Education head	—	0.8	—	—	4.9	—
15 Social class head	—	0.7	—	—	2.1	—
16 Occupation head	—	0.7	—	—	—	—
17 Ethnicity	—	—	—	—	0.8	—
18 Religion	—	—	—	—	—	1.2
Predisposing—beliefs						
19 Value of health services	—	—	—	—	—	1.0
20 Value of MDs	—	2.2	—	—	—	—
21 Knowledge of disease	—	—	—	—	—	0.8
22 Response threshold	—	0.7	—	—	—	0.7
Enabling—family						
23 Family income	—	—	—	—	1.6	—
24 Insurance	0.6	—	—	—	*	*
28 Regular care	—	—	2.4	—	—	—

Enabling—community						
33 Residence	—	—	—	—	—	1.2
34 Region	—	—	—	—	1.0	0.8
35 MD ratio	—	1.0	—	—	—	1.9
36 Hospital bed ratio	—	3.0	—	—	1.0	—
Illness—perceived						
37 Disability days	8.8	—	4.8	4.6	—	0.9
38 Symptoms	—	—	1.4	1.9	—	—
39 Perceived health	1.0	—	—	1.0	—	—
40 Worry about health	3.5	10.9	7.6	0.7	—	—
41 Pain frequency	—	—	—	0.7	—	—
42 Dental symptoms	*	*	—	*	4.9	—
Illness—evaluated						
43 Diagnosis	*	—	*	14.0	*	*
44 Symptoms	*	—	*	—	*	*
Total (R^2)	14.8	32.6	16.3	23.4	18.4	10.1

* Indicates predictor not included in analysis.
— Indicates predictor did not contribute to variance explained.
aIncludes only predictors which contributed to variance explained in at least one AID analysis.

Table 2–3.   Relative Importance of Predictors in Explaining Utilization by Type of Service in MCA Analyses[a]

	Service					
	Hospital		Physician		Dental	
Type predictor	1 Contact	2 Volume	3 Contact	4 Volume	5 Contact	6 Volume
			Beta squared			
Predisposing—demographic						
7 Age	0.005	0.089	0.008	0.008	0.033	0.016
8 Sex	—	—	—	*	—	—
9 Marital status	0.004	0.012	—	—	—	0.010
10 Family size	—	—	0.017	0.009	0.002	0.006
11 Birth order	—	—	—	—	0.005	—
12 Past hospitalization	0.006	0.006	—	—	—	—
Predisposing—social structure						
14 Education head	—	0.007	0.004	—	0.014	—
15 Social class head	—	0.007	—	—	0.011	—
16 Occupation head	—	0.003	0.001	—	0.009	*
17 Ethnicity	*	—	—	0.001	0.002	—
18 Religion	0.001	—	—	—	—	0.018
Predisposing—beliefs						
22 Response threshold	—	0.015	—	—	—	—
Enabling—family						
23 Family income	0.001	0.003	0.002	0.001	0.017	0.002
25 Enrollment	—	0.002	—	—	—	—
26 MD office coverage	—	—	0.001	—	*	*
27 Dental coverage	—	—	—	—	—	—
28 Regular care	—	—	0.029	0.005	—	—
29 Group practice	—	—	—	—	—	0.006
31 Travel time	0.009	—	—	—	—	—

Enabling—community						
33 Residence	0.001	0.006	*	0.001	0.003	*
34 Region	–	–	–	–	0.003	0.006
35 MD ratio	–	0.011	0.004	–	–	0.010
Illness—perceived						
37 Disability days	0.040	–	0.025	0.016	–	–
38 Symptoms	–	–	0.013	0.005	–	–
39 Perceived health	0.007	–	–	0.002	–	–
40 Worry about health	0.041	0.072	0.027	0.007	–	–
41 Pain frequency	–	–	–	0.005	–	–
42 Dental symptoms	–	–	–	–	0.053	0.012
Illness—evaluated						
43 Diagnosis	–	–	–	0.077	–	–
44 Symptoms	0.003	–	–	–	–	–
Adjusted R^2	0.140	0.219	0.194	0.246	0.207	0.070

* Value < 0.0005.

– Indicates not included in analysis.

[a]Includes only predictors found in at least one MCA analysis.

judgment would differ with a better specified model. Secondly, it does not take into account the appropriateness or continuity of care provided for a hospitalized episode of illness. A broader definition of equity would include this quality aspect and might also lead to a different conclusion.

Physician Utilization

Physician services, like hospital services, seem to be largely determined by illness levels, according to Tables 2–1 through 2–3. Disability days, worry about health and symptoms reported are all important predictors of who will see a physician over the course of a year. The importance of illness in predicting physician contact is not unexpected. What is less expected is the seemingly negligible predictive power of most predisposing and enabling variables. Given the expectation that patient judgment about when to see a doctor would, in part, be socially and economically determined, and the knowledge that a considerable proportion of doctor–patient interaction is for preventive and elective services, it was expected that non-illness determinants would be more important.

The one enabling variable found to be important in influencing physician contact (in all three analyses) is regular source of care. People without any regular source are least likely to see a doctor, while those who report specialists as their regular source are most likely to visit a physician during the year. This finding reinforces the idea that an established entry into the health service system may be influential in motivating people to use the system. In addition the MCA analysis suggests that, independent of the other variables listed in Table 2–3, persons in smaller families are more likely to see a physician than persons in larger ones.

The illness variables were even more important for predicting volume of visits to a physician than for predicting whether or not a physician was seen. However, both multivariate analyses indicate that the evaluated illness measure in this case is more important than the perceived one: physicians' rating of severity of treated conditions is a better predictor of the number of visits made than are patients' reports of disability days, perceived health or worry, although the latter variables are also important. This finding suggests that, once a person is in the medical care system, the way the physician views the illness may be essential to understanding the subsequent care provided.

The multivariate analyses suggest little of major importance apart from these illness measures. The MCA analysis does indicate that number of visits is directly correlated with age and inversely correlated with family size.

The findings from the analysis of physician visits, like those from the analysis of hospitalization, show a reasonably equitable system. Most of the variance in use is explained by illness levels, the criteria by which we defined an equitable system of distribution. Some inequity is suggested for people without a regular source of care. This is a fairly mutable variable given sufficient motivation and resources. Through the establishment of health centers, outreach programs, use of new types of health providers and some redistribution of medical manpower, it does seem possible to provide regular entry into the health service system for those with none. These data suggest that such a process would establish greater equity with respect to who sees a physician.

Dental Utilization

Seeing a dentist appears to depend on most of the major components of the model. Tables 2–1 through 2–3 show symptoms to be important, but social structural variables as a group appear even more important. Higher education and social class along with being white all contribute to a higher probability of seeing the dentist. Also, both multivariate analyses show adolescents, middle-aged adults and higher income persons to be more likely to see a dentist.

The multivariate analyses of volume of dental visits have lower R^2s than any other analyses. Furthermore, few patterns consistent with the theoretical framework emerge. The AID analysis suggests some complex interactions involving beliefs about health. The MCA estimates indicate that, controlling for other factors, Jews and Catholics appear to be higher users, as do people who live in the Northeast and in areas with high physician-population ratios. The physician measure may serve as a proxy for the availability of dentists, since areas with larger numbers of physicians also tend to have more dentists (no measure of dentist availability was employed in this study). Better measures of dental health and some judgment of severity of condition for dental conditions comparable to that provided for conditions treated by physicians would probably improve the R^2 (Newman 1971). Further, it must be noted that the measures of belief are oriented toward medical rather than dental issues. Measures of beliefs specifically related to dental utilization might conceivably increase our understanding of this area.

The dental contact analysis suggests inequity in the system. Considerable variance in utilization is explained by social structure and the enabling variables. Equitable distribution would require a reduction of this variance. However, the low mutability of the social structure variables (social class, occupation and ethnicity) suggest that equity will be difficult to achieve. The income differences and the apparent influences of supply suggest that some movement toward equity might be achieved by dental care financing and service programs. However, more of the variance appears to be related to fundamental class differences which cannot be easily rectified by social programming.

LEVELS OF EQUITY FOR SELECTED SUBGROUPS IN THE POPULATION

A major concern of the national study (Andersen et al., 1975) is to compare the utilization patterns of certain subgroups with the rest of the population. Of special interest is the care received by the elderly, nonwhites, low income groups and those living in inner city and rural areas. Tables 2–4 and 2–5 show these comparisons in two ways. The unadjusted estimates show utilization rates disregarding the other characteristics of the group being examined. The adjusted estimates indicate what the utilization rate of the group would be if it had the same characteristics as the sample as a whole (Andrews et al. 1973:7) [7].

For example, the first column in Table 2–4 shows a familiar relationship: the elderly are much more likely to enter the hospital during a given year than are younger persons. The second column shows the expected use for each age group if its members had the same distributions of marital status, past hospitalization, ethnicity, religion, family income, travel time, residence, disability days, perceived health, worry and symptom severity as the general population.

Components of inequity and excess for population subgroups can be studied by examining the relationship of the unadjusted and adjusted scores of subgroups in the MCA analyses to scores for the total population. Figure 2–1 illustrates the various adjustment possibilities and the related components of inequity and excess.

The areas labeled "unexplained equity" and "unexplained excess" indicate differences which remain between utilization rates of subgroups and the total population after social structure, beliefs, enabling determinants, illness levels and demographic characteristics have been taken into account. Arrows marked "explained inequity" and "explained excess" illustrate the difference attributable to social structure, beliefs and enabling determinants; while "explained apparent inequity" and "explained apparent excess" show the portion of this difference attributable to illness and demographic determinants.

Inequity in health service distribution occurs when individuals receive services primarily according to their place in the social structure, their beliefs or enabling characteristics. Even though we "explain" this inequity (or excess) then, it remains "real." The inequity may be only "apparent," however, if the lower use rate can be explained by varying age structure (demographic) or illness levels. For example, lower use rates for an ethnic group consisting of predominantly younger persons in reasonably good health may be only "apparent inequity." "Excess" utilization is indicated if a subgroup has higher utilization rates than the rest of the population. However, like inequity, it may be only "apparent excess." One example would be higher utilization rates by the elderly which could be attributed to the larger number of symptoms and disability days they experience.

Adjusting subgroup utilization scores may result in a *greater* difference in use between a subgroup and population. This increase either in the direction of more inequity or more excess is labeled "latent" [8]. For instance, a subgroup with lower rates of use than the population (inequity) may have even lower adjusted rates if they experience more illness than the rest of the population (explained latent inequity).

A complete elaboration of the various relationships between subgroup and

Figure 2–1. Inequity and Excess Utilization for Subgroups in the Population

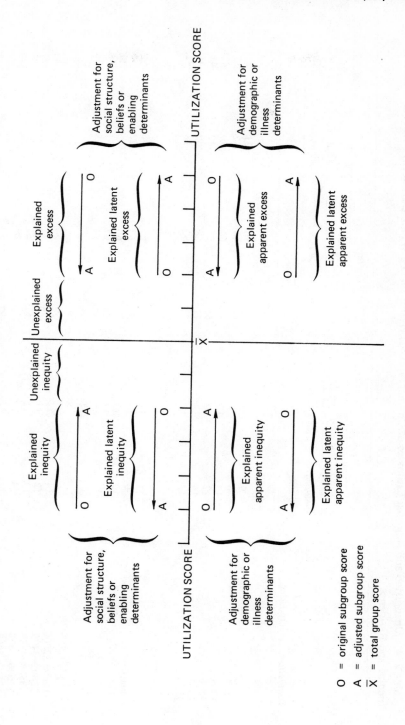

O = original subgroup score
A = adjusted subgroup score
X̄ = total group score

Table 2–4. Unadjusted and Adjusted Estimates of Contact With the Health Service System During 1970 by Age, Ethnicity, Income and Residence

	Contact					
	1 Admitted to Hospital		3 Saw MD		5 Saw Dentist	
	Unadjusted	Adjusted	Unadjusted	Adjusted	Unadjusted	Adjusted
Population characteristics			*percent*			
7 Age						
Under 6	9	9	75	70	21	21
6–15	6	9	55	59	57	55
16–44	13	13	65	64	50	47
45–64	12	10	65	59	40	41
65–74	15	12	72	68	30	41
75 or over	19	17	72	67	18	32
17 Ethnicity						
White	11	11	67	65	48	48
Black	9	10	54	63	23	34
Mexican, Puerto Rican	12	13	53	60	25	37
American Indian	10	12	55	69	31	46
Oriental	4	7	52	54	38	38
23 Family income						
Under $2000	14	12	66	63	24	33
$2000–3499	12	11	59	61	23	31
$3500–4999	13	11	61	61	34	39
$5000–7499	13	12	63	64	35	39
$7500–9999	12	12	64	65	44	44
$10000–14999	10	11	68	68	50	45
$15000 or over	8	9	66	66	61	52

33 Residence

SMSA central city	10	10	63	64	41	43
Other SMSA urban	11	12	69	66	54	49
Other urban	13	13	66	66	44	45
Rural nonfarm	11	11	64	65	41	42
Rural farm	10	9	56	63	39	46
Total population	11	–	65	–	45	–

Table 2-5. Unadjusted and Adjusted Estimates of Modal* Volume of Services Used by Those Receiving Services During 1970 by Age, Ethnicity, Income and Residence

Population Characteristic	Volume					
	2 Hospital Days		4 MD Visits		6 Dental Visits	
	Unadjusted	Adjusted	Unadjusted	Adjusted	Unadjusted	Adjusted
7 Age						
Under 6	4.6	3.0	3.9	4.0	1.8	2.6
6–15	3.7	3.7	2.4	3.3	2.5	3.1
16–44	6.3	7.6	4.1	4.4	2.7	2.4
45–64	11.9	11.0	5.0	4.2	3.0	2.6
65–74	14.2	12.7	5.8	4.5	2.9	2.7
75 or over	19.9	15.8	6.1	4.5	2.3	2.3
17 Ethnicity						
White	8.3	8.4	4.1	4.0	2.7	2.7
Black	8.0	7.4	4.0	4.2	2.9	2.8
Mexican, Puerto Rican			5.2	5.2	2.6	2.7
American Indian	6.8	5.6	4.5	4.3	2.0	2.5
Oriental			3.0	3.7	2.1	2.3
23 Family income						
Under $2000	12.8	8.0	5.5	3.9	2.6	2.6
$2000–3499	10.9	7.5	4.9	3.7	2.6	2.5
$3500–4999	9.8	8.0	5.1	4.1	2.6	2.6
$5000–7499	8.6	7.8	4.2	3.9	2.7	2.7
$7500–9999	6.4	7.8	4.1	4.2	2.4	2.5
$10000–14999	6.9	8.3	3.9	4.3	2.7	2.7
$15000 or over	8.4	9.7	3.5	4.1	2.9	2.8

33 Residence

SMSA central city	8.5	8.1	4.2	4.0	2.8	2.7
Other SMSA urban	9.0	9.4	4.1	4.2	2.9	2.7
Other urban	6.0	6.6	3.9	3.9	2.5	2.7
Rural nonfarm	8.1	8.2	3.9	4.0	2.4	2.6
Rural farm	10.0	7.6	4.2	4.2	2.4	2.8
Total population	8.2	—	4.1	—	2.7	—

*The scores shown in this table were obtained by first averaging the square roots of actual experience. This gave maximum likelihood estimates of the square root of the experience since the distribution of square roots is approximately normal. These values were then squared giving maximum likelihood (i.e., modal) estimates of units of use shown in the reading. See for example Goldberger, (1964:131). The author is indebted to Richard Foster for pointing out these relationships.

total population scores illustrated in Figure 2–1 has not been attempted here. However, Figure 2–1 provides a preliminary framework to assist in the examination of health service equity for the aged, poor, minority groups and residents of central city and rural areas.

Subgroup Contact Measures

Hospital Admissions. The unadjusted scores (Table 2–4) suggest excess hospital admissions for persons 65 and over, but when adjustment is made for their higher illness levels, their admission rate moves closer to that of the general population. However, after all the variables shown in Table 2–3 are taken into account there remains unexplained excess, particularly for the group 75 years old and over. This suggests that the elderly do not experience inequities with respect to getting into the hospital.

The unadjusted scores for ethnic groups suggest some inequities, particularly for blacks and Orientals. Much of this is removed by the adjustment process which mainly involves age: these groups tend to be younger, and the young are less likely to be hospitalized. It is difficult to make a case that these minorities experience inequity in hospital admissions, with the possible exception of the Oriental population, but in the latter case the small number of observations makes the results suspect.

Low income persons appear to have excess hospital admissions, according to the unadjusted rates in Table 2–4. These excesses are explained by adjustments for age and illness, and the resulting "flat distribution" suggests neither excessive nor inequitable use by the poor.

Unadjusted rates for hospital admissions for inner city and rural farm residents are below the national level. This difference is not removed by the adjustment process. Consequently, it might be argued that these subgroups do experience inequity in being admitted to hospitals.

Seeing a Physician. Older people are more likely to see a physician than any other age groups except young children. The adjusted scores show that this discrepancy is reduced by taking into account the higher levels of illness reported by older people. However, the adjusted scores still show higher proportions of the aged seeing physicians than the rest of the population.

The unadjusted estimates suggest considerable inequity for the minorities in seeing physicians which can be largely explained by the lack of a regular source of care. When this difference is taken into account the proportion of blacks and other minorities seeing physicians is much closer to that for the white population. In this case we have rather clear documentation of inequity largely attributable to lack of an enabling resource, i.e., an identified entry into the health service system.

The unadjusted proportion of individuals seeing physicians shows relatively little variance across income levels. The adjusted scores are quite similar but do suggest that the relatively high contact of the lowest income group may in part reflect higher illness levels.

The rural farm population is less likely to see a physician than is the rest of the population. The adjustment brings the farm rate close to that for the population as a whole. The adjustment in this case seems to be primarily in terms of illness level: the rural farm population reports less illness. Consequently, the inequity is largely apparent. The findings also suggest relatively little inequity for inner city residents with respect to seeing a physician.

Seeing a Dentist. Normative judgments about the appropriate relationship between age and use of dental services differ from those for hospital and physician use since older children and young adults are normally considered to "need" more care than the youngest and oldest age groups. Table 2–4 suggests that people 65 and over see a dentist much less frequently than the general population, but much of the inequity can be explained by the lower education, class and family income of older people [9].

Considerable inequity in seeing a dentist is shown for all minority ethnic groups in Table 2–4; however, much of this inequity can be explained (except for Orientals) by the adjustment process. The main adjustment factors are education, social class, occupation and income. Some of this inequity is a function of mutable variables such as income but the major part is related to social structure, suggesting that complete equity will be difficult to achieve through financing mechanisms alone.

Large inequities are found for contact with a dentist by income level. The low contact rate for the lower income groups rises somewhat when age and social structure are taken into account. The most salient finding, however, is the striking difference that remains after adjustment, a difference which suggests that variation by income group largely represents financial barriers which might be overcome by financing mechanisms.

Unadjusted estimates show the inner city and rural populations less likely to see a dentist than other urban residents. The adjustment process accounts for most of the inequity. The lower education, occupation and income levels of the inner city and rural residents largely explain the inequity they experience.

Subgroup Volume Measures

Hospital Days. Hospitalized elderly persons spend much more time in the hospital than younger ones, according to the unadjusted estimates (Table 2–5). The adjustment is primarily for the higher illness level experienced by the older groups which reduces the apparent excess use of these groups. However, the adjusted rate is still quite high, suggesting the possibility of excess use according to our criteria.

The unadjusted hospital days by ethnicity indicate relatively little inequity for these groups. The adjusted figures suggest the possibility of some latent inequity, since adjustment moves the scores away from the total population score.

The low income groups show considerable excess use of hospitals according to the unadjusted scores. This excess vanishes when the greater age and higher illness levels of these groups are taken into account. In fact, the adjusted scores for the low income groups fall below those for the total population.

The rural farm population appears to have excess use of hospitals according to the unadjusted estimates. However, this excess is again explained by the greater age of that group.

Visits to Physicians. Older people seeing a physician have more visits than the rest of the population. Much of this is explained by their higher illness levels. Little inequity is indicated for physician visits with respect to ethnicity. The low income groups appear to be excess users of physician visits. However, adjustments for their greater age and higher illness levels explain that apparent excess. Little difference exists in mean number of visits according to residence.

Visits to Dentists. Table 2–5 suggests relatively little inequity concerning visits to dentists for any of the subgroups under examination. Thus, while Table 2–4 indicated considerable variation across subgroups concerning seeing a dentist at all, Table 2–5 suggests relatively homogeneous use patterns once people are in the dental care system.

SUMMARY

This chapter has proposed a definition of equitable distribution of health services based on the relative importance of various determinants of health service use. It has pointed out that the difficulty of attaining equity, when inequity is found, can be in part assessed by considering the extent to which the determinants of differential use are mutable.

The analysis suggests that hospital services were, by our definition, rather equitably distributed in the population: hospital admission is explained primarily by demographic and need variables. However, length of stay appears affected by social structure, beliefs, and availability of facilities and personnel, in addition to illness level and age.

Physician services were also found to be distributed largely according to illness levels. Severity of illness as evaluated by physicians was particularly important in determining volume of visits. The one enabling factor found important in determining who sees a physician was acknowledgment of a regular source of care. This suggests that inequity could be reduced by a health policy designed to provide all population groups with a place and/or person to serve as a regular source of medical advice and treatment.

Considerable inequity was discovered in dental care. Social structure and income are strongly associated with seeing a dentist. Financing mechanisms might reduce the inequity associated with income differentials, but social structure is more difficult to change. The number of visits to a dentist, given that the individual sees a dentist at all, appears more equitably distributed. However, a relatively small proportion of behavior in this sector was explained by the analysis.

This chapter also undertook more detailed analysis of equity for the aged, minority groups, low income persons, and rural and inner city residents. These groups appear to have greater problems in gaining entry to the system than in receiving care once in the system. For the aged, seeing a dentist is the only measure for which inequity appears substantial. Part of the low contact rate is related to low income, education and social class, but much remains unexplained by the analysis here.

Nonwhite groups experience inequity in getting to see physicians, but have fewer problems with hospital admissions. Once in the system, their use rates are similar to those for whites. An exception occurs in the case of Orientals, who appear to be consistently low utilizers. Low income groups appear to have no major equity problems with respect to hospital or physician services, but some with respect to seeing a dentist. However, those who do see a dentist have volume rates similar to those of the rest of the population.

By the criteria used here, the group most consistently experiencing inequity in entering the system is the rural farm population. They are less likely than the rest of the population to be admitted to a hospital or to see a doctor or dentist. Access problems for inner city residents appear in contrast less serious.

The analysis of the determinants and distribution of health services presented in this chapter offers a general view of health services utilization. However, analyses which concentrate on particular health services, emphasize certain types of determinants, utilize alternative analytic schemes or perhaps imply a different definition of equity may extend or modify these findings and conclusions. That is the task of subsequent chapters.

NOTES TO CHAPTER TWO

1. The figures given are the percent of variation in the dependent variable which can be explained by the independent variable using the dichotomous split of independent variable categories in the appendix which maximizes the variance explained. A minimum value of 0.5 is suggested as a rough guide for considering the variable to have a meaningful influence on utilization (Sonquist and Morgan 1964:119–120).

2. For both the AID and MCA analyses, all volume measures were transformed using a square root transformation to reduce the positive skewness of the dependent variables.

3. The parameters used in the AID analysis were minimum group size for splitting = 25 and split reducibility = 0.006.

4. The tolerance test used to stop the iterations on the MCA program is that all coefficients change by less than 0.01 percent of the grand mean. The maximum number of iterations allowed was 25.

5. For a discussion of the strategy for the joint use of AID and MCA see Sonquist (1970:189–219).

6. An exception to this pattern is ethnicity which will be discussed in the next section. The following section of this chapter addresses explicitly the level of equity for various subgroups in the population.

7. The characteristics controlled for are those determined by the MCA analyses and shown in Table 2–3.

8. The distinctions between explained inequity or excess and explained apparent inequity or excess discussed above also apply here.

9. This group is also, of course, much more likely to be edentulous.

Part II

Predisposing Factors

Chapter Three

Age, Race and Education as Predisposing Factors in Physician and Dentist Utilization

John F. Newman, Jr.

If an implied goal of the American health care system is the equitable distribution of health services, then the influence of some characteristics should be minimized (race and education for example) while that of other characteristics should be maximized (age for example).

Multivariable analysis techniques (AID and MCA) were employed for the study of two forms of the dependent variable for both physician and dentist utilization: practitioner contact and number of visits. Control variables were introduced to discern the true impact of age, race and education on utilization.

With respect to physicians, it was found that (1) differences in physician contact by age, race or education cannot be attributed entirely to differences in levels of illness or family income, while (2) illness levels do account for variations by age, race or education in the number of visits.

For dentists, a pattern similar to physician utilization was observed: (1) the proportion seeing a dentist by age, race and education was not significantly affected by dental illness level, while (2) the number of visits was affected by illness level and income.

The results suggest that different program strategies should be developed depending on whether policy goals are to either increase contact with practitioners or to increase the total number of visits.

INTRODUCTION

The utilization of health services by individuals can be viewed as a function of three major groups of variables: (1) predisposing variables which are not causes of utilization per se such as age, education or health beliefs which are present prior to the onset of illness and influence whether care is sought; (2) enabling variables which facilitate the seeking of care such as income, health insurance or the availability of health resources to the individual; and (3) an individual's illness level (Andersen 1968; Andersen and Newman 1973). In this chapter three key predisposing variables, age, race, and education are analyzed to determine their effect on utilization.

Age is an important variable since it is physiologically based—younger persons have a lower physiological need for medical care while older persons have a much higher need. Both race and education are social structure variables which denote a person's position in a social system. As such, these variables reflect differences in life styles and values which influence behavior.

If an implied goal of the American health care system is the equitable distribution of health services, then public policy issues with respect to age, race and education are indeed important. In terms of desired goals, some characteristics should be minimized in relation to health services use while others should be maximized.

Thus, an implicit goal of the health care system is to maximize age differences in utilization. That is, services received should be maximized for those persons with the highest level of need, in this case the elderly. On the other hand, it seems reasonable to assume that differences in utilization of services by race and education should be minimized if one believes that medical care should be distributed and utilized according to need rather than social position.

This chapter then is concerned with age, race and education in relation to utilization and social policy issues. Physician and dentist utilization are selected for study because they represent: (1) two major entry points into the health care system; and (2) different levels of insurance coverage throughout the population. Currently, 74 percent of the population is covered either by private insurance, Medicare or CHAMPUS for at least some physician care while approximately 11 percent of the population is covered for dental care.

TRENDS IN UTILIZATION

Trends in utilization by age, race and education are represented below as a means of documenting the baseline data for subsequent analysis. These trends, in addition, give rise to policy related issues which will frame the interpretation of the empirical data in the last section of this chapter.

Overall Trends in Utilization

Cross-sectional survey data has in recent years shown a slight increase in the proportion of the population reporting that they saw a physician within the last year—66 percent in 1958 and 68 percent in 1970 (Andersen et al. 1972:9). There have been large increases in the proportion of the population seeing a dentist—34 percent in 1953 and 45 percent in 1970 (Ibid., p. 23). On the other hand the average number of visits per person-year have actually declined for physician visits and have remained about the same for dentist visits (Ibid., p. 12; Newman and Anderson 1972).

However, cross-sectional data and aggregate measures of utilization can only summarize major trends. Since significant variations in utilization by certain population subgroups are obscured by aggregate data, a close examination of the particular variables is necessary.

Utilization by the Aged

Utilization by the aged, those 65 and older, is of particular concern from a public policy standpoint. Since persons 65 and older are less healthy, experience more disability conditions than the rest of the population and generally have relatively low incomes, attempts to reduce barriers to seeking physician care in the form of Medicare and Medicaid legislation have been devised.

In 1963 the percent of the population 65 and older seeing a physician was 68; by 1970 the percentage had increased to 76. With respect to dentist utilization which was not affected significantly either by large increases in private insurance coverage or by legislation, the proportion of persons 65 and over seeing a dentist increased from 19 to 26 percent (Andersen et al. 1972:9, 23).

However, while the proportion of the elderly who have had contact with a physician has increased, the mean number of physician visits has actually slightly declined from 6.8 in 1963 to 6.4 in 1970, although this age group still has the highest mean number of visits. Utilization of dentists by the aged has changed very little since 1963 (Newman and Anderson 1972). Except for children under six, the aged have the lowest mean number of dental visits according to the survey data upon which this chapter is based.

Utilization by Children and Youths

From a policy perspective, the relative mix and distribution of preventive and symptomatic services should depend on the relative needs of the populations served. Unlike utilization by the aged, utilization by children from birth to five years and among youths six to seventeen presumably reflects a greater use of preventive services. Illness and disability levels are lower for these two groups when compared to the rest of the population and to those 65 and older.

Utilization of physicians by children in 1970 was high: (1) 75 percent had contact with a physician and (2) the mean number of visits was 4.2. In contrast, physician utilization by youths was lower, with 62 percent having a visit and 2.2 being the mean number of visits.

Dentist utilization in 1970 as measured by the proportion with a visit was only 21 percent for children. For youths the percentage increased to 56, which was substantially higher than the 46 percent reported for the population as a whole. The mean number of visits for children was, as might be expected, low, (0.5 visits per person-year) since children under three do not normally see the dentist. For youths, the mean was 1.7.

Of particular interest is the finding that low income children and youths have a substantially lower mean number of physician visits than middle or high income children and youths (Andersen et al. 1972:13). For all other age groups, excluding those 65 and over, income and utilization are inversely related. This leads to the conclusion that variables other than income or age may be important predictors of utilization among low income children and youths. Other enabling variables such as the lack of insurance, the availability of services, or even attitudes and values toward health care by low income persons may be possible explanations.

Utilization by Race

Racial differences in physician and dentist utilization continue to be large with whites having substantially greater contact and a higher volume of use than nonwhites. For physician utilization in 1970, 70 percent of the whites in contrast to 58 percent of the nonwhites saw a physician; whites had an average of 4.1 visits while nonwhites had 3.6 visits on the average (Ibid., p. 12). Differences for dentist utilization are quite large. Thus, 47 percent of the whites but only 24 percent of the nonwhites had a dentist visit in 1970 and the mean number of visits in 1970 was 1.5 for whites compared to 0.8 for nonwhites (Ibid., p. 26).

It has been argued that nonwhites utilize services less than whites because they do not have the resources, income or insurance to obtain care. If this is the case, we would expect utilization by nonwhites to be the same as for whites when both groups are at the same income level. However, data for 1970 indicate that whites have a higher level of physician utilization than nonwhites at all income levels (Ibid., p. 14). These differences increased as income level increased. The same finding is applicable to dentist utilization for the survey period.

Thus, it appears that policy decisions based only on changing income barriers to health care may be only a partial solution if a desired goal is to minimize utilization differences according to race.

Utilization by Educational Level

In the utilization model presented at the beginning of this chapter, education is classed as a predisposing variable. Accordingly, differences in education may predispose individuals to use health services differently due to variations in health knowledge, values or attitudes. Education then would be viewed as a measure of social rather than economic class differences.

If, for example, educational level was found to directly influence utilization, then policy decisions might be directed toward (1) increasing the general educational level of the population or (2) developing preventive health education programs for specific low education subgroups. This latter strategy is based on the assumption that utilization depends in part on preventive attitudes and beliefs which are present in upper but not in lower educational groups.

For physician care there is a direct but weak association between the educational level of the household head and utilization (Wilder 1972: Table 10). For dental care there is a strong, direct association between education and utilization (Newman and Anderson 1972). A partial explanation for the differences between physician and dental care may be that an individual's use of a physician occurs on occasions where illness is viewed as a serious problem. Hence, persons respond in a similar way regardless of education. Dental care on the other hand may be viewed as less serious in nature (Newman and Anderson 1972), so that utilization is highly discretionary and influenced more by attitudes and values. The relation between attitudes and dental use is in fact stronger than that for physician use. For a more complete discussion of this issue the reader is referred to Chapter Five of this volume.

Summary

To summarize, there are differences in utilization by age, race and education for both physician and dentist utilization when each variable is considered separately. This finding is true not only with respect to the percent of the population seeing a physician or dentist but also with respect to mean number of physician or dentist visits.

However, several issues remain unresolved: (1) What levels of physician or dentist contacts by age, race and education are observed when other predisposing variables are included in the analysis? (2) What levels of physician or dentist contacts are observed when predisposing, enabling and illness variables are included? and (3) What is the relative importance of age, race and education in terms of predicting contact when predisposing, enabling and illness variables are included?

These issues are important because of the necessity of developing appropriate strategies according to the mutability of the variables in question. Since age, race and education are low in mutability (Andersen and Newman 1973:116–118), if their effect on utilization is relatively small when other variables are considered, an argument can be made for focusing on these other variables which are more amenable to manipulation. Thus, maximizing utilization by age and minimizing utilization differences by race or education may not be important.

ANALYSIS

Overview

The plan of this analysis is to present data on physician and dentist utilization separately. Similarities and contrasts in findings are discussed at a later point. The analysis involves two stages.

The first stage focuses on predicting whether a practitioner was seen or not. The second stage is directed toward accounting for variations in the number of visits. The analysis is conducted through the use of the Automatic Interaction Detector (AID) program developed by Sonquist and Morgan (1964).

AID is a multivariate technique which combines elements of regression analysis and analysis of variance. The program operates in a stepwise manner to reduce the unexplained sum of squares for the independent variables. This results in selecting the "best" dichotomous independent variable in each step of the analysis.

Variables

The physician contact and visit variables are based on respondent reports and verified by attending physicians and hospitals. For the analysis of number of visits, inpatient hospital visits were excluded. Both analyses of dentist use will be based on respondent reports only.

Predisposing variables from the social survey are: (1) the individual's sex and age; (2) the individual's race and the education level of the head of the household for each person (social structure variables); (3) the belief variables defined in four scales—value of physicians, value of health services, knowledge about health and reaction to symptoms.

The two scales, value of health services and value of physicians, and the knowledge variables are equivalent to Andersen's (1968) measures developed to predict family utilization patterns. The construction of the four belief variables was based on assigning the head of the household's responses to every member of the household. If the head had no response, the response of the head's spouse was assigned to every member [1].

Enabling variables used in the analyses were (1) total family income, (2) employment status of the head of the household and (3) the presence or absence of insurance coverage of the individual. Both income and employment status were from the social survey while insurance coverage is a best estimate variable.

The illness level variables for physician utilization were (1) the number of disability days reported by the individual and (2) symptom severity which is the weighted sum of the individual's reported symptoms [2]. For dentists two symptom measures were used: toothache and sore or bleeding gums.

Percent Seeing a Physician

In this stage of the analysis the focus is on whether or not a person saw a physician in 1970. As shown in Table 3-1, when only predisposing variables were used, the proportion of the variance explained, R^2, was 2.5 percent as compared to 11 percent when all variables (predisposing, enabling, illness) in the model were included as predictors. Looking only at the predisposing variables, it is clear that the demographic and social structure variables are more important predictors of care than the four belief variables.

When all potential variables are used in the analyses, disability days and symptom severity are the two most important variables. Of the predisposing variables, only education is important.

Figures 3-1 and 3-2 were produced as part of the AID analysis, indicating the interaction between the predictor variables. The analysis for the predisposing

Table 3–1. **Relative Importance** *(R²)* **of Variables in Predicting (1) the Percent Seeing a Physician and (2) the Number of Physician Visits**

Variables	Percent seeing a physician		Number of visits
	Predisposing variables	*All variables*	
Predisposing			
Age	0.016		0.019
Sex			
Race			
Education of head	0.009	0.006	
Value of health services			
Value of physicians			
Reaction to symptoms			
Health knowledge			
Enabling			
Income	–		
Insurance	–		
Employment status of head	–		
Illness			
Disability days	–	0.070	0.057
Symptoms severity	–	0.033	0.014
R^2	0.025	0.109	0.090

– not included in the analysis.

Figure 3–1. Analysis of the Percent Seeing a Physician: Predisposing Variables

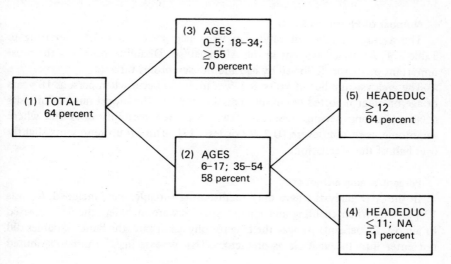

Figure 3–2. Analysis of the Percent Seeing a Physician: All Variables

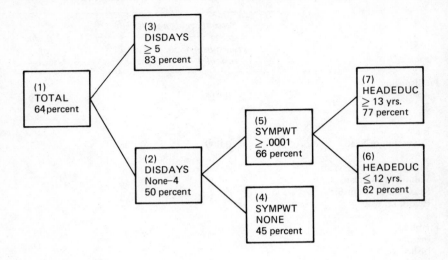

variables, Figure 3–1, indicates that the highest level of utilization (70 percent) occurred for children from birth to age five and adults 18 to 34 and 55 and older. Utilization was lowest (51 percent) for persons aged 6 to 17 and 35 to 54 in households where the head had not graduated from high school.

Considering all variables, as is done in Figure 3–2, the percent seeing a physician was highest, 83 percent, when persons reported five or more disability days. In contrast, utilization was lowest, 45 percent, where no symptoms were reported and where disability days ranged from none to four.

Number of Physician Visits

The average number of physician visits per person was 3.4. Referring to Table 3–1, R^2 was 9 percent in the AID analysis. Disability days was the most important predictor, followed by age and the symptoms variable.

The greatest number of visits, 8.7, was found to occur when persons 18 years of age or older reported ten or more disability days. The lowest number of visits occurred among persons reporting fewer than ten disability days and where symptoms were not severe (0.7199 or less) [3]. This group represents slightly over half of the population.

Percent Seeing a Dentist

In the AID analysis where only predisposing variables were included, R^2 was 12 percent. When enabling and illness variables were included, the R^2 increased to almost 17 percent. As was the case for physician care, the belief variables did not enter into the analysis as predictors. The increase in R^2 can be attributed

Figure 3–3. Analysis of the Number of Physician Visits: All Variables

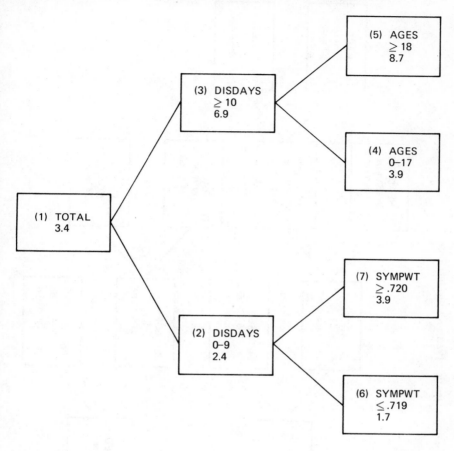

entirely to the effect of the illness variable, toothache. Education of the head still appears to account for a larger proportion of the variance than toothache, however.

For the predisposing variables, as shown in Figure 3–4 the highest level of utilization, 77 percent, occurs for persons between the ages of 6 and 64 in families where the head of the household is a college graduate. Utilization is lowest among persons from one to five and those 55 and older in families where the head did not graduate from high school.

Differences by race are substantial. Even when education is relatively high (12 to 15 years, group 6) only 27 percent of the nonwhites have made a dentist visit compared to 57 percent for whites. This percent is only slightly greater than the 24 percent figure reported by nonwhites where heads of households have less than 12 years of education (group 8).

Figure 3-4. Analysis of the Percent Seeing a Dentist: Predisposing Variables

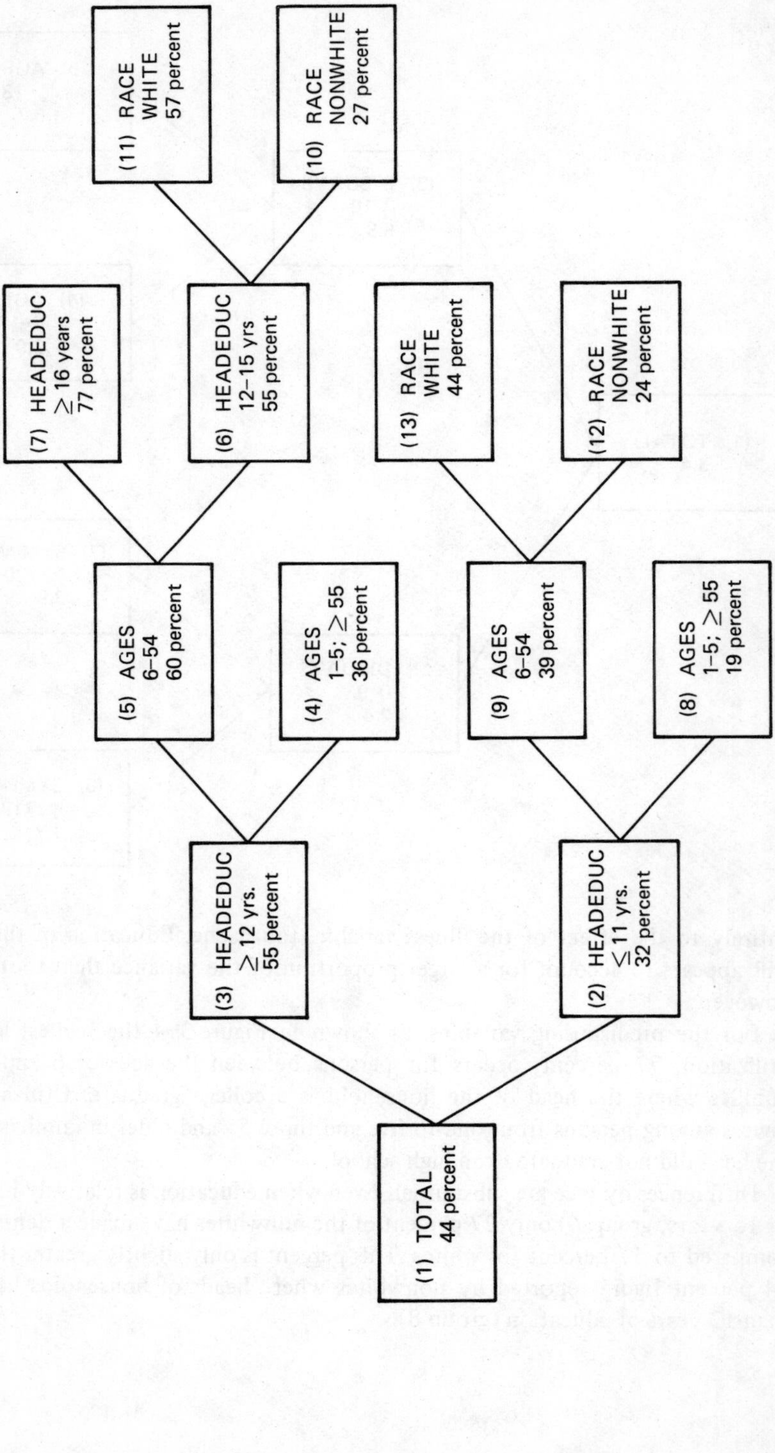

(1) TOTAL
44 percent

(2) HEADEDUC
≤ 11 yrs.
32 percent

(3) HEADEDUC
≥ 12 yrs.
55 percent

(4) AGES
1-5; ≥ 55
36 percent

(5) AGES
6-54
60 percent

(6) HEADEDUC
12-15 yrs
55 percent

(7) HEADEDUC
≥ 16 years
77 percent

(8) AGES
1-5; ≥ 55
19 percent

(9) AGES
6-54
39 percent

(10) RACE
NONWHITE
27 percent

(11) RACE
WHITE
57 percent

(12) RACE
NONWHITE
24 percent

(13) RACE
WHITE
44 percent

The effect of the dental symptom, toothache, on utilization is depicted in Figure 3–5. In this instance, the highest proportion of persons seeing a dentist, 77 percent, is found among those reporting the symptom. However, utilization is almost as high for another group. This includes people from homes headed by college graduates less than 55 years of age. In this group, fully 75 percent had seen a dentist. The lowest utilization, 16 percent, was found among children one to five years and adults 55 and older when the head had not graduated from high school. As was the case for physician use in Figure 3–4, low levels of utilization were evident for nonwhites (groups 12 and 14) regardless of the educational level of the head of the household.

Number of Dentist Visits

As shown in Table 3–2 the proportion of the variance explained for number of dentist visits was approximately 6 percent. The most important predictors in descending order were toothache, family income, age and education of household head.

The AID diagram on number of visits indicates that the average number of

Table 3–2. Relative Importance (R^2) of Variables in Predicting (1) the Percent Seeing a Dentist and (2) the Number of Dentist Visits

	Percent seeing a dentist		Number of visits
Variables	*Predisposing variables*	*All variables*	
Predisposing			
Age	0.038	0.033	0.008
Sex			
Race	0.017	0.019	
Education of head	0.065	0.064	0.006
Value of health services			
Value of physicians			
Reaction to symptoms			
Health knowledge			
Enabling			
Income	—		0.019
Insurance	—		
Employment status of head	—		
Illness			
Disability days	—		
Toothache	—	0.052	0.031
Bleeding gums	—		
R^2	0.120	0.168	0.064

— not included in the analysis.

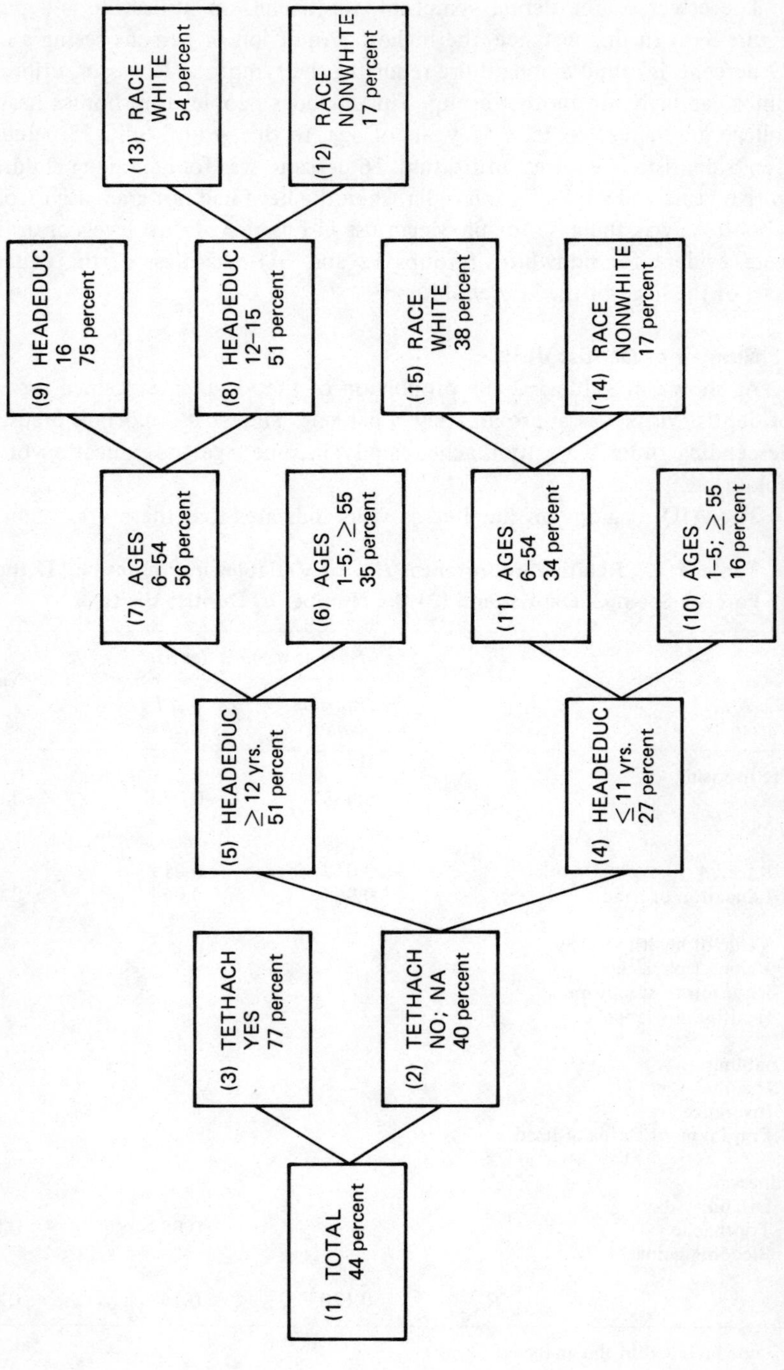

Figure 3-5. Analysis of the Percent Seeing a Dentist: All Variables

visits per person was 1.4. The presence of a toothache results in the highest mean number of visits, 2.8. In the absence of a toothache, the highest number of visits per person, 2.3, occurred for persons six years of age and older where family income was $11,000 or more and educational level was relatively high. The average number of visits was only 0.9 when a toothache was not reported and where the family income was less than $11,000.

EXTENDED ANALYSIS

The preceding analysis found for both the percent seeing a physician and the percent seeing a dentist that educational level of household head and age were the two major predictors to emerge when all the predisposing variables were included. In addition, for the dentist analysis, race emerged as a predictor. It seems, therefore, that other predisposing variables and particularly those relating to attitudes and beliefs are not significantly related to seeing a physician or a dentist for all care considered as a whole [4].

Subsequent analysis in which enabling and illness variables were included along with the predisposing variables indicated that the illness measures were the most important predictors both for seeing a physician and seeing a dentist. For the physician analysis, education level of household head was the only nonillness predictor. In the dentist analysis, age, race and education of household head were nonillness predictors.

Similarly, the analysis of the number of visits revealed that the illness measures were the most important predictors. Age was the only nonillness predictor for physician visits, while for dentist visits age, education and family income were predictors.

Although the AID analysis identifies the pattern of interaction among a set of variables meeting the criteria for inclusion in the analysis, it does have some limitations. For example, the procedure for determining the "best" binary split depends on the percentage reduction of the unexplained sum of squares. Thus, if two variables with almost identical percentages emerge, the one with the higher percentage will be included, reducing the other variable's probability of being included at a subsequent step. In addition, AID does not allow for detailed analysis of variables and category values for variables.

The AID program has identified the potential predictors for each of the analyses shown in Tables 3–1 and 3–2. For subsequent analysis the Multiple Classification Analysis (MCA) program will be used (Andrews et al. 1973). More specifically, the MCA analysis will help to answer the question of how the other predictor variables identified in the separate analyses influence the percent seeing a practitioner or the number of visits by age, education and race.

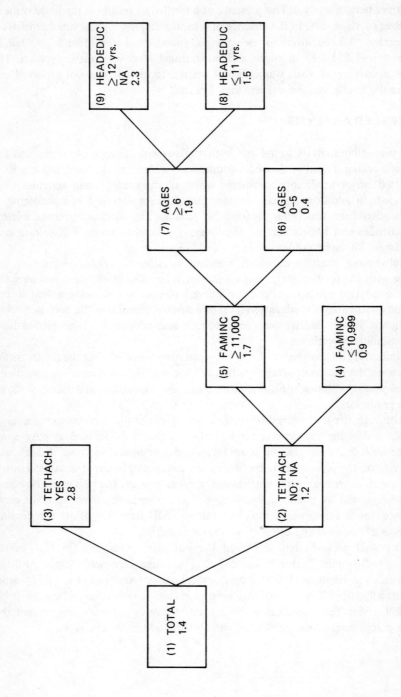

Figure 3–6. Analysis of the Number of Dentist Visits: All Variables

**Percent Seeing a Physician and Number
of Physician Visits**

Disability days and symptoms severity, because they are predictors of the
percent seeing a physician and the number of physician visits (Table 3–1), are
used as control variables in separate analyses for (1) age, (2) education and
(3) race.

The results for the percent seeing a physician are presented in Table 3–3.
Disability days and symptoms severity have relatively little impact on the effects
of age or education on seeing a physician. The same is true for whites, but
adjusting for the effects of disability days and symptoms severity increases the
likelihood of seeing a physician for nonwhites.

While the two variables had only minimal influence on the percent seeing a
physician, considerably greater variation was observed for the number of physician visits. Specifically, increases of 0.52 and 0.60 of a visit were found for ages
0 to 5 and 6 to 17 respectively (Table 3–4). Conversely a substantial decrease in
visits occurred for those 55 to 64 (0.92 visits decrease) and those 65 and over
(1.11 visits decrease) when disability days and symptoms severity were taken
into account.

**Table 3–3. The Percent Seeing a Physician by (a) Age, (b) Education of Head
of Household and (c) Race: (1) Unadjusted Percentages, (2) Adjusted for Disability Days and Symptoms Severity**

Variable	Unadjusted (percent)	Adjusted (percent)
Total population–65 (percent)		
Age		
0– 5	72	74
6–17	57	59
18–34	69	69
35–54	63	60
55–64	70	67
65 and over	73	74
Education of head		
Less than 7 years	58	57
7–8	59	60
9–11	61	62
12	67	66
13–15	71	68
16 and over	74	76
Race		
White	67	66
Nonwhite	53	59

Table 3–4. The Number of Physician Visits by (a) Age, (b) Education of Head of Household and (c) Race: (1) Unadjusted Visits, (2) Adjusted for Disability Days and Symptom Severity

Variable	Unadjusted	Adjusted
Total population—3.4 visits		
Age		
1–15	3.13	3.65
6–17	1.68	2.28
18–34	4.07	4.25
35–54	3.25	3.16
55–64	5.09	4.18
65 and over	5.29	4.18
Education of head		
Less than 7 years	3.72	2.95
7–8	3.23	2.98
9–11	3.13	3.17
12	3.29	3.40
13–15	4.06	2.79
16 and over	4.69	2.67
Race		
White	3.52	3.49
Nonwhite	2.75	2.98

With respect to education, the adjusted visits were considerably lower for all categories except families whose head had attended or graduated from high school, where slightly higher values were observed. While values for whites showed little change, the mean number of visits by nonwhites increased by 0.24 visits.

Thus it seems that the two illness variables account for a considerable amount of the initial relationship between age and visits and education and visits. In terms of race, the illness variables account for increases in visits by nonwhites but not for whites.

Percent Seeing a Dentist and Number of Dentist Visits

According to the findings in Table 3–2, the dental illness measure, toothache, appeared to be the most important variable in predicting whether a dentist was seen. However, as shown in Table 3–5, the presence or absence of a toothache makes virtually no difference in the effects of age, education and race on seeing a dentist. A small increase of 3 percent between unadjusted and adjusted percentages did occur for children ages one to five.

On the other hand, for the number of dentist visits, toothache and family income were stronger predictors. Examining toothache and income in relation to

Table 3–5. The Percent Seeing a Dentist by (a) Age, (b) Education of Head of Household and (c) Race: (1) Unadjusted Percentages, (2) Adjusted for Toothache

Variables	Unadjusted (percent)	Adjusted (percent)
Total population–45 (percent)		
Age		
1–5	21	24
6–17	57	56
18–34	52	51
35–54	47	46
55–64	34	35
65 and over	26	27
Education of head		
Less than 7 years	25	25
7–8	29	29
9–11	39	38
12	49	49
13–15	53	54
16 and over	70	71
Race		
White	48	48
Nonwhite	24	22

age, the number of visits was reduced by 0.5 for persons 65 and older between the unadjusted and adjusted values (Table 3–6). Small increases were observed for ages one to five and 55 to 64 while small decreases occurred for persons 6 to 54.

With respect to education, visits (adjusted for toothache and family income) increased 0.24 for levels of education less than seven years and decreased by 0.26 visits where education was 16 years or greater. The number of visits by nonwhites increased by 0.14 visits while for whites there was a decrease of 0.02 visits.

SUMMARY

The differences in the proportion of the population seeing a physician according to age, educational or racial categories cannot be attributed to differences in levels of illness, i.e., disability days or symptoms severity. The overall effect of controlling these variables is relatively small, indicating that age, race and education exert an independent effect on the percent of the population seeing a physician.

The number of physician visits by age, education or race, however, are signifi-

Table 3–6.   The Number of Dentist Visits by (a) Age, (b) Education of Head of Household and (c) Race: (1) Unadjusted Visits, (2) Adjusted for Toothache and Family Income

Variable	Unadjusted	Adjusted
Total population–1.4 visits		
Age		
1–5	0.46	0.56
6–17	1.75	1.68
18–34	1.64	1.54
35–54	1.60	1.46
55–64	1.13	1.26
65 and over	1.83	1.28
Education of head		
Less than 7 years	0.81	1.08
7–8	0.94	1.07
9–11	1.35	1.27
12	1.43	1.42
13–15	1.79	1.71
16 and over	2.07	1.81
Race		
White	1.48	1.46
Nonwhite	0.79	0.93

cantly affected by introducing disability days and symptoms severity into the analysis. Based on Table 3–4, there was a substantial shift in mean number of visits for most of the variable categories, notably in the higher age and educational groups. As a result of adjusting category values, differences within age, educational and racial categories became less pronounced, indicating that the effect of disability days and symptoms severity accounts in large part for variations in utilization.

In the analysis of the percent of the population seeing a dentist, it was found that the illness variable, toothache, had no impact on the three predisposing variables. However, the AID analysis, Figure 3–5, did reveal that high utilization occurs both when a symptom is present and through the interaction of the three predisposing variables when no symptom is present. Apparently, various combinations of age, education and race contribute significantly to whether a dentist is seen or not.

With respect to the number of dental visits, the combined influence of family income and the presence or absence of a toothache reduced the variation in the mean number of visits between categories for the three predisposing variables. This implies that the effects of income and toothache on visits accounts in part, but not entirely, for the observed unadjusted differences by age, education and race.

From a policy perspective, it is not clear how utilization can be maximized according to age or minimized according to education or race. The traditional strategy of educational appeals through the mass media may be ineffective (see Chapter Five). Further, with respect to those population subgroups who are low users of health care services, as identified by specific age, racial or educational categories, it is by no means clear that everyone in those groups should have higher levels of utilization (the discussion of equity in Chapter Two addresses this issue). We may wish to reduce utilization for some categories—for example, those with no symptoms—to a minimal preventive level in order to redirect the delivery of services. In any event, strategies would have to be developed to reach the appropriate target population within the subgroups.

For dental care, it seems obvious that not seeking care indicates a lack of dental symptoms as well as the influence of age, race and education as depicted in Figure 3—5. Inasmuch as dental problems are not viewed as serious by the American public (Newman and Anderson 1972), traditional methods of mass public education through schools or the media will probably not be effective here either.

It seems evident that illness levels are associated directly with more dentist. visits independent of the effects of age, education or race. Hence, attention should be given to identifying population subgroups with high levels of illness and lower than expected levels of utilization. Current work in the direction of identifying illness levels has been undertaken by Kessner (1973). It may be that broad based health intervention programs would initially be effective. However, some means of maintaining contact with the health care system would need to be implemented. Whatever the public policy goals, it is clear that refinement of intervention approaches are necessary due to the complexity of factors which influence utilization.

NOTES TO CHAPTER THREE

1. Coefficients of reproducibility were 0.86 and 0.84 for the health services and physician scales respectively using Guttman Scale Analysis. A low score on the value of health services and value of physicians scales represented little belief in health services or physicians. Low scores on the knowledge scale indicated minimal health knowledge and on the symptoms scale low scores meant a tendency to seek care immediately.

2. Weights for each of the 20 symptoms were assigned by a panel of physicians separately for five age groups. The symptom severity index for each individual is calculated by summing the weights of the reported symptoms. See Appendix, variable 44 for further explanation.

3. The seven categories for symptom severity are: (1) none; (2) 0.001 through 0.4399; (3) 0.4400 through 0.7199; (4) 0.7200 through 1.0399; (5) 1.0400 through 1.6899; (6) 1.6900 through 2.7499; (7) 2.7500 through 11.6699. The meaning of these units is given in the Appendix, variable 44.

4. It should be noted, however, that the belief variables were oriented to physicians rather than dentists. Until equivalent dentist measures are developed and tested, the issue remains unresolved.

Chapter Four

Physician Utilization and Family Size

*Judith Kasper**

Previous research suggests a relationship between physician use and family size with persons in large families having lower levels of use than persons in small families. The influence of family size on fact of physician contact and mean number of visits was evaluated for both adults and children, controlling for regular source of care, disability days, perception of health and worry about health. The effects of family size on adults' physician use was negligible. For children, however, family size influenced likelihood of seeing a physician and to a lesser degree mean number of visits. Children in large families became even less likely to see a physician if they were also low income, rural or inner city residents, or 13 to 17 years of age. This analysis suggests that children living in large families are subject to inequity in use of physician services which changing financing mechanisms alone may be unable to eliminate.

Among the variables which may predispose individuals to seek medical care is family size. Analyses of utilization which have included it, such as Andersen's in Chapter Two of this volume, generally suggest that persons in large families are less likely to see a physician than those in small families. It is not clear, however, how much of the influence of family size on physician use is attributable to intercorrelations with variables such as income, race and residence. Previous research, which will be discussed in more detail, suggests that family size may be a more important element in children's physician use than adults'. The purpose of this chapter is to evaluate the influence of family size on both physician contact and volume of visits for adults and children in relation to other predisposing and enabling components of use.

*I wish to thank Ron Andersen, Lu Ann Aday and Gretchen Fleming for their careful reading of and comments on this paper.

PREVIOUS RESEARCH

Studies of the family have a long history in sociological research and an interest in family size has figured in many of them. Although modern researchers of the family evidence more concern for the determinants of family size, there is still a considerable body of information about the consequences of size on other aspects of family life. Bossard and Boll (1945; 1956, 1960) were among the early researchers who pointed out differences between children in small versus large families. Their depiction of the small family suggests that these children receive more individual attention, and more planning for their education and careers, and that interaction in such families tends to be more democratic and cooperative. In large families, on the other hand, there is more emphasis on the needs of the group than those of individuals, conformity to family decisions is valued, and organization of tasks and abstract rules of behavior are more common.

One might speculate from these types of findings that differences in family size which mean more parental attention for some children than others and varying degrees of flexibility in family routine would have consequences for the health behavior of family members. In fact, studies of health utilization behavior have reported differences in physician use by family size. The National Health Survey of 1963–64 showed physician visits per person per year in two person families was 5.7, in contrast with a family of five or more who reported a little less than four visits per person (NCHS 1969: series 10, no. 55). Ronald Andersen (1968) found in his study of families' use of health services that next to need, family composition variables (age of head, sex of head, marital status of head, family size) had the highest correlation with use. The best single predictor of physician use among these variables was family size. Although large families used more care than smaller ones, the amount of care received by each family member decreased as size of family increased. Similar findings are reported in a comparative study of the Swedish and American health systems:

> in each country young persons living in smaller families are more likely to
> see a doctor than those living in larger families. Family size . . . is found to
> be a very important predictor of who will see a doctor among those under
> 21 (Andersen, Smedby, and Anderson 1970:98).

This finding persists despite the differences in organization and delivery of services between these two countries. More recently, Andersen and Kasper (1973) investigated the relationship between family size and whether children saw a physician during the year. The inverse relationship between seeing a physician and family size was not substantially reduced by controlling separately for poverty level (above or below), residence or race.

Many of the results just mentioned focus on the experience of children or of all family members considered together. Evidence concerning the influence of family size on the utilization of adult family members appears less clear. Two studies (Robertson et al. 1967; Hare and Shaw 1965) indicated that increasing family size raises the likelihood of parents seeing a physician possibly due to the strain of managing a large family. Generally, however, there are fewer indications that family size is an important indicator of adult physician utilization.

What these studies tell us is that there seems to be an inverse relationship between children's use of physicians and their family size, although it is not clear whether this relationship would disappear if other variables associated with family size were controlled. Whether family size influences adult physician utilization and whether it influences adult use as it does children's use is also unresolved. The findings presented in the next section will address both of these issues.

DATA AND VARIABLE DESCRIPTIONS

Physicians are usually the first point of contact with a health care system and a considerable amount of discretion exists with regard to the decision to contact a doctor (Andersen 1968; and Chapter Two). Whether or not a person saw a physician during the survey year is meant to distinguish those who had some contact with the health care system from those who had none. Volume of visits, on the other hand, differentiates among those who have gained access to the system (persons with no visits are excluded). Expressed as mean number of visits, this variable compares heavy users of physician services with those who had only one or two visits per year. The discussion in Chapter Two suggests that family size might be a more important determinant of physician contact than of volume of visits, since decisions about return visits involve the physician and therefore are less discretionary.

The data used in this analysis are from the 1970 national health survey conducted by the Center for Health Administration Studies and National Opinion Research Center. The mode of analysis is MCA (Multiple Classification Analysis). Since both the survey and this analytic technique are described in Chapters One and Two of this volume, they will not be discussed here. The dependent variables in this analysis, physician contact and volume of visits, are discussed above. In addition to family size, four other independent variables are presented in the tables—family income, residence, age and race [1]. Income, race and residence were chosen because it was thought that effects of family size might be explained if large families are primarily low income, nonwhite, or rural and inner city dwellers. These are also three of the population subgroups for which there is a great deal of concern regarding the equity of their utilization patterns (see Chapter Two). Age was included since young children have higher rates of use than older children (NCHS 1971: series 10, no. 62) and family size might affect these age groups differently. In addition, the age of adults is one indication of stages in the family life cycle and might be expected to be associated with family size [2]. Four covariates or control variables are included in each of the tables as well; these are regular source of care, perception of health, worry about health and disability days. Perception of health and worry about health are perceived measures of health status, while disability days is a clinical measure (these distinctions are made by Newman, see Chapter Nine). By controlling these variables, the differences in physician use by family size which are attributable to need or differences in illness levels can be removed. Similarly, persons with a regular source of medical care are more likely to see a physician, so it was desirable to control for differences in regular source of care by family size. The physician utilization behavior of adults and children was analyzed separately on the basis of previous studies which indicated that the effects of family size might be quite different for these two groups. The results of these analyses follow.

FINDINGS

Tables 4–1 and 4–2 show the percent of children and adults, respectively, who saw a physician during the year by family size and the other independent variables. There seems to be little relationship between physician contact and family size for adults. In fact, the variables which contribute most to explaining why adults see a physician are those which measure need and regular source of care (R^2 or variance explained increases from 0.01 to 0.166 with the introduction of these variables). For children, however, family size, income and age appear to influence whether they see a physician regardless of need and regular source of care. The independent variables account for about half of the total variance explained (0.087 of 0.171). Adjusting for the covariates and other independent variables, 78 percent of the children in small families see a physician during the year, compared to 67 percent in medium sized families and 59 percent in large families.

In examining volume of physician visits among children and adults who had one or more physician visits, family size is a weaker predictor of the mean number of physician visits (Tables 4–3 and 4–4, respectively). Almost all of the total variance explained (0.130 for children and 0.137 for adults) is attributable to differences in need and regular source of care rather than the independent variables.

Findings from Tables 4–1 through 4–4 indicate that family size has little impact on either physician contact or volume of visits for the adult population. For children, the correlation between mean number of physician visits and family size is low (0.09) when other independent variables and covariates are controlled. Family size, though, appears to have more influence (Beta = 0.12) on whether children have physician contact, even when need, regular source of care, income, residence, age and race are controlled.

Table 4–1. Percent of Children Seeing a Physician During the Year

	Unadjusted percentage	Eta[a]	Percentage adjusted for independents	Beta	Percentage adjusted for independents and covariates[b]	Beta
Total population—65 (percent)						
Family size						
Small	82		83		78	
Medium	69		68		67	
Large	55	0.19	56	0.18	59	0.12
Family income						
Low	50		52		56	
Medium	62		62		61	
High	73	0.17	73	0.16	71	0.13
Residence						
Rural	62		62		63	
Inner city	60		64		64	
Other urban	72	0.11	69	0.06	67	0.04
Age						
1–5	75		73		74	
6–12	64		66		64	
13–17	58	0.13	58	0.12	59	0.11
Race						
White	67		66		65	
Nonwhite	51	0.12	59	0.05	63	0.02
R^2				0.087		0.171

[a]Eta is the zero order correlation between the independent and dependent variable, while the betas are the correlations once control variables have been introduced.
[b]For all six tables, the covariates are regular source of care, worry about health, perception of health and disability days.

Table 4–2.   Percent of Adults Seeing a Physician During the Year

	Unadjusted percentage	Eta	Percentage adjusted for independents	Beta	Percentage adjusted for independents and covariates	Beta
Total population—69 (percent)						
Family size						
Small	71		71		71	
Medium	70		70		68	
Large	61	0.07	62	0.06	63	0.06
Family income						
Low	68		67		64	
Medium	69		69		68	
High	69	0.01	70	0.02	71	0.05
Residence						
Rural	68		68		69	
Inner city	67		67		67	
Other urban	71	0.04	71	0.03	70	0.03
Age						
18–34	70		70		72	
35–54	66		67		66	
55–64	73	0.05	72	0.04	68	0.06
Race						
White	70		70		69	
Nonwhite	62	0.05	64	0.04	66	0.02
R^2				0.010		0.166

Table 4–3. Mean Number of Physician Visits for Children

	Unadjusted visits	Eta	Visits adjusted for independents	Beta	Visits adjusted for independents and covariates	Beta
Total population—3.8						
Family size						
Small	5.2		5.1		5.0	
Medium	4.0		4.0		3.9	
Large	3.0	0.13	3.2	0.11	3.4	0.09
Income						
Low	3.6		3.6		3.3	
Medium	4.0		4.0		3.9	
High	3.7	0.03	3.8	0.02	4.0	0.03
Residence						
Rural	3.4		3.3		3.4	
Inner city	3.8		4.0		4.0	
Other urban	4.2	0.07	4.2	0.06	4.1	0.05
Age						
1–5	4.8		4.7		4.9	
6–12	3.6		3.7		3.6	
13–17	3.2	0.11	3.2	0.10	3.2	0.12
Race						
White	3.9		3.9		3.9	
Nonwhite	3.2	0.04	3.3	0.03	3.4	0.03
R^2				0.031		0.130

Table 4-4. Mean Number of Physician Visits for Adults

	Unadjusted visits	Eta	Visits adjusted for independents	Beta	Visits adjusted for independents and covariates	Beta
Total population—6.0						
Family size						
Small	6.8		3.4		6.6	
Medium	5.0		5.5		5.3	
Large	5.3	0.09	5.8	0.04	5.4	0.07
Family income						
Low	8.2		7.5		5.8	
Medium	5.9		6.0		5.9	
High	5.4	0.09	5.6	0.07	6.2	0.02
Residence						
Rural	5.4		5.3		5.5	
Inner city	7.3		7.2		6.8	
Other urban	5.6	0.09	5.8	0.08	5.9	0.06
Age						
18–34	5.2		5.3		6.0	
35–54	5.8		6.0		5.8	
55–64	8.3	0.11	7.8	0.09	6.8	0.04
Race						
White	5.9		6.0		6.0	
Nonwhite	6.9	0.03	6.1	0.00	6.0	0.00
R^2				0.027		0.137

The effects of family size are difficult to sort out not only because of possible intercorrelations with other independent variables affecting physician use (a problem which MCA handles by allowing us to look at the effects of a variable first by itself, then adjusted or controlling for other independent variables and covariates) but because of possible interactions with these other variables. In other words, the effects of family size may be different within categories of variables such as income or race. Perhaps large family size inhibits physician contact more seriously when combined with low income as opposed to high income, for instance. Tables 4–5 and 4–6 show the effects, combining family size with each of the other four independent variables, on physician use by children.

Combining income with family size, we find that the largest discrepancy in physician contact by family size is within middle income families (Table 4–5). Controlling for need, regular source of care and the other three independent variables (race, residence and age) only a 9 percent difference separates large and small families in the high income group. For low income families, the gap increases to 17 percent, while for medium income families there is a 29 percent difference between children in small families, 81 percent of whom saw a physician, compared to 52 percent in large families who saw a doctor. Children in large, low income families were least likely to see a physician (48 percent) followed by children in large, medium income families (52 percent). By comparing Table 4–1 to Table 4–5, we see the independent effects of the variables versus their combined effects. Fifty-nine percent of children in large families saw a physician, 56 percent of those in low income families saw a doctor (Table 4–1); while only 48 percent in large, low income families had physician contact during the year (Table 4–5). Similarly, the percentage drops to 52 percent for middle income children in large families (Table 4–5), compared to 61 percent for income considered alone and 59 percent for large families regardless of income. Using the combined variable, rather than income and family size separately, increased the amount of variance explained from 0.171 to 0.175 (the amount explained by the independent variables increases from 0.087 to 0.094); the correlation between family size combined with income and physician contact was 0.18 compared to 0.12 for family size alone and 0.13 for income (Table 4–1).

The combined effects of family size and residence indicate that family size differences in seeing a physician are greatest for those in the inner city (24 percent difference between small and large families), followed by rural (17 percent) and then other urban residents (15 percent). Seventy-nine percent of children in small, inner city families saw a doctor compared to 55 percent in large families. Children in large, inner city families were least likely to see a physician, followed by children in large rural families (57 percent). Tables 4–1 and 4–5 show being in a large rural family compares less favorably with the effects of large families or rural residence alone (59 percent and 63 percent

Table 4–5. Percent of Children Seeing a Physician During the Year by Family Size Combined with Income, Residence, Age, and Race*

	Unadjusted percentage	Eta	Percentage adjusted for independents	Beta	Percentage adjusted for independents and covariates	Beta
Income and family size						
Low						
small family	62		65		65	
medium family	57		59		61	
large family	38		42		48	
Medium						
small family	91		89		81	
medium family	66		65		64	
large family	48		49		52	
High						
small family	85		83		79	
medium family	75		74		71	
large family	68	0.27	68	0.24	70	0.18
R^2				0.094		0.175
Residence and family size						
Rural						
small family	75		76		74	
medium family	67		66		66	
large family	53		53		57	
Inner city						
small family	80		85		79	
medium family	70		72		70	
large family	48		50		55	
Other urban						
small family	89		88		81	
medium family	61		68		66	
large family	67	0.22	66	0.21	67	0.15
R^2				0.095		0.174

	(1)	(2)	(3)	(4)
Age and family size				
1–5				
small family	90	90		85
medium	78	78		77
large	63	64		66
6–12				
small family	81	85		80
medium family	73	71		68
large family	52	53		56
13–17				
small family	74	76		72
medium family	57	55		56
large family	55	55		59
R^2	0.23	0.23	0.094	0.18
				0.175
Race and family size				
White				
small family	84	85		79
medium family	71	69		67
large family	58	57		60
Nonwhite				
small family	63	71		73
medium family	55	62		65
large family	46	51		58
R^2	0.21	0.19	0.088	0.12
				0.171

*Each of these four combined variables was entered in a separate MCA analysis with the remaining three independents and regular source of care, perception of health, worry and disability days as covariates. For example, family income and family size were analyzed with age, race, residence and the covariates. Age and family size were analyzed with race, residence and income, plus the covariates. Only the combined variables are presented here, since the other independent variables in each procedure were unaffected by combining two variables.

respectively see a doctor). The percentage seeing a physician for inner city children is 64 percent (Table 4–1), but for those in large inner city families, 55 percent (Table 4–5). Interestingly, the effects of other urban residence and a large family are no worse than simply being other urban (67 percent). However, 81 percent of the children in small other urban families saw a physician compared to independent effects which showed 78 percent of those in small families saw a doctor and 67 percent of children living in other urban areas had physician contact (Table 4–1).

Age plus family size shows that family size makes the most difference in whether six to twelve year old children see a physician, with 80 percent of children in small families seeing a doctor when need, regular source of care and other independent variables are controlled, and only 56 percent in large families. Young children one to five years are most likely to see a physician when compared with their counterparts in large, medium and small families, but 85 percent of these young children see a physician if their families are small in contrast to 66 percent for those in large families. Table 4–1 indicates 78 percent of those in small families regardless of age and 74 percent of the one to five year olds independent of family size see a physician. In Table 4–5, the combined effects of family size and young age mean 85 percent of one to five year olds see a physician. The combination of race and family size appears to add less to the data presented in Table 4–1. The difference between small and large families' physician contacts is only slightly higher for whites (19 percent versus 15 percent for nonwhites). Sixty percent of children in large white families saw a physician, compared to 58 percent in large nonwhite families.

Table 4–6 shows the combined effects of family size and the other four independent variables on mean number of physician visits for children. Results were similar to those reported for Table 4–5 although not as striking. The combination of low income and large family meant 3.1 mean visits for children, compared to 3.4 for the effect of large family and 3.3 for low income considered separately (Table 4–3). The number of visits for high income children in small families was 5.4, inflated above the 5.0 average for small family children and 4.0 average for high income (Table 4–3). Two visits separated children from small versus those from large families with high incomes, while the difference for low and medium income families was 1.2 visits. (The larger difference for high income children results from the considerably higher number of mean visits for small family, high income children).

Table 4–6 shows less than a one visit difference between children in large and small families who lived in "other urban" areas. Children in large families with rural or inner city residences, however, averaged approximately two visits less than children from small families who lived in these areas. The combination of rural residence and a large family meant 2.8 average visits for children, compared to 3.4 average visits for the effects of family size and rural residence separately (Table 4–3). Two and one-half visits separated one to five year olds in small families from those in large families, but the difference was less than a visit for six to twelve year olds and 1.4 visits for older children 13 to 17. Like children in high income, small families, one to five year olds in small families have an average of 6.6 visits, much higher than other groups. (This figure also exceeds the five average visits reported for small families and 4.9 for younger children in Table 4–3). While nonwhites had fewer average visits when compared with whites by family size, the difference between large and small families for both white and nonwhite children was approximately the same (1.5 and 1.6 visits respectively).

One other point can be made with regard to these tables. Differences in physician use by family size are not necessarily "inequitable" if they are linked to need (Chapter Two). Although we have tried to control for differences in need, another way to evaluate levels of use is by comparing them to the mean. The mean percent of children seeing a physician is 65 percent (Table 4–1), so, for instance, the fact that only 70 percent of the children in large, high income families saw a physician compared with 79 percent in small families does not seem a serious maldistribution of services. Similarly, 67 percent of the children in large, other urban families saw a physician, much lower than the 81 percent in small families but still above the population mean. On the other hand, the interaction effects in Table 4–5 indicate that for large, low and middle income families; large, rural and inner city families; large families with children aged 6 to 17; and both white and nonwhite large families, the percent of children seeing a physician ranged from 5 percent to 17 percent below the mean. The same test may be applied to Table 4–6 with similar results. Large nonwhite and large rural families are both slightly over a visit below the population mean.

In summary, while Table 4–1 indicates family size does affect whether children see a physician, Table 4–5 shows that the impact can be greater or less when the effects of family size are compounded by income, residence, age and to a lesser degree race. Children in small families who are most likely to see a physician become even more likely to see a doctor when they are also high income, other urban, one to five year old or white. Conversely, children least likely to see a physician—those who live in large families—become even less likely to see a doctor if they are also low income, rural or inner city residents, older or nonwhite. Even when need and regular source of care are controlled, children in small families are more likely to see a physician than children in large families. Table 4–3 shows family size also affects the mean number of physician visits for children who saw a doctor, although the effects are less than for contact, perhaps due to the less discretionary nature of repeated physician visits. Table 4–6, like Table 4–5, suggests family size is a more important determinant of how many times a physician is seen when considered in combination with the characteristics of income, residence, age and race. Children in small families have more physician visits than those in large families in every case (controlling for need and regular source of care). This suggests that although the number of visits is

Table 4–6. Mean Number of Physician Visits for Children by Family Size Combined with Income, Residence, Age and Race*

	Unadjusted visits	Eta	Visits adjusted for independents	Beta	Visits adjusted for independents and covariates	Beta
Income and family size						
Low						
small family	4.6		4.7		4.3	
medium family	3.6		3.7		3.3	
large family	2.8		3.2		3.1	
Medium						
small family	5.4		5.3		4.8	
medium family	4.1		4.0		3.8	
large family	3.3		3.4		3.6	
High						
small family	5.4		5.2		5.4	
medium family	4.0		4.0		3.9	
large family	2.9	0.13	3.0	0.12	3.4	0.09
R^2				0.031		0.130
Residence and family size						
Rural						
small family	4.8		4.7		4.8	
medium family	3.6		3.6		3.4	
large family	2.4		2.4		2.8	
Inner city						
small family	6.0		6.0		5.8	
medium family	3.8		3.9		3.6	
large family	3.0		3.2		3.7	
Other urban						
small family	5.0		4.9		4.6	
medium family	4.3		4.3		4.2	
large family	3.7	0.15	3.7	0.14	3.8	0.12
R^2				0.033		0.132

Age and family size			
1–5			
small family	6.6	6.6	6.6
medium family	4.6	4.6	4.8
large family	3.6	3.8	4.0
6–12			
small family	3.9	3.9	3.8
medium family	4.1	4.0	3.7
large family	2.9	2.9	3.2
13–17			
small family	4.5	4.4	4.3
medium family	3.1	3.1	2.9
large family	2.8	2.8	3.1
R^2	0.17	0.17 / 0.034	0.16 / 0.132
Race and family size			
White			
small family	5.3	5.2	5.1
medium family	4.0	4.0	3.8
large family	3.1	3.2	3.6
Nonwhite			
small family	4.4	4.3	4.3
medium family	3.8	3.7	3.8
large family	2.6	2.5	2.7
R^2	0.13	0.12 / 0.031	0.10 / 0.130

*Each of these four combined variables was entered in a separate MCA analysis with the remaining three independents and regular source of care, perception of health, worry and disability days as covariates. For example, family income and family size were analyzed with age, race, residence and the covariates. Age and family size were analyzed with race, residence and income, plus the covariates. Only the combined variables are presented here, since the other independent variables in each procedure were unaffected by combining two variables.

less discretionary, there may be a limit to the number of times large families can reorganize routine functions and amass resources to make return visits to a physician. One test would be whether children in large families are less likely to keep appointments than those in small families.

CONCLUSIONS AND POLICY IMPLICATIONS

Family size is not a mutable variable which could be manipulated by policy makers to alter utilization patterns. However, changes in fertility patterns, resulting from family planning programs or simply changing demographic trends toward smaller families, may have implications for utilization. With the decline in average family size in the United States we might expect the physician utilization patterns of children in small families to become more prevalent—i.e., an increasing percentage of contacts and more visits per child—although the reduced number of children may mean fewer absolute contacts and number of visits. There will remain, however, a considerable number of children in large families who will have lower rates of physician use.

One interesting issue with regard to parents of large families is whether they "learn" on early children and then substitute home for physician care as their families grow larger. There is some indication from this analysis that reducing financial barriers to care would alter the use patterns of children in large families. But if differences in physician use are due to structural constraints on time and parental attention present in large families but not in small, it will be more difficult to get these children into the health care system and maintain repeated contact with them, even though enabling variables such as income and insurance coverage are altered. While it is clear that family size is not *the* most important variable in determining whether children see a physician or how often, it does appear to be one of the more important predisposing variables and a source of inequity in children's use of physician services.

NOTES TO CHAPTER FOUR

1. Family size has three classifications—small is one to three persons, medium is four to five persons and large is six or more. Family income is categorized as low (below $5,000), medium ($5,000 to below $11,000) and high ($11,000 and over). Rural residence includes both farm and nonfarm residences defined as rural by the census; inner city is residence in the central city of a SMSA; and other urban is urban residence other than central city. Age is self-evident. The nonwhite category of the race variable consists primarily of blacks but includes Orientals.

2. Persons over 65 were excluded from the adult population. In earlier analyses it appeared that including this age group increased the correlation between family size and physician use for all adults, primarily because people over 65 are heavily overrepresented in small families and are also more likely than the rest of

the population to see a physician. The literature on adults argues that any relationship between health behavior and family size is a result of strain which adults in the parental role in large families experience. Since most persons over 65 are less likely to be fulfilling such a role, and their physician experience differs from other adults, they were excluded.

Chapter Five

The Relationship of Attitudes to Discretionary Physician and Dentist Use by Race and Income

Joanna Kravits

Data in this book indicate that there is virtually no relationship between atti-tudes and discretionary health care use considered as a whole. This chapter refines the measure of health care and considers only discretionary health care, for which such a relationship might be expected. This relationship was not found for the population as a whole, indicating that national policy aimed at changing attitudes toward health care would appear to be worthless.

For certain subgroups of the population, however, correlations between attitudes and use of discretionary physician and dental services ranged from 0.20 up to 0.77. These subgroups were blacks and the aged, especially individuals in these groups above the near poverty line. These are groups which appear to experience the greatest barriers to obtaining preventive health care.

It would appear that there are some implications for public policy decisions in the area of attitude change and health care financing for these particular subgroups rather than aiming an attitude change program at the entire popula-tion. Since income turns out to be such a strong factor in obtaining elective physician and dental care, however, it seems as though removing financial barriers to this care by providing first dollar third party payments is a far more direct, though possibly more costly, way of ensuring that the U.S. population obtains more preventive care, if this is actually what is desired.

INTRODUCTION

This chapter will explore a variety of questions linking attitudes to health care behavior for blacks and whites controlling for differences in income between these two groups. Race has long been considered a predisposing condition for receiving health care, as have attitudes. That is, these appear to be attributes of the individual which may make him more or less ready to obtain medical care. Income, in contrast, is considered an enabling characteristic, because it makes access to medical care possible. This chapter considers whether race and attitudes may influence obtaining elective physician and dental care even when income is controlled.

In general, attitudes appear to play a rather small role in influencing actual behavior. This is true regardless of the type of behavior studied. It is particularly true in the health care field where health levels or state of health, income, insurance coverage, race and education are all much more highly correlated with whether a person uses medical care than are attitudes. A pervading explanation is that health care is not an item which is chosen because it is desired but rather one which is obtained as a necessity, largely whether one wants it or not. Under these circumstances, attitudes and beliefs might be expected to exert little influence. Under certain circumstances, however, attitudes and beliefs actually may have a substantial effect upon health care behavior. These circumstances concern discretionary health care, that is, health care that is chosen rather than required.

Studies in the area of public health were among the earliest in the health care field which investigated the influence of attitudes on use. Burns (1951) attempted to determine why some parents would not have their children immunized against diphtheria. Clausen et al. (1954) improved upon Burns' study by comparing parents who refused to allow their children to participate in polio vaccine trials with parents who cooperated. This study found the *education* of the mother accounted for the differences between the participants and the refusers.

Janis and Feshback (1953) investigated the effects of persuasive communications which attempt to motivate people to conform to a set of recommendations by stimulating fear reactions. The main conclusion of this study was that the overall effectiveness of a persuasive communication will tend to be *reduced* by the use of a strong fear appeal if this fear appeal evokes a high degree of emotional tension without adequately satisfying the need for reassurance.

By 1966, Rosenstock (1966) had developed a social-psychological model for the utilization of preventive health services. The model hypothesized that the decision to seek preventive care would not be made unless the individual was psychologically ready to take action and felt the preventive care was feasible, and a cue or stimulus occurred to trigger the response. Rosenstock noted that empirical research for testing his model was absent and that many methodological difficulties lay in the way of examining its usefulness in explaining health care behavior.

Other studies of health attitudes included Schonfield et al. (1963), Suchman (1964), Leventhal et al. (1965), Coe and Wessen (1965), Kegeles (1967), and Fink et al. (1968). Schonfield et al. (1963) continued along the path provided by Burns and Clausen by looking at differences between mothers who did and did not allow their children to participate in a mass tuberculin testing program. He added another group for comparison—mothers who did not participate because they took their children to their own private doctor for the test—and thus controlled to some extent for the influence of income and education. Compared to the refusers who did not have their children tested at all, the participants were more knowledgeable about tuberculosis and more favorably inclined toward physicians. The early participants were the most favorably inclined of any group toward public preventive health measures. Thus, Schonfield et al. indicated that attitudes and knowledge were important variables in explaining preventive behavior, but were not able to produce any statistical measure of the relationship between the two.

Suchman (1964) suggested for the first time that differences in attitudes between groups such as blacks and whites actually did account for differences in their health care use, but again he could provide no empirical data relating attitudes to actual behavior. He did find, however, that differences among various ethnic groups in knowledge of disease, attitudes toward medical care and behavior during illness were related to the form of social organization within the ethnic group.

Coe and Wessen (1965) did a review of the literature dealing with social-psychological factors influencing the utilization of health care facilities. They concluded that many individuals have negative attitudes toward seeking help from physicians due to unpleasant experiences with doctors. Unfortunately, there were no empirical data showing that these negative attitudes led to future lower utilization.

Kegeles (1967) reviewed and criticized studies which have attempted to differentiate the attitudes and beliefs of women who have Pap smears from those who do not. Typically, Kegeles does not advocate that the models upon which these studies are based be discarded but rather that they be treated as hypotheses-generating rather than hypotheses-testing studies. In other words, they should be treated as starting points for other studies.

Fink (1968) utilized the old public health model—comparing participants and nonparticipants as did Burns, Clausen and Schonfield—to look at the reluctant participant in a breast cancer screening program. He found that participants were more likely to have favorable attitudes toward the screening program, to be more concerned with the possibility of having cancer, to report more specific symptoms associated with breast cancer and to be more likely to have seen a physician within the last year than were the nonparticipants. However, the participants were also younger and better educated than the nonparticipants and no attempt was made to do crosscorrelations to see if education would explain the differences.

Thus, over nearly two decades, the position of attitude research among public health psychologists and sociologists has changed relatively little. There was a conviction that attitudes and beliefs were an important determinant of participation in preventive health care and other public health measures, a gradual realization that this relationship was not as simple as it first appeared, a rethinking and discussion of other variables which might affect behavior, and ultimately very little change in the way research was conducted.

Virtually none of the data presented substantiate the theory in strong statistical terms, but enough research has been done to make it appear at least likely that attitudes and beliefs in conjunction with other variables do influence preventive health care behavior. The public health literature is, in this respect, more positive on the subject than other literature dealing with the effect of attitudes on behavior. Wicker (1969), for example, has thoroughly summarized all the empirical studies he could find relating attitudes to behavior in nonhealth care settings. He concluded that correlations are rarely above 0.30 and often near zero.

Data presented in this chapter will attempt to correlate attitudes toward health care with discretionary health care behavior for the population as a whole and for subgroups within the population whose attitudes and discretionary health care behavior differ substantially from that of the majority. Even if there is no correlation between attitudes and discretionary health care behavior for the U.S. population, this may mean only that the population is too heterogeneous to be looked at as a whole and that substantial correlations for important subgroups are being overlooked. In particular, this chapter advances the hypothesis that correlations between attitudes and preventive health care should be higher for blacks than for persons in the mainstream of American medical care and that the difference between racial groups should persist even when income is controlled. Poor blacks should be the group for whom the influence of attitudes is most pronounced since they have the most barriers to overcome in obtaining care.

THE DISCRETIONARY USE VARIABLES

This chapter is concerned only with utilization of outpatient physician services and dental care in relation to health care attitudes. Dental care was not verified, but during the interview the respondent was asked what kind of procedures the dentist had performed so that services could be used as a reasonable proxy of dental diagnoses. Two variables for discretionary care use were constructed. One was derived from the services for which a dentist was seen and separated those individuals seeing a dentist for discretionary dental care services (check up, teeth cleaned, X-rays, orthodontia, fluoride treatments, gum treatments, crowns or capping) from those seeing a dentist for any mandatory services (teeth extracted, dentures, bridge work, fillings or inlays). A dental consultant made these decisions (Chapter Ten explains the development of diagnostic severity codes for dental care). A two part variable was constructed from this breakdown, excluding from the analysis those individuals who had mandatory dental work done and considering only those individuals who appeared not to need dental work. These were divided into two groups: those who saw a dentist for preventive care and those who did not see a dentist at all. Undoubtedly in this latter group there were some individuals who did need dental care and who might have fallen into the mandatory category if they had seen a dentist, but it was impossible to separate these out.

The same system was followed with regard to developing a variable for discretionary utilization of physician care except that, instead of using services, the diagnoses for which the individual had seen the physician were examined and the verification data were incorporated. (For a discussion of the actual development of the scale for physician care see Chapter Ten.)

Whenever a physician verification was received, the physician diagnosis was taken over that of the respondent; for those cases with no physician verification, the respondent's diagnosis was taken. A respondent, of course, could have more than one diagnosis. Each diagnosis was rated for its severity by a panel of five physicians—three internists, a psychiatrist and a recent medical school graduate. The four point medical need index ran as follows:

1 = preventive care *or* care from a physician would make no difference for this condition (check ups, eye refractions, common cold)
2 = symptomatic relief available from physician (headache, varicose veins, hemorrhoids, removed mole)
3 = should see a physician (otitis media, essential hypertension, strabismus, asthma)
4 = must see a physician (cancer, diabetes mellitus, heart failure, broken bone, ulcerative colitis, schizophrenia)

When the panel disagreed, the modal score was taken for the diagnosis. Each individual seeing a physician was assigned a score for each diagnosis for which he was seen. All individuals in the study were then placed into one of the three categories: did not see a physician, saw a physician for discretionary diagnoses only (no diagnostic score above two on the medical need index), or saw a physician for at least some mandatory care (one or more scores of three or above on the medical need index). As with dental care, those individuals who saw a physician because they were sick enough to require some mandatory care were excluded from the analysis, leaving a two part variable: individuals who were not seriously ill but who saw a physician for preventive or elective care and individuals who did not see a physician at all.

DIFFERENCES IN ATTITUDES

The attitudes discussed in this portion of this chapter consist of ten questions which appeared on the Health Opinions Questionnaire. When a questionnaire had been filled out by both the head of the family and spouse, the head's questionnaire was chosen and these attitudes were attributed to all family members including children so that the entire universe of the sample could be used for relating attitudes to discretionary utilization. Because of the large size of the sample, most of the attitudinal differences discussed are significant at least at the 0.05 level.

In general, blacks and low income individuals have more negative attitudes than the remainder of the population. Race and income interact on some of the questions to the extent that *higher* income blacks actually have more negative attitudes than do *lower* income whites. This same phenomenon was found for the utilization of discretionary physician and dentist services: that is, higher income blacks were more similar in some of their use to lower income blacks than they were to lower income whites. Race appears to make the main difference on some questions, while on others income is the main determinant of differences. The attitude questions were originally asked as a four part variable, but strongly agree and tend to agree have been combined into "agree" while strongly disagree and tend to disagree have been combined into "disagree" for purposes of this analysis. Table 5-1 shows the differences for the ten attitudinal questions by race and income.

Turning to these actual attitude questions, Table 5-1 indicates that although the differences are small, blacks are more apt than whites to believe that you can get over most diseases without aid and this difference persists even when income is controlled. Low income people of both races are more apt to believe this than higher income people, but it is striking that *higher* income blacks are more apt to believe this than are low income whites. This is the beginning of a pattern which indicates that blacks are more skeptical of organized medical care than are whites.

The next question indicates that blacks are more apt than whites to believe that good health is a result of strong will power, which tends to substantiate the previous statement. Controlling for income, however, we find that, below the poverty line, race makes virtually no difference. Above the poverty line, however, blacks are still influenced by this idea, which may keep them away from doctors and hospitals.

The next question provides more support for the hypothesis that blacks are more negative than whites about medical care. They certainly believe more strongly in home remedies as opposed to prescribed drugs than do whites. When income is controlled for both, income and race appear to make a difference but, again, high income blacks are still slightly more likely to endorse this item than are low income whites.

Blacks also tend to feel that no matter how well a person follows his doctor's orders, he has to expect a good deal of illness in his lifetime. This finding is especially striking in that the data are not age adjusted and the black population is considerably younger than the white. Income also makes a much greater difference here than in the previous tables. The same is true of the next question, in which blacks are more negative to doctors and feel that they understand

Table 5–1. Distribution of Response to Attitude Questions by Race and Income

Attitude question	White			Black			All races		
	Above near poverty	Below near poverty	Total	Above near poverty	Below near poverty	Total	Above near poverty	Below near poverty	Total population
	percent								
1. If you wait long enough, you can get over most any disease without getting medical aid.									
Agree	13	17	13	19	19	19	13	18	14
Disagree	87	83	87	87	81	81	87	82	86
2. Good personal health depends more on an individual's strong will power than on vaccinations, shots and vitamins.									
Agree	26	37	30	38	39	39	26	38	29
Disagree	74	63	70	62	61	61	74	62	71
3. Some home remedies are still better than prescribed drugs for curing illness.									
Agree	27	41	30	43	51	47	28	44	33
Disagree	73	59	70	57	49	53	72	56	67

Table 5-1. continued

Attitude question	White			Black			All races		
	Above near poverty	Below near poverty	Total	Above near poverty	Below near poverty	Total	Above near poverty	Below near poverty	Total population
					percent				
4. No matter how well a person follows his doctor's orders, he has to expect a good deal of illness in his lifetime.									
Agree	39	57	43	47	66	57	40	60	45
Disagree	61	43	57	53	34	43	60	40	55
5. A person understands his own health better than most doctors do.									
Agree	32	44	34	39	53	46	32	45	36
Disagree	68	56	66	61	47	54	68	55	64
6. Modern medicine can cure most any illness.									
Agree	53	51	53	53	59	56	54	52	53
Disagree	47	49	47	47	41	44	46	48	47

7. The medical profession is about the highest calling a man (sic) can have in this country.									
Agree	61	74	64	65	76	70	62	74	65
Disagree	39	26	36	35	24	30	38	26	35
8. Most doctors are more interested in their incomes than in making sure that everyone receives adequate medical care.									
Agree	39	38	39	61	50	56	40	40	40
Disagree	61	62	61	39	50	44	60	60	60
9. Choosing your own doctor is about the most important thing in getting good medical care.									
Agree	79	83	80	87	77	82	79	82	80
Disagree	21	17	20	13	23	18	21	21	20
10. The care I have generally received from doctors in the last few years was excellent.									
Agree	86	83	85	85	86	86	86	84	85
Disagree	14	17	15	15	14	14	14	16	15

their own health better than a doctor does. Income also has a considerable effect, independent of race.

The findings for the sixth question appear to disagree with all of the previous ones. Up until now, blacks have been shown to be more negative to medical care and doctors and more likely to stay away, but in this case low income blacks say they think modern medicine can cure most any illness. Perhaps this is due to their relative unfamiliarity with the health care system or perhaps they think "modern medicine" is something different from what they themselves are exposed to. Another hypothesis is that this question is related to knowledge of the limitations of modern science so that low income people would be expected to have a more positive response than people of higher income and blacks a more positive response than whites.

The next question, "The medical profession is about the highest calling a man (sic) can have in this country," also appears to elicit an unusual response but for a different reason. Doctors appear to be quite popular with the American public despite all the adverse publicity the health care system has been getting, and they seem to have a particularly positive image among blacks. In fact, it is the white middle class which is the most negative to medicine as a "high calling." The suspicion is strong that this question reflects relative aspirations rather than attitudes toward the health care system.

This hypothesis appears to be borne out by the eighth question in which blacks are most apt to agree that doctors are more interested in their incomes than in making sure that everyone receives adequate medical care. This is a strong racial difference and it is the *higher* income blacks who feel most negative. When these two questions are combined, the conclusion appears to be that blacks would like to be physicians themselves but also dislike them and the way they operate within the system. Whites aren't so impressed with physicians, but they don't feel they're being taken advantage of by them either. Higher income blacks are, of course, paying for physician care out of their own pockets and so have more reasons to be negative than lower income blacks.

The ninth question is one of the few which shows no clear-cut differences by either race *or* income. This seems rather odd because a priori, one might expect that high income whites feel much more strongly about choosing their own doctor than low income blacks since they are more likely to do this than blacks. Perhaps, again, this is an example of blacks realizing that there is something the matter with the care they receive and assuming that it would improve if they could choose their own doctor rather than go to a clinic. The last question also indicates no clear-cut differences—the implication is strong that most of the American public is satisfied with the medical care they themselves receive and this is almost totally unrelated to race or income. One rather cynical hypothesis is that there may be a strong negative relationship between the amount of care received and how good the respondent thought the care was—that is, the respondents who received little or no care are the ones who thought it was excellent.

In general then, with a few exceptions, the poor and the black have more negative attitudes toward preventive care and the value of medical care and also have considerably lower utilization of discretionary physician and dental services as indicated in Chapter Ten. The question crucial to this chapter is whether a causal connection can be demonstrated between these two facts: that is, whether negative attitudes toward health care are correlated with less use of discretionary health care services. This is the crux of the final portion of this chapter.

THE RELATIONSHIP OF ATTITUDES TO HEALTH CARE USE

Are attitudes related to discretionary health care use for the population as a whole, and, if they are not, are they related for groups which have both negative attitudes and low discretionary care use, namely the black and the poor? To answer the first question, correlation coefficients were computed for each of the ten attitude questions to examine their relationship to discretionary physician and dentist use for persons using discretionary care or no care at all. People using mandatory care were excluded from the analysis. Since physician and dentist use had been constructed as dichotomous rather than continuous variables, Kendall's Tau and Gamma were used for the correlations.

Table 5–2 shows correlations which are in the expected direction for seven of the ten attitude questions. Given the large sample size, most correlations are statistically significant. However, statistical significance in these cases does not necessarily indicate public policy relevance when the correlations are negligible. The three questions which have correlations in a direction opposite to the expected are the same three questions which were discussed in the previous section as showing attitudinal differences between blacks and whites which were the opposite of the trend for most of the questions. The correlations for the population as a whole are rather low between attitudes and health care behavior, although perhaps not unduly low considering the usually disappointing results in the literature. The highest correlation is between disagreement with the statement, "No matter how well a person follows his doctor's orders he has to expect a good deal of illness in his lifetime," and seeing a dentist for preventive care; this correlation is 0.24. The next two highest correlations, 0.17 and 0.16, are also for preventive dental care. The highest correlation for the population as a whole for preventive physician care is 0.15 for disagreement with the statement, "Some home remedies are still better than prescribed drugs for curing illness."

This discussion has covered the U.S. population as a whole and has shown that attitudes appear to have only a weak, although fairly consistent, connection with preventive health care behavior. What of the various subgroups of the population, however? Is this weak connection consistent throughout, or do attitudes have a stronger connection with preventive health care behavior for some groups than for others? In order to answer this question, the correlations

Table 5–2. Correlation Between Attitude Questions and Seeing a Physician or Dentist for Elective Care Versus Not Seeing Him At All

Attitude item	Seeing a physician for elective care versus not seeing him at all		Seeing a dentist for elective care versus not seeing him at all	
	Tau C	Gamma	Tau C	Gamma
1. If you wait long enough, you can get over most any disease without getting medical aid (correlations should be negative).	−0.05	−0.08	−0.05	−0.11
2. Good personal health depends more on an individual's strong will power than on vaccinations, shots and vitamins (correlations should be negative).	−0.08	−0.12	−0.08	−0.17
3. Some home remedies are still better than prescribed drugs for curing illness (correlations should be negative).	−0.10	−0.15	−0.06	−0.14
4. No matter how well a person follows his doctor's orders, he has to expect a good deal of illness in his lifetime (correlations should be negative).	−0.07	−0.11	−0.11	−0.24
5. A person understands his own health better than most doctors do (correlations should be negative).	−0.07	−0.11	−0.06	−0.13
6. Modern medicine can cure most any illness (correlations should be positive).	0.00	0.00	0.00	0.01
7. The medical profession is about the highest calling a man (sic) can have in this country (correlations should be positive).	−0.08	−0.13	−0.07	−0.15
8. Most doctors are more interested in their incomes than in making sure that everyone receives adequate medical care (correlations should be negative).	−0.02	−0.04	−0.02	−0.04
9. Choosing your own doctor is about the most important thing in getting good medical care (correlations should be positive).	−0.08	−0.14	−0.06	−0.16
10. The care I have generally received from doctors in the last few years was excellent (correlations should be positive).	−0.05	−0.09	−0.00	−0.00

were recalculated for each of the race and income categories discussed in earlier sections of this report. The results are shown in Table 5–3. Only correlations of 0.20 or higher are shown. Questions which have no correlations of this magnitude are omitted entirely. This cutoff level was chosen for two reasons: (1) correlations of this magnitude are significant at the 0.01 level for even the smallest group discussed (the blacks, both above and below poverty considered separately), and (2) these correlations are higher than those found for the U.S. population as a whole for this study and also for most of the other public health related studies reviewed.

It is immediately apparent from Table 5–3 that:

1. Attitudes appear to have no influence upon the preventive or discretionary care behavior of the mainstream of Americans—that is, whites above the near poverty line, who account for almost three-quarters of the population.
2. Attitudes have more of an effect on poor whites, but only on their use of discretionary dental care.
3. Attitudes are most closely connected with the discretionary care of blacks, and particularly for blacks *above* the near poverty line. This effect is much more clearly pronounced for dental care than for physician care even though most of the questions are overtly connected with physician care.

One variable which has not yet been discussed but which should figure prominently in any analysis of the effect of attitudes on discretionary care use by subgroups of the U.S. population is age. Individuals over 65 use relatively little discretionary care, particularly dental care, but like blacks and individuals below the poverty level, they are less positive in their attitudes toward organized health care and face some of the same barriers to obtaining preventive care. Although a detailed consideration of the effects of age is beyond the scope of this chapter, the questions which produced high correlations for the poor and the black were reanalyzed controlling for age.

This reanalysis, controlling for race, income and age simultaneously, produced correlation coefficients which ranged upwards to the 0.70s. Table 5–4 shows the results of this analysis. Using these results, the conclusions drawn from Table 5–3 can be modified as follows:

1. Attitudes still appear to have no relationship to behavior for higher income white Americans under 65, but for several questions they correlate with preventive physician and dental care for the white above poverty level aged.
2. For poor whites, the most marked effect of attitudes upon discretionary care behavior is also for individuals above 65, but again only for their use of discretionary dental care.
3. The relationships for blacks are extremely complex when age is controlled for. The combination of being old and black and *above* the near poverty line

Table 5–3. Correlation of Response to Attitude Questions With Seeing a Physician or Dentist for Elective Care Versus Not Seeing Him At All by Race and Income

Attitude question	White			Black			All races		
	Above near poverty	Below near poverty	Total	Above near poverty	Below near poverty	Total	Above near poverty	Below near poverty	Total population
1. If you wait long enough, you can get over most any disease without getting medical aid (negative).									
Physician Gamma					-0.21				
Dentist Gamma					-0.34	-0.28			
2. Good personal health depends more on an individual's strong will power than on vaccinations, shots and vitamins (negative).									
Dentist Gamma				-0.21	-0.25			-0.23	
3. Some home remedies are still better than prescribed drugs for curing illness (negative).									
Dentist Gamma		-0.22			-0.23			-0.24	
4. No matter how well a person follows his doctor's orders, he has to expect a good deal		-0.21			-0.39			-0.34	

Statement	Measure	(1)	(2)	(3)	(4)	(5)	(6)	(7)
of illness in his lifetime (negative).	Physician Gamma	−0.20	−0.21	−0.30		−0.23	−0.21	
	Dentist Gamma			−0.61		−0.38		−0.24
5. A person understands his own health better than most doctors do (negative).	Physician Tau			−0.22				
	Physician Gamma			−0.35		−0.21		
	Dentist Gamma			−0.52	−0.34	−0.47		
6. Modern medicine can cure most any illness (positive).	Dentist Gamma			0.38				
7. Most doctors are more interested in their incomes than in making sure that everyone receives adequate medical care (negative).	Physician Gamma			−0.25			−0.23	
	Dentist Gamma			−0.57		−0.32		
8. The care I have generally received from doctors in the last few years was excellent (positive).	Dentist Gamma			0.33				

Table 5–4. Correlation of Response to Attitude Questions With Seeing a Physician or Dentist for Elective Care Versus Not Seeing Him At All by Age, Race and Income

Attitude question	White			Black			All races		
	Above near poverty	Below near poverty	Total	Above near poverty	Below near poverty	Total	Above near poverty	Below near poverty	Total population
1. If you wait long enough, you can get over most any disease without getting medical aid (negative).									
Physician Under 65		−0.24		−0.73	−0.21	−0.33			
Over 65		−0.24		−0.73	−0.23	−0.24		−0.23	
Dentist Under 65					−0.31				
Over 65		−0.53	−0.31	*	*	*		−0.57	
2. Good personal health depends more on an individual's strong will power than on vaccinations, shots and vitamins (negative).									
Physician Under 65				0.27	−0.24				
Over 65				0.40	−0.21				
Dentist Over 65		−0.60		*	*	*			
3. Some home remedies are still better than prescribed drugs for curing illness (negative).								−0.60	−0.32

		C1	C2	C3	C4	C5	C6	C7	C8	C9
Physician	Over 65	-0.26	-0.27	-0.29	-0.37	-0.22	-0.33	-0.26	-0.27	-0.27
Dentist	Under 65		-0.64			-0.22	*		-0.65	
	Over 65				*					
4. No matter how well a person follows his doctor's orders, he has to expect a good deal of illness in his lifetime (negative).										
Physician	Under 65				-0.30	*	-0.23			
	Over 65				-0.29		-0.37			-0.22
Dentist	Under 65				-0.60	*	*			
	Over 65			-0.22	*					
5. A person understands his own health better than most doctors do (negative).										
Physician	Under 65				-0.36	-0.33	-0.23		-0.74	
Dentist	Under 65				-0.51		-0.46			-0.23
	Over 65				*	*	*			
6. Modern medicine can cure most any illness (positive).										
Physician	Over 65	-0.25		-0.26	0.77	-0.42		-0.25	-0.28	
Dentist	Under 65	-0.25		-0.26	0.39					-0.28
	Over 65				*	*	*			

Table 5–4.   continued

Attitude question	White Above near poverty	White Below near poverty	White Total	Black Above near poverty	Black Below near poverty	Black Total	All races Above near poverty	All races Below near poverty	All races Total population
7. Most doctors are more interested in their incomes than in making sure that everyone receives adequate medical care (negative).									
Physician Under 65			-0.31	0.26					
Over 65	-0.49		-0.31	-0.75	-0.28	-0.39	-0.51		-0.32
Dentist Under 65		-0.20		-0.57		-0.34		-0.25	
Over 65		-0.22		*	*	*		-0.23	
8. The care I have generally received from doctors in the last few years was excellent (positive).									
Physician Over 65	-0.22			0.73		0.25			
Dentist Under 65				0.32		0.20			
Over 65	-0.35			*	*	*	-0.33	-0.30	

All correlations are Gamma. Tau is always in the same direction as Gamma but usually lower.

* Less than 25 unweighted individuals.

produces the strongest relationship between attitudes and discretionary physician use with four questions correlating highly on this variable (0.77, 0.75, 0.73, 0.73). Thus correlations with physician care use which did not show up when race and income alone were considered now appear for the aged only.

Simply being black and above the near poverty line correlates highly with discretionary dental care use. Relatively well-off blacks over 65 appear to have even higher correlations than their younger counterparts, but there are too few cases in this particular analysis to yield significant results. The correlations with discretionary dental care use for younger blacks above the near poverty line are 0.60, 0.57 and 0.51; with the small number of old, above poverty line blacks correlations of up to 0.84 were achieved but were not significant.

4. Age appears to make little or no difference for blacks below the near poverty line. In general, there is much less correlation between attitudes and behavior for this group than for blacks *above* the near poverty line.

CONCLUSIONS

How do the findings in this chapter support the hypothesis previously suggested that the correlation between attitudes and discretionary health care would be expected to be higher for two groups in the population, the poor and the black, since these groups had more barriers to overcome in obtaining elective and preventive health care? The data appear to bear out these expectations about the black population but it is black individuals *above* the near poverty level who seem to show the highest correlations between attitudes and discretionary health care behavior. Furthermore, age was shown to be an important variable which must be considered along with race and income in order to pinpoint the group with the highest correlations between attitudes and behavior, namely blacks above the near poverty line and individuals over 65.

If the concept that attitudes are important in obtaining discretionary health care only when there are barriers to overcome is correct, then the idea that being above the near poverty line is necessary for attitudes to make a difference seems a contradiction in terms. It is obvious that being black is a barrier to obtaining elective medical care in a variety of ways: discrimination against blacks which is still strong in many parts of the country, and the rural and ghetto location of blacks where physician accessibility for elective care is poor seem to be the most important barriers for this group. For the aged, sheer effort in terms of seeking care for minor illnesses or check ups would appear to be a significant barrier, plus to a lesser extent the two barriers mentioned above for blacks since the aged also tend to live in doctor poor areas and to be discriminated against by doctors, although in more subtle ways.

Using the barrier concept in terms of access to the system, it seems impossible at first to reconcile the income findings. Income is tremendously important, but in the opposite direction of what had been predicted. The above and below near poverty levels were set up to take into account eligibility for welfare and for Medicaid so that most people below the poverty line were eligible for these programs while practically no one above the poverty line was. Added to this is the fact that, although coverage for Medicare is virtually universal, there was in 1970 a $50 deductible and 20 percent coinsurance requirement which makes it apparent that the barrier to obtaining physician care is a more subtle one than was originally perceived. Dental care is usually covered by Medicaid as well, but not usually by private insurers (11 percent of the population were covered in 1970) or by Medicare.

Attitudes appear to make a difference *only if the individual has to pay for elective care at least in part out of his own pocket.* Those below the near poverty line had, in effect, no financial barrier to care since their care was almost entirely subsidized. The literature had led this researcher to believe that, since this low income group had more negative attitudes toward health care and lower elective health care use, these two variables would be correlated, but this does not appear to be the case. Previous findings had in fact already hinted at this in indicating that while the poor did go to the doctor less than the nonpoor, when they did go they were almost as apt to go for elective care only as the nonpoor. The measure of elective care finally used in this chapter for correlating attitudes and behavior was seeing a physician or dentist for elective care only versus not seeing him at all, and on this measure, where the two groups were reasonably equal, income appeared to make a difference only when the individual had to pay. Thus, it was the *above* poverty group, given the organization of U.S. medical care in 1970, which experienced the barrier.

In summary, then, the following points emerge from this large scale analysis attempting to relate attitudes to discretionary health care behavior:

1. There is relatively little relationship between attitudes and discretionary health care behavior for the U.S. population as a whole.
2. There is however, a strong and consistent relationship, as measured by correlations, for certain subgroups of the population between attitudes and discretionary health care behavior.
3. These subgroups are blacks, particularly blacks *above* the near poverty level who are not eligible for free elective medical care but must pay at least some of the costs for elective medical and dental care out of their own pocket, and individuals over 65.

It would appear that there are some implications for public policy decisions in the area of attitude changes and health care financing. Specifically, a policy of attitude change aimed at the U.S. population as a whole would appear to be worthless. However, a selective policy of attitude change aimed at blacks and the aged might change behavior in these groups in the direction of obtaining more elective care. Since income is such a strong factor in obtaining this care, however, it seems as though removing financial barriers by providing first dollar medical and dental coverage rather than having the population pay for elective care out-of-pocket is a far more direct, although perhaps more costly, way of ensuring that the U.S. population obtains more elective type care, if this is indeed what is desired.

Part III

Enabling Factors

Chapter Six

Utilization of Physician Services Across Income Groups, 1963–1970

Lee Benham and
Alexandra Benham

To investigate relative changes over time in utilization of physician services across income groups in the U.S. we construct a measure of long term or permanent income for education-age groups and then estimate parameters for two models, one which treats utilization as a function of permanent income and age, and a second which also includes health status variables among the independent variables.

The estimates of the model suggest that utilization by low income groups increased relatively between 1963 and 1970 and that by 1970 the relationship between income and utilization was weak. Furthermore, when measures of health status are included in the specification, essentially no association between income and utilization appears for 1970. The U.S. thus appears to have moved toward greater equality of utilization across permanent income groups during this period.

Concern is frequently expressed about the equity of utilization of medical services in the U.S. Many individuals, particularly those who advocate further government medical programs, feel that there have been significant inequities, with many persons receiving too few medical services. One expressed aim of the major government medical programs introduced in the 1960s was to reduce inequities in utilization. This chapter investigates patterns of utilization of physician services in 1963 and in 1970 as a means of examining some aspects of this question.

There is, of course, no consensus concerning the meaning of equity in medical utilization. Equality of utilization across income groups is one standard which has frequently been proposed. The analysis which follows deals primarily with relative utilization across income groups, and it also examines the income-utilization relationship when levels of illness are taken into account. The usual approach in this arena, that of examining individuals' utilization patterns as a function of their current personal income or their current family income, has serious difficulties. Individuals whose health is currently poor tend both to use more medical services and to have lower current income, both absolutely and with respect to their own long term or permanent income, than do individuals whose health is currently good. This implies that if equality of utilization across permanent income classes existed, at any point in time we would observe the groups with lower current incomes using more services. Therefore, in investigating the relationship between permanent income and utilization, some account must be taken of this impact of health status on current income (Andersen and Benham, 1970).

The situation is further complicated because levels of illness may differ across permanent income groups; individuals with lower permanent income are likely to have poorer health. This adds another dimension to the concept of equity, to the extent that utilization rates across income groups do not indicate utilization rates by level of illness. If the poor utilize the same level of services as the rich but are sicker than the rich, the poor are utilizing fewer services per "sickness."

In the following analysis we construct a measure of permanent income and then examine utilization patterns across permanent income groups, first using a simple model which treats utilization of physicians' services as a function of permanent income and age. A second model is then constructed by adding health status variables to the set of independent variables; this permits estimation of the impact of permanent income on utilization taking into account the level of illness. Our presumption is that ill persons in high income groups will obtain more physician services than comparably ill persons in low income groups.

To construct a measure of permanent income, aggregation techniques are used on the basic data from the 1963 and 1970 surveys conducted by the Center for Health Administration Studies. For each of the survey years, individuals are classified into one of 28 education-age cells on the basis of their education (0–8, 9–11, 12 and 13+ years of schooling completed) and age (23–29, 30–36, 37–43, 44–50, 51–57, 58–64 and 65–71 years of age); median family income for each cell is then computed and used as the measure of permanent income for members of the cell [1]. Education is strongly associated with lifetime earnings, and age is used to capture life cycle differences in earnings across education categories. Education and age are relatively unaffected by current health status, at least for the categories considered here. This measure of permanent income should therefore be a reasonably good one, relatively unaffected by the transient changes in individuals' income resulting from temporary changes in their health.

Individuals' utilization of physician services is defined here as number of nonobstetrical physician visits during the previous year. For the education-age cells, two utilization measures are computed because of the nature of distribution of utilization of these services. A small number of very high utilizers of physician services occur in the sampled population, with the consequence that mean estimates within the cells are sensitive to the presence of these individuals. Therefore, we calculate the mean number of physician visits for individuals within the cell and also the percent of individuals within the cell having one or more physician visits.

The following models are then estimated:

1. $\text{MD VISIT}^{i,j}_k = \beta_0 + \beta_1 \ \text{INCOME}^{i,j} + \beta_2 \ \text{AGE}^{i,j} + \mu^{i,j}$

2. $\text{MD VISIT}^{i,j}_k = \beta_0 + \beta_1 \ \text{INCOME}^{i,j} + \beta_2 \ \text{AGE}^{i,j}$

$$+ \beta_3 \ \text{SYMPTOMS}^{i,j} + \beta_4 \ \text{DISDAYS}^{i,j} + \mu^{i,j}$$

where: the superscripts i, j denote respectively the education and age categories defining cell i, j; $k = 1, 2$; and

MD VISIT_1 = mean number of nonobstetric visits to physicians during previous year by individuals within cell,

MD VISIT_2 = percent of individuals within cell who had one or more nonobstetric visits to physicians during previous year,

INCOME = median family income within cell during the previous year,

AGE = mean age within cell,

SYMPTOMS = mean number within cell of symptoms that individuals reported they experienced during previous year (from a list of 20 symptoms) [2],

DISDAYS = mean number within cell of disability days individuals had during previous year.

The β_1 coefficients provide estimates of the relationship between median family income and medical utilization by cell in the two years in question. If permanent income is not related to utilization patterns, β_1 should not be statistically different from zero. Furthermore, any changes in the utilization patterns across income groups between 1963 and 1970 should be reflected in changes in the β_1 estimates.

MODEL ONE RESULTS

The 1963 and 1970 estimates for the first model are shown in Table 6–1. For 1963, mean physician visits (Equation 1) are positively and significantly related to median family income. The magnitude of the coefficient indicates that a 10 percent increase in permanent income—i.e., in median family income—is associated with a 2.7 percent increase in physician visits; in other words, the elasticity

Table 6–1. Estimates of the Effect of Median Family Income on Utilization of Physician Services for 28 Age-Education Groups in 1963 and 1970

(*t* statistic in parentheses)
[elasticity calculated at the mean in brackets]

Dependent variable: utilization of medical services[a]	*Median family income*[b]	*Mean age*[b]	*Constant*	R^2	*N*
Mean number of visits to physicians in 1963	0.00021 (2.3) [0.27]	0.06621 (5.0)	0.57539	0.52	28
Mean number of visits to physicians in 1970	−0.00008 (1.0) [−0.16]	0.07362 (4.1)	1.78280	0.47	28
Proportion of individuals visiting physicians in 1963	0.00118 (2.2) [0.12]	0.23988 (3.0)	46.49101	0.32	28
Proportion of individuals visiting physicians in 1970	0.00070 (1.7) [0.10]	0.34134 (3.8)	44.70018	0.37	28

[a]Excluding obstetric services.
[b]For year corresponding to year of dependent variable.

is 0.27 [3]. Thus, groups with low permanent incomes obtained substantially fewer physician services than did high income groups in 1963. Equation 2 shows the comparable estimates for 1970. The change over the seven year period is striking; in 1970 mean physician visits and median family income are related negatively. These results indicate a substantial relative increase from 1963 to 1970 in low income groups' utilization of physician services measured as mean number of visits.

The second measure of utilization, the percent of individuals in the cell with one or more physician visits during the previous year, is used in Equations 3 and 4. The β_1 coefficient is positive in 1963, indicating that a larger proportion of individuals in low income groups did not see a physician at all during the year. The β_1 coefficient is also positive in 1970, but both the magnitude and the elasticity are smaller than in 1963. We are less confident of a change in utilization across income groups between 1963 and 1970 using this measure of utilization, but the suggested direction of change appears to be the same as for the previous measure.

The estimates for the first model thus suggest that from 1963 to 1970 there was an improvement in the relative level of utilization of physician services by groups with low permanent income and a reduction in the importance of income in determining utilization patterns.

MODEL TWO RESULTS

Table 6–2 presents the results for the second model, which includes two health status variables: number of symptoms and number of disability days during the previous year. The β_1 estimates in this case are estimates of the relationship between income and utilization taking into account these aspects of health status. In this case, in both 1963 and 1970, median family income is related to mean number of physician visits positively but not significantly.

Using mean physician visits as the dependent variable, we can be somewhat more confident that utilization is positively associated with income in 1963 than in 1970. The differences here across years are less dramatic than for the first model. Thus the relationship between utilization and income is weakened in both years, and the difference between 1963 and 1970 is reduced, when health status is taken into account.

If the percent of individuals (by cell) visiting physicians is used as the dependent variable, the β_1 coefficient for 1963 (Equation 3) is positive and of approximately the same magnitude as in the first model [4]. In contrast, for 1970 the β_1 coefficient is essentially zero, while it was positive in the first model. Thus when health status is taken into account, there appears to have been a larger decline over time in the importance of income in determining whether an individual sees a physician than when health status is not taken into account.

The results shown in Table 6–2 are surprising in that we expected income to appear as a more significant determinant of physician utilization, with a higher elasticity, when health status measures were included [5].

CONCLUSIONS

This analysis has offered some estimates of the relationship between permanent income and utilization of physician services in 1963 and 1970. The estimates suggest that utilization by low income groups increased relatively during this period, and that by 1970 the relationship between income and physician utilization was weak. When measures of health status were included in the specification, essentially no association was found between income and utilization for 1970. There thus appears to have been a considerable change during this period, a change at least concurrent with the introduction of Medicare and Medicaid. To the extent that equity is defined in terms of equality of utilization across income groups, it appears that the U.S. moved in the direction of greater equity during this period.

One caveat is in order here. The link between utilization of physician services

Table 6–2. Estimates of the Effect of Median Family Income and Health Status on Utilization of Physician Services for 28 Age-Education Groups in 1963 and 1970

(t statistic in parentheses)
[elasticity calculated at the mean in brackets]

Dependent variable: utilization of medical services[a]	Median family income[b]	Mean age[b]	Mean numbers of symptoms reported[b]	Mean numbers of disability days[b]	Constant	R^2	N
Mean number of visits to physicians in 1963	0.00022 (1.4) [0.28]	0.06344 (2.3)	0.05891 (0.07)	0.00619 (0.1)	0.42786	0.52	28
Mean number of visits to physicians in 1970	0.00005 (0.6) [0.10]	0.05336 (3.1)	−0.02734 (−0.05)	0.13807 (2.4)	−0.28510	0.63	28
Proportion of individuals visiting physicians in 1963	0.00111 (1.5) [0.11]	0.21105 (1.3)	−2.25787 (0.5)	0.29348 (0.76)	50.14903	0.34	28
Proportion of individuals visiting physicians in 1970	0.00019 (0.4) [0.03]	0.40127 (4.2)	−3.05324 (1.0)	−0.19697 (0.6)	56.49328	0.45	28

[a] Excluding obstetric services.
[b] For year corresponding to year of dependent variable.

and adults' health status has not been firmly established (see Chapter Twelve). If it cannot be established, we need to question the importance of attaining equality of utilization.

NOTES TO CHAPTER SIX

1. This measure of permanent income is therefore not the usual one which takes into account full life cycle earnings but is simply a long term (seven year) average family income.

2. These symptoms are listed in Aday and Andersen (1975:84).

3. Elasticity is defined here as relative change in utilization of physician services/relative change in income. See Stigler (1966:329). These elasticities were calculated at the means of income and physician utilization.

The estimated elasticity for 1963, (0.27), is close to that which was obtained for 1963 using an instrumental variables technique. The elasticity obtained there from the simple relationship between permanent income and a broad measure of physician use was 0.31 (Andersen and Benham, 1970:90).

4. The standard error of β_1 in Equation 3 is larger in Table 6–2 than in Table 6–1.

5. When this question was investigated in an earlier study using individual data for 1963, the inclusion of health status variables tended to increase the income elasticities (Andersen and Benham, 1970:90).

Chapter Seven

Effects of Insurance on Demand for Medical Care

Charles E. Phelps *

Demand curves (and expenditure curves) are estimated for hospital stays, physician office visits and surgical expense using members of the 1970 survey who reported actual utilization of those services, focusing on the effects of insurance on demand for the services. Physician office visits are most influenced by insurance, and surgical expense least influenced. Tables show predicted levels of demand and expenditure at various coinsurance levels. For hospital and physician services, coinsurance affects expenditure more than amounts of service, implying that persons with better insurance chose more costly providers of care. The current distribution of insurance shows that the largest possible increases in coverage are for physician office visits, the service most sensitive to coverage. It is concluded that coverage of such services without a deductible could increase demand for physician visits considerably above current capacity. How the system would respond and equilibrate is discussed.

As universal provision of health insurance becomes an important political topic in this country, questions arise as to what the consequences of various financing proposals might be. Will increased insurance coverage improve access of the poor to the health system? How would the introduction of universal insurance affect the delivery system and its ability to meet demands placed upon it? How much will various financing plans cost in the short run and in the long run? These are but some of the issues facing legislators discussing these issues, but this set of questions can be answered to a considerable extent by analysis of the *demand* for medical care, defined here as the number of people trying to obtain medical services. How demand changes with different levels of insurance coverage is the central focus of this chapter. Demand will be analyzed by type of care, and

*This study was supported by Grant Number HS 01029–01 from the National Center for Health Services Research and Development. I would like to extend my thanks to Bryant Mori for his efficient and careful computational assistance.

estimates will be made not only of demand for services but of expenditure levels under various levels of coinsurance.

THEORY OF DEMAND FOR MEDICAL SERVICES

The basic theory of demand for medical services used here follows that of Grossman (1972), Phelps and Newhouse (1974a) and Newhouse and Phelps (1974). The theory specifies that a person's health is valuable to him (that is, his health enters his utility function), and that additional medical services will improve a person's health. The person (together with his doctor) decides how much medical care to buy on various occasions (normally, when the person becomes ill), the amount of care being a function of variables that can be classified as predisposing variables (or "tastes"), enabling variables (which are the central focus of this chapter) and need variables (the level of illness the person has). The demand for medical services is derived from a more basic demand for health. Medical care (and all other goods and services) are chosen (according to this model) to maximize the person's utility, subject to the constraint that his total expenses must not exceed his budget. The key aspect of health insurance is that it reduces the price of medical care in the budget constraint, so that instead of paying the "market price" per unit of care, the consumer pays Cp, where C is the coinsurance rate specified in his insurance policy. Since the price of care is lower to the consumer, he will (on average) purchase more medical care (and fewer "other goods and services") with insurance than without it [1].

In this chapter, estimates of demand for medical care will be presented using this basic model. A brief summary of the variables in these estimates follows.

Enabling Variables

Coinsurance. For each person using care, a coinsurance rate is computed to reflect the portion of expenses paid for by the person out-of-pocket for each type of care received (hospital admissions, hospital length of stay, surgical procedures, physician office visits). The calculation uses data from the insurance policies held by the person (where possible) as well as actual expenditure data. For each demand equation, a separate coinsurance rate is computed. These variables are:

Hospital length of stay coinsurance. For persons who actually entered the hospital, explicit expenditure data can be used to calculate the actual coinsurance rate facing the person as decisions are made about extending the stay one more day. If the person's insurance policy contains a deductible, that is taken into account in the calculation with the formula $C =$ (Out-of-Pocket − Deductible)/(Total Expense − Deductible) [2]. This coinsurance rate reflects the rate paid once the deductible has been met, as is appropriate for decisions about staying in the hospital one extra day, given an admission.

Surgical expense coinsurance.   The average coinsurance rate (Out-of-Pocket Expense)/(Total Expense) is used for surgical expense.

Physician office visit coinsurance.   Most persons covered for physician office visits either have Medicare (with a $50 deductible per illness period in 1970), Medicaid (typically with no deductible) or major medical insurance (typically with a deductible of $50 to $100 per year). A small number of persons in the sample (under 10 percent of those covered by private insurance) have physician office visit coverage under a basic medical policy, typically with no deductible. If the person has not met an applicable deductible, he is treated as having no third party coverage (i.e., C is set to 1.0) [3]. If he has met the deductible, a coinsurance rate is calculated similar to that for hospital length of stay, namely C = (Out-of-Pocket − Deductible)/(Total Expense − Deductible). This formulation allows calculation of a coinsurance rate for persons with multiple payment sources (e.g., Medicare plus a private insurance supplementary policy) reflecting actual amounts paid. Naturally, such a calculation can be made only for persons who actually had some medical visits during 1970.

Income.   Income is normally thought of as an enabling variable, in the sense that more income allows people to acquire more goods and services of whatever nature they desire. Grossman (1972) has shown that income may also be interpreted as a predisposing variable, in the sense that persons with higher *wage* incomes have a stronger desire to remain healthy (each unit of time is more valuable to them) than persons with low wage rates. This leads to consideration of wage income and nonwage income separately as predictors of demand, with the basic effect of nonwage income being interpreted as an enabling effect, and any higher effect of wage income on demand interpreted as showing both the enabling and predisposing aspects of wage income. (It should also be noted that higher income leads persons to purchase better health insurance, so that higher incomes produce a secondary effect of lower out-of-pocket prices for medical care because of the better insurance policies.) Actual reported incomes from the household survey are used in these estimates.

Waiting and Travel Time as a Price.   When purchasing medical care, persons must spend not only money but also time to acquire the care. Thus higher time costs, just as higher money costs, can be expected to reduce demand for medical services, holding everything else constant. The most appropriate fashion to use time and travel costs is to multiply the actual time spent receiving service by the value of the time to the person receiving care, so that the "time price" is measured in dollars per unit of care. The time value, unfortunately, is difficult to measure. For persons working for an hourly wage, with no sick leave, the appropriate value is simply their wage rate—they forego the equivalent of an hour's wage to receive an hour of medical care. For persons working on a salary, the concept is more difficult to measure, and for persons with sick leave from work, or with disability insurance (for more prolonged sicknesses such as those involving hospitalization), the appropriate value is best measured by the costs to the patient. Sick leave and disability insurance insure the time costs of medical care just as health insurance insures the money costs of care. Unfortunately, there are no good measures of these concepts in the 1970 survey, so the estimated wage rate per week is used as the best available proxy for a person's time value. This wage rate is multiplied by values reported in the survey for travel time and waiting time, and the resultant time-cost variables are used in the physician office visit demand curves [4].

Appointment Delay as a Price. The survey also reports the customary delay to appointment experienced by patients when they requested to see their customary source of care. This delay to appointment is not a direct cost in the same sense that travel and waiting times are, because the delay time (typically measured in days between when an appointment is made and when the office visit is actually made) can be used for other purposes in many cases. For patients whose ability to function is limited by their illness, and whose illness could be cured (or the symptoms relieved) by immediate physician contact, the delay does indeed exact a price in the usual sense, the price being the value of the foregone productive time. For other patients, however, the delay simply postpones access to the physician. This may still reduce demand for care if many of the illnesses treated for this group are self-limiting in nature, so that the illness goes away before the physician visit may be obtained. In either case, additional delay to appointment should reduce demand for care, just as any other form of a higher price for care should, and we can expect demand to fall for patients facing longer appointment delays.

Need Variables

Three sets of variables are employed to characterize the person's need for medical care. The demand curve for care can be pictured as shifting outward for increasing levels of need, as portrayed in Figure 7–1. The actual variables used to portray need are:

Disability Days. The household interview reports the number of disability days for each respondent during the year 1970. This variable is used directly.

Self-Perceived Health Status. Each respondent was asked to assess his health in general as excellent, good, fair or poor. These variables were spread into four dummy variables (set equal to Good = 1 if the person reported "good health," Fair = 1 if the person reported "fair health," Poor = 1 if the person reported "poor health" and "Deceased" similarly; each variable is set to zero otherwise) so that each dummy variable reflects the additional amount of care associated with each level of health, relative to persons in "excellent" health (whose average demand is contained in the constant term of the regression).

Figure 7–1. Demand for Medical Services as a Function of Coinsurance and "Need"

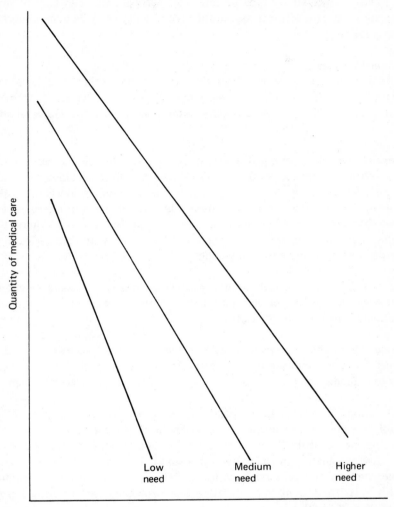

Frequency of Pain. Respondents assessed how often each person in the household experienced pain—very often, fairly often, seldom or not at all. These responses were categorized in three dummy variables (very often, fairly often, seldom) in a fashion similar to the self-perceived health status measure, each showing additional demand for care relative to persons who reported experiencing no pain at all.

Each of these sets of variables should show persons with more disability, more pain or poorer health using more medical care, although their relative importance may differ by type of care (e.g., the pain variables may be more important for doctor office visits, but the disability days may be more important for hospital care).

Other Variables

The demand curves estimated for all services contain other variables serving primarily as "controls," since they are known to influence demand for medical care, but there is no particular economic interpretation for them. These variables are:

Sex. A variable is set equal to one if the person is female and zero if male. The coefficient estimated on this variable shows the additional amount of medical care used, on average, by females relative to males, holding constant all other factors in the estimated demand equation. Thus, for example, if the coefficient for the "Sex" variable is 0.50 in a physician visit equation, this would mean that females demanded, on average, one-half visit more per year than males, if all other descriptive characteristics were equal.

Age of Person. Although health variables standardize to some extent for illness levels, age of the person is included as a further control on level of illness, since the two are strongly correlated.

Race. A variable set equal to one is included in the estimates for nonwhite persons; this may indicate differences in environment, medical supply availability or in predisposing variables such as attitudes toward the medical system.

Education. The demand equations include a person's education as a final control variable. While education has often been interpreted as a "taste" or "predisposing" variable, thought to increase demand for medical care, there is an alternative explanation provided by Grossman (1972). His model proposes that people combine medical services with their own activities and time to produce "health." To the extent that education makes people more efficient at such "production of health," it implies that less medical care (i.e., doctor and hospital services) would be required to reach the same level of health. Thus this model— the "household production of health" model—would predict that better education would lead (all else held equal) to less use of medical services per se. The demand estimates presented in this chapter test this theory directly.

Interaction Effects

It is of considerable policy interest to know not only the average response of demand to changes in insurance coverage, but how that response varies for different people. Of particular interest are estimates of any price interaction with income (this will alter the distributional effects of any insurance plan), the extent of illness (this will show whether coinsurance changes demand more for the very sick or the not so sick) and also how the price response changes over different price levels (this is important in assessing shifts between no insurance and some relatively generous insurance). The estimated demand equations test for these interactions by specifying demand curves of the following form:

$$y = a_o + a_1 (\text{Coinsurance}) + a_2 (\text{Income}) + a_3 (\text{Income} \times \text{Coinsurance}) \qquad (7.1)$$

$$(\text{plus other variables}),$$

so that the effect of coinsurance on demand is given by

$$dy/dC = a_1 + a_3 (\text{Income}).$$

The theory specifies that a_1 should be negative (lower coinsurance leads to higher demand) and the sign of a_3 should tell if the effect of insurance differs across income groups. If a_3 is positive, then lower income people are more responsive to coinsurance (they will increase their purchases of care more than higher income persons as coinsurance falls). The converse is true if a_3 is negative. Similar interactions can be estimated for illness severity. If the coefficient on the (illness $\times$ coinsurance) variable is positive, that means sicker individuals are less sensitive to coinsurance changes. Finally, an interaction with the coinsurance rate itself (a term for coinsurance squared) will show whether the effects of coinsurance differ at various levels of coinsurance. If the coefficient on coinsurance squared is positive, then people become less sensitive to coinsurance as coverage becomes more complete, since the basic effect of coinsurance on demand should be negative.

Exclusions of Persons from the Sample

These demand estimates contain several important exclusions of persons from the sample not found in other sections of this book. The exclusions are made so the remaining observations will have data conforming to conditions necessary for accurate estimation of demand curves, as will be explained below [5].

The first exclusion necessary is for persons who obtained part or all of their medical care under special circumstances, not representative of their usual source of care and with special financing provisions. Major categories of exclusion were for persons receiving part or all of their care at work or school clinics, workman's compensation cases or employment related physical examinations. For many of these persons, their only care during the year may have been a free employment or school physical examination. To infer that they could receive all the care they wished at zero price is incorrect. Further, if they have had one additional physician visit at $20, it would be incorrect to infer that they could receive all the care they wished at $10 per visit. Since the data do not allow separation of the "special" visits (and their costs) from the "normal" visits, they are deleted.

Persons on welfare and Medicaid present a special problem. Typically, they pay nothing for care received while on the Medicaid program, but that program has many limitations on demand ("nonprice rationing") that reduce demand for those persons below what it would be if they had an insurance policy with $C = 0$. To include either Medicaid recipients or other persons receiving "special circumstance" care makes correct inferences about the effects of insurance impossible—such an estimate would associate small demands (say, for the rationed Medicaid persons) with low coinsurance rates, thus biasing the estimate. Thus all recipients of Medicaid and other free care are excluded from the analysis involving physician outpatient care.

Persons with large incomes (over $75,000) or sickness levels (as indicated by over 100 disability days) are excluded on grounds that the functional form used in the regression estimates cannot account for these extreme observations and that their inclusion may overwhelm the response pattern shown by the remainder of the sample.

DEMAND FOR HOSPITAL CARE

The results described below are derived from a linear regression with the dependent variable (days per admission) in linear form and with the independent variables entered in interacted or quadratic form. Equations were estimated both with ordinary least squares (OLS) and with simultaneous equation methods (using two stage least squares [TSLS]). The results in general suggest accepting the linear OLS equation used. None of the interaction terms (testing whether the coinsurance effect varied by income, illness or level of coinsurance) were significantly different from zero. Simultaneous equation (TSLS) methods with insurance variables jointly determined gave estimates near zero of the effects of insurance, with very low precision. Equations with the dependent variable in logarithmic form gave nearly identical results to those with a linear dependent variable, except that the precision was slightly higher for some coefficients. Table 7–1 shows the linear equations from which the reported results were derived. The estimated income elasticity for length of stay is negative, implying that higher income may lead to a life style that helps avoid hospital stays [6]. As predicted by the household production model, education has a negative effect on demand. Holding constant other factors, better educated households are able to produce the commodity "health" using fewer market inputs (in this case, hospital days). This contrasts with usual hypotheses that education is a predisposing variable leading to more care being sought. A considerable amount of variance is explained by illness and pain variables, particularly the disability days measure and the "very often experiencing pain" measure. Age is positively associated with length of stay, consistent with a depreciating stock of health as a person ages (Grossman 1972), and also with the hypothesis that the marginal product of medical care falls with age (requiring more days to achieve the same "cure").

Estimates of the expense per admission are shown in Table 7–2. These differ from the length of stay equations in that differences in the price per day will also affect the dependent variable. To the extent that the equations differ, one may impute the difference to the effects of the explanatory variable on the price per day in the hospital. The linear dependent variable OLS equation is presented, since the simultaneous equation methods and alternative forms of the explanatory variables gave no additional information. The coinsurance elasticity was slightly higher than the length of stay elasticity, suggesting that price per day increases with better insurance, although the estimated effect is small. Using predictions from the equation in Table 7–2, one can show the estimated expenditure per admission at various coinsurance levels, holding all else constant. In 1970 the mean expense per admission in this sample was $650 at an average coinsurance level of 5.83 percent. Extrapolating to full coverage, expense per admission would be $675.5 or an increase of 4 percent in resource use. At a coinsurance rate of 20 percent, expense would be $589.2, and at no coverage the figure is $245.5, indicating that fully insured persons would use over two and one-half times the resources per admission as those with no insurance. This is an extrapolation beyond the range of most of these data, however, and should be viewed with caution.

The other information necessary to understand how insurance affects demand for medical care is the effect of insurance on the rate of hospital admissions. The sum of that effect plus the change in expenditures per day shows the total effect of insurance on changes in resource use for hospital stays. Unfortunately, the data in the 1970 survey do not allow direct computation of a coinsurance rate for those in the sample who did not actually have a hospital admission in 1970. It is therefore impossible to estimate a true demand curve for hospital admissions, because the coinsurance variable cannot be formulated. The most helpful approximation derivable from these data is to estimate demand for hospital admissions as a function of age, health status, income and other variables in the demand curve (as in Table 7–1) plus a variable set equal to one if the person carries hospital insurance and equal to zero otherwise. A similar variable is established for persons on Medicare. The estimated coefficient shows the additional number of hospital admissions per year for these types of persons above the quantity chosen by persons without insurance. Private hospital insurance and Medicare are separated to see if there are differential effects because of the structure of the insurance. Most private hospital insurance contains no deductible, whereas there is a deductible equal to one day's hospital care in Medicare. Since almost every hospital admission would lead to total expense beyond such a deductible, there should be little effect on admissions, but the estimated coeffi-

Table 7–1. Hospital Length of Stay

Variable	Hospital days (no interactions) Coefficient (t ratio)	Elasticity	Hospital days (including interactions) Coefficient (t ratio)	Elasticity (t ratio)
Coinsurance	-0.0413 (2.35)	-0.03	-0.0151 (0.28)	—
Coinsurance squared	—		0.138 E-04 (0.02)	-0.035* (1.83)
Coinsurance × disability days	—		-0.293 E-03 (0.40)	
Coinsurance × income	—		-0.283 E-05 (0.78)	
Income	-0.4793 E-04 (1.06)	-0.06	-0.250 E-03 (2.40)	-0.14* (2.13)
Income squared	—		0.745 E-08 (2.14)	
Disability days	0.0875 (8.66)	0.25	0.0909 (8.06)	0.25* (8.78)
Wage income	-0.0903 (0.41)	-0.03	-0.0577 (0.26)	-0.02
Education (recoded)	-0.322 (2.87)	-0.18	-0.287 (2.52)	-0.15
Age	0.0862 (6.62)	0.39	0.0796 (5.96)	0.36
Sex (1=female)	-0.0895 (0.17)		-0.071 (-0.13)	—

Race (1=nonwhite)	0.4462 (0.58)	0.298 (0.38)
Good health	0.158 (0.26)	0.289 (0.49)
Fair health	0.586 (0.80)	0.626 (0.85)
Poor health	−0.0011 (−)	0.046 (0.05)
Deceased	3.623 (2.34)	3.689 (2.38)
Pain very often	2.665 (3.27)	2.64 (3.22)
Pain fairly often	0.7364 (0.99)	0.734 (0.97)
Pain occasionally	−0.149 (0.25)	−0.138 (0.22)
Welfare received (1=yes)	1.018 (0.92)	0.692 (0.62)
Constant term	4.407 (5.07)	5.307 (5.20)
R^2 (Adjusted)	0.256 (0.243)	0.261 (0.244)
F (d.f.) (significance)	19.247 (16, 894) (P < .00001)	15.682 (20, 890) (P < .00001)
Std. Error of Y: X	6.44 days	6.43 days

* Elasticity calculated at means of interaction variables.

Table 7-2. Hospital Expense Per Admission

Variable	Coefficient (t ratio)	Elasticity
Coinsurance	−4.297 (2.09)	−0.04
Income	0.4098 E−05 (0.0)	0.0
Wage	28.535 (1.10)	0.10
Disability days	8.364 (7.08)	0.30
Education (recoded)	−14.165 (1.08)	−0.09
Age	3.099 (2.04)	0.18
Sex (1=female)	5.488 (0.08)	
Race (1=nonwhite)	56.147 (0.62)	
Good health	−11.160 (0.16)	
Fair health	−71.395 (0.83)	
Poor health	−164.43 (1.43)	
Deceased	290.10 (1.60)	
Pain very often	251.740 (2.65)	
Pain fairly often	−29.842 (0.34)	
Pain occasionally	−85.702 (1.23)	
Welfare care (1=yes)	80.573 (0.62)	
Constant term	380.09 (3.75)	
R^2 (Adjusted)	0.130 (0.115)	
F (d.f.) (significance)	8.369 (16, 894) (P < .00001)	

Note: No interaction terms significant; hence, only the linear equation is presented.

cient on Medicare should be slightly lower, if anything, than that for the private insurance variable. Demand curves were estimated for hospital admissions on a sample of 10,122 persons, with the average probability of admission for the sample being 8 percent. Hospital coverage was held by 74 percent of the sample, and an additional 8.2 percent were covered by Medicare [7].

The results of the estimation are summarized in Table 7–3. The coefficient on the private insurance variable was 0.033 ($t = 5.37$), and for Medicare the coefficient was 0.028 ($t = 2.41$). Average admissions for the entire sample were 7.9 per 100 person years [8].

Thus persons with the average amount of health insurance in the U.S. in 1970 are estimated to demand 60 percent higher hospital admissions than persons without insurance, holding constant age, sex, race, income, health status variables and education. Since most private insurance in fact covers almost all hospital expense (the average amount covered is over 90 percent for those with admissions), these estimates can be taken as a fair approximation of the shift in demand for admissions between no coverage and full coverage. Taken together with results from Table 7–2 (see also Table 7–8), these suggest that the resource use in hospitals for persons with full coverage is substantially greater than for those without any insurance.

SURGICAL EXPENSE

For those who had a surgical operation in 1970, it was possible to compute a coinsurance rate for the procedures performed, and therefore to estimate a demand curve for surgery. Since the "number" of procedures is only a weak indicator of the actual amount of service performed, estimates were made only for surgical expense. The estimated effect of coinsurance is small (elasticity of –0.04), similar to that found for hospital expense but less precise. The coefficient on surgical coinsurance is significant at the 0.2 probability level, so that there is a one in five chance that the true coefficient is actually zero. Health status indicators account for the majority of explained variance, with the estimated effects of income and education being near zero. (The predicted demands at various levels of coinsurance are shown in Table 7–9.) These results suggest that decisions about surgery are even less sensitive to insurance than hospitalization, and considerably less sensitive than other types of care. These estimates do

Table 7–3. Demand for Hospital Admissions

Insurance status	Admission rate per 100 person-years	Ratio to rate for insured persons
Persons with insurance	8.3	1.0
Persons on medicare	8.3	1.0
Persons with no insurance	5.1	0.6

Table 7-4. Surgical Expense Per Operation

Variable	Coefficient (t ratio)	Elasticity	Average value in sample
Coinsurance	−0.534 (1.24)	−0.04	22.55
Income	0.00287 (1.00)	0.10	$10,728.50
Wage	−6.299 (0.42)	−0.05	$2.43
Education (scaled)	7.039 (0.94)	0.10	4.36
Age	0.877 (0.95)	0.10	35.73
Sex (1=female)	−122.59 (3.29)		0.57
Race (1=nonwhite)	−44.053 (0.77)		0.07
Welfare care (1=yes)	−14.54 (0.14)		0.022
Good health	21.014 (0.42)		
Fair health	24.014 (0.46)		
Poor health	91.674 (1.06)		
Deceased	140.04 (1.00)		
Pain very often	−16.420 (0.30)		
Pain fairly often	−81.865 (1.63)		
Pain occasionally	−36.422 (0.91)		
Disability days	2.944 (4.75)	0.24	25.87 days
Constant term	260.73 (4.25)	−	−
R^2 (Adjusted)	0.139 (0.103)		
F (d.f.) (significance)	3.778 (16, 373) (P < .00001)		

not include any effect of insurance on the decision to seek surgery or not, but simply the expense conditional on surgery being performed.

Similarly to estimating demand for hospital admissions, it is possible to estimate a demand curve for surgical procedures as a function of whether or not the person had surgical insurance. Again, it was not possible to compute actual coinsurance rates for persons without actual expenses, so the zero-one variables for private insurance and for Medicare were again established to reflect source of coverage. The estimates are summarized in Table 7-5. The estimated coefficient on the private insurance variable was 0.017 ($t = 3.73$) and the estimate for the Medicare variable was insignificantly different from zero (0.001, $t = 0.08$). If the effects of private insurance and Medicare are restricted to be identical in the estimation, the coefficient is 0.014 ($t = 3.33$) [9]. Average frequency of surgery in this sample is 3.8 percent.

Recall that persons receiving welfare or free care for surgery are omitted from this sample, causing the apparently low estimate for Medicare persons (although age has been held constant in these estimates, so that the insurance variable should not reflect effects of age on demand). Using the more precise estimates of the effects of private insurance on demand, it is clear here, as for hospital admissions, that insurance exerts a strong effect on the demand for surgical procedures. Since the average proportion of surgical expense covered is high (over 75 percent for persons with surgical expense), these estimates show most of the difference in surgical procedures that would occur between no coverage and full coverage.

DOCTOR OFFICE VISITS

Doctor office visits are less frequently covered by private insurance than are hospital services, but in 1970 there were still sufficient numbers of persons with insurance coverage to allow estimation of demand curves for MD office services. A major complication in these estimates was the presence of persons with special coverage for some services, but not for others. Major categories include persons receiving employment physicals; chest X-rays; services through school, industrial or armed forces clinics; and persons on welfare or Medicaid. For persons on Medicaid, the problem is that eligibility is uncertain, and demand does not

Table 7-5. Effects of Insurance on Demand for Surgical Procedures

Insurance status	Estimated surgical procedures per 100 person-years	Ratio to rate for insured persons
Persons with private insurance	4.1	1.0
Persons with medicare	2.4	0.58
Persons with no insurance	2.4	0.58

follow usual patterns because of administrative "rationing." Inclusion of these persons in the sample obscures true relationships between coinsurance and utilization. Similarly, persons receiving care in special circumstances cannot have a coinsurance rate calculated accurately. For example, if the person has no insurance, but obtained a single physician visit as a pre-employment physical, the coinsurance (using the methods of calculation adopted for this paper) would be zero and demand would be one visit. To attribute the one visit to a zero coinsurance rate clearly does not represent the person's true situation. If the person has some mixed combination of free "unusual" visits and nonfree "normal" visits, it is even more difficult to infer what has really happened. Hence, all such persons are deleted from the sample before analysis.

The equations were estimated with 3596 persons who had between one and 30 physician visits, under 100 disability days, incomes under $75,000, and did not receive Medicaid or have any "special conditions" physician visits. The results are shown in Table 7–6. The estimated effect of insurance on demand is large—demand for visits is over twice as high at full insurance as with no insurance. Health status variables accounted for a large amount of the explained variance; those with worse self-perceived health status and those with more frequent pain used noticeably more services. Disability days similarly increased demand for care. These variables show the importance of standardizing for health levels when estimating demand for care. Other control variables were also important: age showed a positive association with use, and demand was about one-half visit lower for nonwhites than whites holding constant other factors. Family income had a slight negative effect (significant at the 0.22 level only) on demand, similar to the effect of income on hospital days. Demand was significantly lower for those persons facing higher waiting times to appointments, but travel and office waiting times showed a positive association with demand, contrary to the expectation that those variables would act as a price, reducing demand for care as they rose.

Expenditures for physician services is even more responsive to coinsurance than is use of physician services, which can only happen if better insurance leads persons to choose not only more services per person, but to use more expensive providers when they do use services. Expense is estimated to be three times higher at full coverage than with no coverage (compared with the doubling of demand between those two coverage levels—see Table 7–10). The third column of Table 7–6 shows equations predicting expense for physician visits at various coinsurance levels.

These equations were also estimated with various interactions between insurance coverage and income, health status, and at different coinsurance levels. The results were uniformly that the interactions were not significant in the demand equations, and these equations are not presented [10].

The estimates shown in Table 7–6 give the demand for physician care for those who actually obtained care. Additionally, there may be an effect of insurance on the decision to seek any doctor care during the year. As for hospital and surgical care, the data restrict us to estimate this simply by observing the difference in seeking doctor care or not for those with and without insurance. Unlike hospital care, however, it is true that the deductible on Medicare is smaller than the deductible for most private insurance covering physician office visits (the Medicare deductible in 1970 was $50, where the most common deductible for private major-medical policies—the most common source of physician office visit coverage—was $100). Thus there is reason to believe here that the effect of Medicare may be greater than the effect of private insurance in these estimates. As before, persons who received free physician office care during the year are restricted from the sample. The results are shown in Table 7-7. The coefficient for private insurance coverage was insignificantly different from zero, (-0.0037, $t = 0.33$), and the coefficient for Medicare was 0.11 ($t = 4.45$) [11]. Thus the smaller average deductible increases the proportion of persons seeking doctor care during the year significantly. If the estimates are restricted so that the effects of private insurance and Medicare are the same, the estimated coefficient is small (0.015, $t = 1.50$).

Thus it appears that the decision to seek physician care at any time during the year is substantially less sensitive to current types of insurance coverage than is the decision to be hospitalized or to have surgery. This effect is almost certainly due to the presence of a deductible in the insurance policies covering physician office visits, so that initial visits even for persons with insurance are likely to be paid entirely out-of-pocket. For those with ongoing expense, the effects of insurance come through additional numbers of visits once physician treatment has been initiated, as the equations in Table 7-6 show.

SUMMARY OF DEMAND RESULTS

The estimated demand equations for hospitals, surgical and physician office care can be summarized best by showing the predicted values of demand for each of these services at various coinsurance levels. In these computations, all other variables in the equation are assumed to have the average value in the sample. Tables 7-8A, 7-9A and 7-10A show the fitted demand values for each type of medical care (taken respectively from Tables 7-1 through 7-6) at coinsurance levels of zero (full coverage), 20 percent, 50 percent and 100 percent (no coverage). Estimates of the effect of insurance coverage on the expensiveness of the provider chosen are obtained by dividing predicted expense at each level by predicted volume of care. For both hospital care and physician office visits (Tables 7-8A and 7-10A), the price per unit of service rises as insurance improves, the largest estimated effect being for hospital care. The rate of hospital admissions, surgical procedures and the probability of seeing a doctor during the year are also significantly affected by insurance coverage [12] (Tables 7-8B, 7-9B and 7-10B).

Table 7–6. Physician Office Visit Demand Curve

Variable	Visits		Expense	
	Coefficient (t ratio)	Elasticity	Coefficient (t ratio)	Elasticity
Coinsurance	-0.0561 (9.25)	-1.38 at $\overline{C}$ -0.18 at C = 25%	-0.6426 (7.86)	-1.61 at $\overline{C}$ 0.19 at C = 25%
Income	-0.1079 E-04 (1.20)	-0.03	0.351 E-03 (2.91)	0.11
Appointment delay	-0.0771 (2.20)	-0.04	1.000 (2.12)	0.05
Travel time × wage	0.00175 (1.33)	0.02	0.0550 (3.11)	0.07
Wait time × wage	0.00107 (1.87)	0.03	-0.0021 (0.27)	–
Disability days	0.0699 (12.93)	0.12	0.4940 (6.78)	0.09
Good health	0.5748 (3.71)		2.533 (1.21)	
Fair health	1.9524 (8.67)		14.230 (4.69)	
Poor health	2.76 (6.16)		25.308 (4.20)	
Deceased	-0.1870 (0.14)		-12.623 (0.70)	
Pain very often	1.637 (4.78)		16.244 (3.52)	
Pain fairly often	1.499 (5.46)		8.691 (2.35)	

Pain occasionally	0.3807 (2.51)		7.571 (3.71)	
Welfare care (1=yes)	-0.4733 (0.52)		-5.550 (0.46)	
Education	0.0477 (0.77)	0.05	3.847 (4.59)	0.38
Age	0.0167 (3.47)	0.13	0.3613 (5.59)	0.29
Sex (1=female)	-0.0813 (0.58)		0.8376 (0.44)	
Race (1=nonwhite)	-0.4307 (1.64)		1.0439 (0.29)	
Constant term	7.0194 (9.14)		44.305 (4.28)	
R^2 (Adjusted)	0.1946 (0.1904)		0.1070 (0.1022)	
F (d.f.) (significance)	45.485 (19, 3576) ($P < .00001$)		22.545 (19, 3576) ($P < .00001$)	
Std. error of Y:X	3.924 visits		$52.85	

Table 7–7.   Effects of Insurance on Decision to Seek Physician Care

Insurance status	Proportion seeing a physician in 1970 (percent)	Ratio to persons with private insurance
Persons with private insurance	48	1.0
Persons with medicare	59	1.23
Persons with no insurance	48	1.0

Table 7–8A.   Hospital Days and Expense Per Admission: Fitted Values From Regression Equations

Coinsurance	Length of stay (days)	Expense	Implicit price/day (Col. 2 ÷ Col. 1)
C = 0 (full coverage)	8.42	$675.14	$80.18
C = 0.2	7.59	589.20	77.63
C = 0.5	6.35	460.30	72.49
C = 1.0 (no insurance)	4.29	245.45	57.21
Level in 1970	8.18	650.09	79.41

Table 7–8B.   Hospital Admissions Per 100 Person-Years

Level of coverage	Admissions per 100 person-years
Average level of coverage in 1970	8.3
No coverage	5.1

Table 7–9A.   Surgical Expense Per Case: Fitted Values From Regression Equation

Coinsurance	Expense
C = 0	$325.42
C = 0.2	314.74
C = 0.5	298.73
C = 1.0	272.04
Level in 1970	313.38

Table 7–9B.   Surgical Procedures Per 100 Person-Years

Level of coverage	Surgical rate per 100 person-years
Average level of coverage in 1970	4.1
No coverage	2.4

Table 7–10A.   Physician Office Visits and Expense: Fitted Values From Regression Equations

Coinsurance	Number of visits	Expense	Implied price per visit (Col. 2 ÷ Col. 1)
C = 0	9.07	$97.38	$10.74
C = 0.2	7.95	84.53	10.63
C = 0.5	6.27	65.25	10.41
C = 1.0	3.46	33.13	9.51
Level in 1970	4.00	39.23	9.81

Table 7–10B.   Persons Seeking Physician Office Care

Level of coverage	Percent seeing physician
Average private insurance in 1970	48
Medicare	59
No coverage	48

IMPLICATIONS FOR POLICY

Several questions can be posed about the effects of insurance on the health care system and upon the American people that can be tentatively answered from these analyses. First, what will happen to the distribution of services? Universal insurance could markedly improve the access of some persons to the health care system and the demand estimates show that lower coinsurance will increase demand extensively for medical services. Whether universal insurance would increase demand for any group of people depends as well on current levels of insurance and financing. For persons with relatively complete health insurance coverage, universal insurance would change little. For persons without private insurance, one must ask how universal insurance would change things relative to the effects of Medicaid and other free or reduced care public programs. As an example, consider demand for physician office visits by various income groups. Table 7–11 tabulates 1970 coverage for such care by income. There is a considerable discrepancy in private coverage across income groups (particularly for persons not in the labor force). This occurs because most private insurance held

Table 7–11. Families With Doctor Office Coverage

Income (% of sample)	Group	Nongroup	Private (subtotal)	Medicare	Medicaid	Public (subtotal)	Total
Under $3000 (18.5%)	0.05	0.03	0.08	0.39	0.10	0.49	0.57
$3000–4999 (12.3%)	0.17	0.02	0.19	0.23	0.06	0.29	0.48
$5000–6999 (12.4%)	0.24	0.03	0.27	0.11	0.02	0.13	0.40
$7000–9999 (18.2%)	0.35	0.02	0.37	0.04	0.01	0.05	0.42
$10,000–14,999 (12.8%)	0.42	0.01	0.43	0.01	—	0.01	0.44
$15,000 + (16.9%)	0.41	0.03	0.44	0.03	—	0.03	0.47
All incomes (100%)	0.28	0.02	0.31	0.13	0.03	0.16	0.47

in 1970 was obtained through employer work groups, which provide insurance much cheaper than individual insurance contracts. But many of the people without private coverage have some governmental program covering their medical expenses. Persons over 65 had coverage under Medicare in 1970 and this category has since been broadened to include those individuals receiving Social Security disability payments. The 1970 CHAS—NORC Survey can give some indication of how many additional people are covered by Medicaid and similar programs, by simply looking at the number of people who had doctor visits and received Medicaid. This understates the actual extent of Medicaid "coverage" in 1970, because some eligible persons will not have become sick, and hence will not have applied for or received any Medicaid payments. Yet as shown in Table 7—11, when persons receiving Medicaid or welfare medical payments are included, the apparent disparity in coverage is shifted. Including Medicare and Medicaid, the group with lowest coverage is that just above common Medicaid limits—the "near poor." Since the demand estimates were tested for interactions between income and coverage (none were found), the evidence suggests that the differences in demand between insured and uninsured persons should hold for lower income persons as well as others. Thus, under universal insurance, the largest gains in physician use would come from the "near poor" group, chiefly under age 65.

A different question also arises. If the coverage of a large number of persons is shifted through universal insurance and demand therefore increases, could that demand be met by the delivery system? For hospital care, this does not appear to be much of a problem, since coverage is quite extensive for the entire population as Table 7—12 shows, either through Medicare and Medicaid or private insurance. Universal insurance, even without any coinsurance provisions, would therefore not be likely to increase demands beyond a point where the current delivery system could match the demands.

For physician office visits, the picture appears quite different. First, consider the composition of coverage of those with insurance for physician office visits. Analysis of verified insurance policies from this study shows that most private coverage for MD office visits is through major medical insurance rather than "basic" coverage. Most major medical plans, of course, contain some deductible provision which must be met before payment begins. For persons with minor illnesses, the deductible will typically not be met by expenses for one or two physician office visits and these persons are to some extent better described as having no insurance for such visits. For more serious illnesses, particularly those involving hospitalization or repeated visits to the doctor, the patient can plan on the deductible being met, and would be likely to immediately act as if the insurance were paying for services.

Thus the question about the delivery system's ability to meet demands generated by universal insurance will largely depend upon the characteristics of the plan. If a deductible is present of a size similar to those in current major

Table 7–12. Families With Health Coverage

Income (% of sample)	Group	Nongroup	Private (subtotal)	Medicare	Medicaid	Public (subtotal)	Total
Under $3000 (18.5%)	0.13	0.08	0.21	0.47	0.12	0.59	0.80
$3000–4999 (12.3%)	0.39	0.12	0.51	0.23	0.08	0.31	0.82
$5000–6999 (12.4%)	0.55	0.10	0.65	0.10	0.02	0.12	0.77
$7000–9999 (18.2%)	0.77	0.09	0.86	0.02	0.02	0.04	0.90
$10,000–14,999 (21.8%)	0.87	0.05	0.93	0.01	—	0.01	0.93
$15,000 + (16.9%)	0.81	0.12	0.93	0.02	—	0.02	0.95
All incomes (100%)	0.61	0.09	0.70	0.14	0.04	0.18	0.88

medical insurance plans (or under Medicare), demand will be increased some but not nearly to the extent that would occur under a plan with no deductible. If there are large overall shifts in demand (defined, again, as the number of people trying to see a doctor), it is likely that the current delivery system would not be able to absorb the increase. Nonprice rationing devices would automatically enter to reduce demand until it equaled observed utilization. For example, Canadian experience suggests that delays for appointments doubled when universal insurance was introduced in Canada (Enterline et al. 1973). A similar experience resulted in Sweden when copayments for doctor visits were removed (Rodgers 1973).

The demand estimates from the 1970 survey (see Table 7–6) show how increased waiting time between appointments and visits (appointment delay) reduces demand for care, holding constant other factors. Appointment time varied for the sample from zero days (about one-third of the sample) to over one month (coded 7 in the data). The estimates show that demand differences between those two levels of delay are over one-half of one visit (on average) per person per year, or greater than a 15 percent reduction from average demand in 1970 [13]. Thus, one way a medical system can equilibrate if there is a large demand increase is by delays in setting up appointments which ration available care.

The estimates presented in this chapter support the contention that increased insurance coverage could lead to increases in demand for medical services over a broad range of services. The estimated demand for physician office visits more than doubles under full coverage insurance relative to no insurance (see Table 7–10A). Similar changes were estimated for hospital length of stay (Table 7–8A), with smaller changes forecast for surgical expense (Table 7–9A). The increases in use that would actually occur depend heavily on the current distribution of insurance (public and private) in the country. Counting Medicare and Medicaid, it appears that the largest gains in coverage from a universal health insurance program would be for the low income group in terms of hospital insurance and for the near poor in terms of physician ambulatory care. Thus these groups would benefit most from introduction of universal insurance even if the universal plan made no special provisions for low income persons.

NOTES TO CHAPTER SEVEN

1. Except for minor differences, the elasticity of demand with respect to coinsurance (the percent change in demand relative to a percent change in coinsurance) is equal to the elasticity with respect to the price of care itself. See Phelps and Newhouse (1974a).

2. The policy is assumed to pay $(1-C)$ percent of all expenses above the deductible (D). Thus benefits $(B) = (1-C) (E-D)$ where E = total expense. Thus $C = (E-D-B)/(E-D) = (\text{Out-of-Pocket}-D)/(E-D)$. Obviously, if $D = 0$, $C = \text{Out-of-Pocket}/E$, i.e., the average coinsurance.

3. While this theoretically may introduce some bias into the estimated price elasticity, there is no way of correcting for the problem in these data. See Keeler, Newhouse and Phelps (1974).

4. The travel and waiting time variables refer to physician office visits only.

5. The number of persons excluded in each equation is available from the author upon request.

6. Note that the interaction of income and income squared shows that higher income first reduces demand, and then (at still higher levels) increases it. This is consistent with Fuchs' (1974) hypothesis that high income, while making better health accessible, may also lead to worse health because of life styles associated with that income.

7. As in the other estimates in this chapter, persons receiving free care for hospitalization were deleted from this sample. Because persons on Medicare are more highly represented in that group, the fraction of this sample with Medicare is therefore lower than for the U.S. population as a whole.

8. The demand for hospital admissions equations are available from the author upon request.

9. The estimated demand for surgery equations are available from the author upon request.

10. In the expenditure equation one interaction was significant at the 0.1 probability level—this interaction showed that the response to insurance (the demand elasticity) became smaller for sicker persons, suggesting that in terms of physician office visit expense, better insurance coverage will change demands of relatively sick persons less than slightly sick persons.

11. The estimated equations are available from the author upon request.

12. For other estimates of these effects, see Feldstein (1971), Davis and Russell (1972), Rosett and Huang (1973), Newhouse and Phelps (1974), Newhouse, Phelps, and Schwartz (1974), and Phelps and Newhouse (1974 a, b).

13. The coefficient on appointment delay in the demand equation was -0.077 ($t = 2.20$). Hence the difference in demand between zero days delay and seven days delay is $7 \times (-0.077) = -0.57$ visits per year. The average for the sample in this equation was four visits per year, so demand (holding constant other factors) would be $0.57/4.0 = 14$ percent lower with the longest waiting times than with no waiting time.

Chapter Eight

Utilization of Health Services and the Availability of Resources

J. Joel May

In the face of current efforts at improving the performance and effectiveness of health planning, at reconfiguring the health services delivery system and at developing some form of guarantee of access to the system for all citizens, the question of the effect of the availability of health resources on utilization patterns is of utmost importance. While there is a fair amount of empirical evidence that such effects exist, none of the work to date has attempted to estimate these effects in a full model of health services utilization which includes all sociodemographic, family, belief and illness factors which influence demand for health care as well as price and resource variables. The present work attempts this. Based on the findings, the author concludes that (1) the supply of resources does appear to have an independent effect on demand in addition to the influences of other factors and (2) the impact is neither a simple one nor is it unidirectional.

The relationship between the supply of hospital and medical resources and their utilization has long been debated. The question is important in light of the current efforts both to reorganize the health care delivery system and to regulate or direct the growth and evolution of the components of the system. While the primary motivations for these efforts are controlling the costs of producing care, the prices charged for it and the amounts of capital invested, there are many who feel that a different pattern or mix of resources will result in improved access, more desirable patterns of movement through the system and assurances of higher quality. A major part of the justification for these efforts is the belief that utilization patterns are affected by the supply and availability of resources and that by changing the mix or volume of services available, utilization patterns can be modified or improved.

THE PROBLEM

The issue of whether or not there is a relationship between the availability of resources and their use is not uniquely confined to the hospital and health care field. Economists have wrestled with the problem in many other areas: an increase in the number of filling stations is associated with increased consumption of gasoline; an increase in the number of barber shops with the frequency of haircuts; etc.

Milton Roemer and Max Shain (1959) are generally credited with having first suggested that the more hospital beds there are, the more use will be made of them. They found a high degree of correlation between the number of short term hospital beds and the average daily census. At the same time, there was virtually no association between the supply of beds and occupancy rates. They concluded that beds are occupied at approximately the same rate regardless of the ratio of beds to population. Elsewhere, Roemer (1961) demonstrated that the demand for hospitalization responded to supply by describing a county in upstate New York in which a new hospital of 200 beds was built, representing an expansion of 42 percent in the bed supply. Within three years, the number of patient days of hospital care in the county had increased 28 percent. He claimed that there were no other changes in the community that might account for the rise in hospital use. A study of the demand for hospital beds in England (Airth and Newell 1962) also led the authors to conclude that the difference in hospital use between the two areas studied could only be attributed to a difference in the supply of beds.

Although Hassinger (1973) and others appear to feel that the relationship between resources and utilization is, at best, tenuous, the weight of empirical evidence suggests utilization rates are, indeed, higher where resources are plentiful. Klarman has concluded, "Today, most students of hospital care believe that for the purposes of policy formulation (or planning) it is best to assume that, under prevailing conditions (particularly payment by third parties for substantial volumes of hospital care), the supply of beds does influence use" (Klarman 1965:141).

Some recent work has addressed this subject. Chiswick (1973) studied admissions per thousand population, bed supply, and occupancy rates in 192 Standard Metropolitan Statistical Areas. He found a positive and significant relationship between hospital admissions per thousand population and (1) beds per thousand and (2) number of surgical specialists per thousand [1].

May used three "utilization" measures in his work on the impact of health planning. In passing, he noted a positive and significant relationship between the variables used by Chiswick and admissions per thousand (and a negative and significant relationship between total physicians per thousand population and admissions per thousand) (May 1973:36).

Controlling for a variety of "nonresource" variables [2], May found a significantly positive relationship between average length of stay and (1) beds per thousand population, (2) hospital size, and (in some instances) (3) the presence of a medical school. Similarly, in his regressions on outpatient visits per thousand (with the same control variables), he reports a positive and significant relationship with number of physicians per thousand population. In the admissions per thousand population regressions, the inclusion of the "resource" variables improved the fit of the model greatly. The coefficient of multiple determination (R^2), which measures the fraction of variance in the dependent variable which is explained by the model, was increased from approximately 0.35 to 0.83. In the average length of stay equations, the R^2 increased by about 0.20 with the inclusion of the "resource" variables; and in the outpatient visits per thousand equation, by about 0.22 (Ibid., p. 46–49).

Thus, a fair amount of evidence that there is, indeed, a demonstrable association between resources and their utilization exists. To date, however, much of the research has not come to grips with a study of the mechanisms behind these relationships. As a result, the findings are inconclusive.

There are three alternative explanations for the phenomena observed which flow directly from economic theory. At the simplest level, it may be the case that an increase in the supply of resources (hospitals, physicians, etc.) serves to depress the money price of health care resulting in an increase in the quantity of care demanded at the prevailing (lower) prices. If so, the notion of "supply increasing demand" is completely compatible with and is explained by traditional economic theory.

Secondly, it may be that an increase in the availability of resources, even if they do not reduce the money price (as would be the case, for example, in a totally "free care" situation such as Great Britain) may cause a reduction in waiting times for treatment, make possible earlier admissions to hospitals, and in general reduce the amount of time involved in obtaining care. If all money prices throughout the economy were held constant and only the adjustment described were allowed to take place, the result would be a *relative* decrease in the total "price" of health care vis-à-vis other goods and services and an observed increase in utilization.

Finally, an increase in the availability of resources in one geographic area relative to the surrounding areas may result in "in-migration" of patients seeking treatment or hospitalization and thus give the appearance of an increase in utilization, especially if utilization levels are measured from the perspective of the provider (hospital occupancy rates, admission rates, etc.) [3].

In this chapter variables representing both money costs and time costs will be included to control for the effects of changes in these factors resulting from greater availability of resources. The purpose is to isolate the effects of movement along the demand schedule resulting in different quantities demanded as prices vary from shifts in the demand schedule itself. If only changes of the former kind are observed, the notion of "supply increasing demand" is completely compatible with accepted economic theory.

If, on the other hand, an increase in the supply of health care resources actually causes the demand schedule to shift upward (increases the number of hospital beds or physicians visits demanded at *every* price), then the market for health care clearly behaves differently from other markets which have been studied by economists.

Feldstein states:

> This [an actual shift in the demand schedule] is probably what at least some writers had in mind when they spoke of "demand" being increased by an increase in bed supply. Both interpretations are consistent with the observation that there is little, if any, relation between the percentage occupancy and bed availability, but neither is implied by it; there has, in fact, been no direct test of the "pure availability effect." Such a test would require estimation of a demand function for hospital care in which both price and availability are explanatory variables. This function could not be tested by observing whether prices are lower where there are more beds per capita, since other factors affecting demand also differ across areas (1971b:31).

DESIGN OF THE STUDY

The purpose of this chapter is essentially to test the proposition that the availability of resources has a causal or associative relationship with the volume of utilization of health services, independent of and in addition to the effect of the price of those services and the many other factors which influence use.

As suggested in the quotation from Feldstein, the difficulty with drawing inferences from the previous work done in this area is the fact that in no case has the requirement that "other factors" be controlled for been met. A model which takes this requirement into account has been provided by Andersen and Newman (1973) in which they not only suggest a series of hypotheses concerning the magnitude of effect of the several factors involved, but also provide a list of variables which they feel could be used to operationalize the concepts. Their model and the list of suggested variables is reproduced in Table 8–1. The resources examined in the present work fall into their "community resources" category.

Using the 1970 household survey data, and linking with it data on the supply of resources in each of the PSUs (primary sampling units) involved, this chapter will examine the partial effects of the availability of a variety of health services resources upon utilization, controlling for the variables suggested by Andersen and Newman (Ibid.). The unit of observation will be the individual. Five different measures of utilization will be considered: (1) total number of visits to

Table 8–1. Factors Influencing Utilization of Hospitals and Physicians' Services: Subcomponents, Their Relative Importance, and Variables which Operationalize Them

| Subcomponent | Relative importance in predicting utilization of | | Variables |
	Hospitals	Physicians	
Predisposing characteristics			
Demographic	Medium	Medium	Age; sex; marital status; past history of illness
Social structure	Low	Medium	Education; race; occupation; family size; ethnicity; religion; residential mobility
Beliefs	Low	Low	Values concerning health and illness; attitudes toward health care; knowledge about disease
Enabling characteristics			
Family factors	Medium	Medium	Income; health insurance; type of regular source of care; access to regular source of care
Community factors	Low	Low	Ratios of health facilities and personnel to population; prices; region of the country; urban-rural character
Illness levels			
Perceived level	High	High	Disability; symptoms; diagnoses; general state of health
Evaluated level	High	High	Symptoms; diagnoses

Source: Andersen, R. and Newman, J. F. "Societal and Individual Determinants of Medical Care Utilization in the United States." *Milbank Memorial Fund Quarterly: Health and Society* 51, no. 1 (Winter 1973), 106–111, 115.

physicians' offices, (2) total visits of all sorts to and by physicians, (3) total number of visits by the individual to hospital outpatient departments, (4) hospitalizations for illness (as contrasted to those for obstetrical care) and (5) the number of days spent in the hospital for those conditions.

The variables used in this chapter are listed, with brief explanations, in Table 8–2. The variables chosen to represent the demographic, social structure, belief and family enabling factors of the individuals involved as well as those representing illness levels correspond as closely as possible, given the data available and the nature of the analytic methodology chosen, to those suggested by Andersen and Newman (Ibid.).

Since the focus of attention in this chapter is the resource variables, full

Table 8-2.   Variables Utilized in This Chapter

Dependent variables

BENOBOFF — The number of visits by the individual to physicians' offices for care other than obstetrical during 1970

MDTOTVIS — The total number of visits to (or by) physicians in all settings for all purposes including obstetrical care during 1970

BENOBOPD — The number of visits by the individual to outpatient departments during 1970

OTHHOSP — The total number of times the individual was hospitalized for other than OB care during 1970

OTHDAYS — The total number of days which the individual spent in the hospital during 1970 for other than obstetrical care

Independent variables

Demographic factors

AGE — The actual age in years of the individual

SEX — A dummy variable which equals 1 if the individual is a male

LIFHOSPX — The number of hospitalizations experienced by the individual prior to the year of the study

Social structure factors

HEADEDUC — The number of years of education of the head of the household

RACE1 — A dummy variable which equals 1 if the individual is nonwhite

SOCCLAS — A measure of the occupational status of the head of the household

FAMSIZE — The number of members in the family

Belief factors

SATISFAC — The heads of families and/or their spouses were asked, "Thinking over the medical care you and those close to you have received over the past few years, how satisfied have you been with each of the following:

1. the overall quality of medical care received
2. waiting time in doctors' offices or clinics
3. ease and convenience of getting to a doctor from where you live
4. the out-of-pocket costs of the medical care received
5. getting all your medical care needs taken care of at the same location?"

The responses were summed with "very satisfied" = 4, "satisfied" = 3, "unsatisfied" = 2, "very unsatisfied" = 1, and "no answer" = 2.5. All family members were given the score for the household head. If there was no response from the household head that of the spouse was substituted

Family factors

FAMINC — Actual total income of the family to which the individual belongs in thousands of dollars

PERINS — A dummy variable which equals 1 if the person is insured and 2 otherwise

Table 8-2.   continued

TRATIME — Travel time to the regular source of medical care in minutes

APTTIME — Elapsed time between initial request and the date of the appointment for medical care in days

Illness levels

DISDAYSX — Number of work-loss days experienced due to illness other than those spent in the hospital during 1970

PERHEAL — An ordinal measure of the state of the individual's health as he perceives it (for a discussion of this variable see Chapter Two)

SYMPWT — A measure of 20 nondental symptoms experienced by the individual weighted by the seriousness of the symptoms as evaluated by a panel of physicians (for a discussion of this variable see Chapter Two)

PAINANX — Each individual (excluding infants) or a proxy family member for that individual was asked about the amount of worry and pain experienced during the past year. For worry the responses were coded: "a great deal" = 4; "some" = 3; "hardly any" = 2; and "none at all" = 1. For pain the responses were coded: "very often" = 4; "fairly often" = 3; "occasionally" = 2; and "not at all" = 1. For both questions "no answer" = 0. The score for each individual was the sum of the responses to the two questions.

Resource variables[a]

MDPOP — The ratio of physicians in patient care per 1000 population for the primary sampling unit (PSU) in which the individual lives

PERCGPS — The fraction of physicians in patient care who are general (or family) practitioners in the PSU

BEDSPOP — The number of community hospital beds per 1000 population in the PSU

BEDSMD — The number of community hospital beds per physician in patient care in the PSU

SIZE — The average size of the hospitals in the PSU

OCCUP — The percentage of hospital beds occupied on average during 1970 in the PSU

MDOFPRIN — Net price per MD office visit[b]

OPDPRIN — Net price per outpatient visit[b]

MDTOPRIN — Net price per MD visit—all sites[b]

OTHTPRIN — Net price per non-OB hospitalization[b]

OTHDPRIN — Net price per non-OB hospital day[b]

---

[a]Data on supply of physicians was obtained from Haug et al. (1971) and data on supply of hospitals, beds and occupancy rates was obtained from American Hospital Association (1971).

[b]Net price is the actual out-of-pocket cost per occasion of service experienced by the individual.

analysis of the findings with respect to the partial effects of the variables representing other subcomponents of utilization will not be presented. In the present chapter they serve the purpose of controlling for the factors which they represent so that the independent effects of resource availability and prices on utilization, holding the other factors constant, can be observed. Further justification for this approach is afforded by the finding that, in general, there was little relationship between the sociodemographic characteristics of the individuals included in the chapter and the supply of resources available to them. (The largest simple correlation coefficient between a resource measure and a population characteristic measure was 0.28 between a net price variable and the dummy variable representing the insured status of the individual.) Thus, in the regression results presented subsequently, only coefficients for the resource and net price variables will be listed and discussed. Since all of the "nonresource" variables have also been included in the analysis, however, the resource effects elicited are all to be considered in the context of the rest of the system "held constant" or controlled for.

For each of the utilization measures, two different populations will be examined. First, all individuals in the study will be included in the regressions, resulting in a dependent variable which takes the value of zero for many (in the case of hospital utilization, most) of the observations and an integer value greater than zero for those individuals who, in fact, utilized the services in question during 1970.

In addition to providing results on all individuals in the study, a second series of findings will be presented for each of the utilization measures employed using subpopulations consisting of all individuals who visited a physician during the year (for the physician visits and outpatient department visits measures) and all individuals who were hospitalized during the year (for the hospital utilization measures). While ordinary least squares (OLS) regressions on the entire population will permit inferences concerning the effect of availability of resources on the likelihood of an individual visiting a physician or being admitted to a hospital [4], the analysis of the subpopulations will allow inferences concerning their association with the volume of such services consumed, given the entry of the individual into the health services system.

In the regression results reported in this chapter, the regression coefficients, the associated t statistics and their elasticities [5] will be given only for the "resource" variables under study. Results on the "control" variables are suppressed in the interest of focusing attention on the variables of interest [6].

THE HYPOTHESES

In Table 8–3, the expected direction of the influence of each of the resource variables on the particular utilization measure involved is presented. The rationale behind the expectation of a positive association between the physician-

Table 8–3. Expected Directions of Relationships Between Measures of Resource Availability and Levels of Utilization

Measures of supply of resources	*Measures of utilization*				
	BENOBOFF	*MDTOTVIS*	*BENOBOPD*	*OTHHOSP*	*OTHDAYS*
MDPOP	+	+	+	−	−
PERCGPS	+	+	−	−	−
BEDSPOP	−	−	−	+	+
BEDSMD	−	−	−	+	+
SIZE	+	+	+	+	+
OCCUP	−	−	−	−	−
Net price	−	−	−	−	−

Source: See text.

population ratio and visits to physicians and outpatient departments is obvious given the subject of this chapter and the literature reviewed above, as is that behind the expectation of a positive association between the supply of beds (per 1000 population and per physician) and the hospital utilization measures. The remainder of the relationships suggested in Table 8–3, however, require some explanation.

Two basic premises lie behind the expected negative relationship between physician-population ratios and hospital utilization. One is that physicians can exercise a fair amount of discretion with respect to the setting in which they provide their care (Anderson and Sheatsley 1967). In fact, in many cases the settings are substitutes for each other. That is, the more hospital care rendered, other things being equal, the fewer the physician visits, and vice versa. The second premise is that physicians have determined for themselves a level of income which they strive to achieve and that they will work longer or shorter hours, seeing more or fewer patients, until they approach the desired income level. The greater the supply of physicians, the lower the prices they can charge and/or fewer the patients any one of them sees. In such a situation they might be expected to attempt to increase their incomes by increasing the number of visits to their offices or by substituting care at these sites for hospital admissions—particularly in those cases for which hospital admission is desirable though not absolutely necessary. Thus, controlling for the availability of other resources and the prices involved, the more physicians, the fewer the hospital admissions expected and the shorter the anticipated stays.

The same arguments hold for general practitioners in relation to hospital utilization measures. In addition, since outpatient departments represent a better substitute for the services of general practitioners than for the services of all physicians (including specialists) as original sources of health care, the association between percent of physicians in general practice and the number of outpatient visits is postulated to be negative. The expectation is that the more general practitioners there are (and thus, the wider the availability of a "good" substitute for outpatient departments), the fewer the visits to the outpatient department.

The converse of the argument offered above in explanation of the relationship between supply of physicians and hospital utilization explains the expected negative relationship between the supply of hospital beds and visits to physicians and outpatient departments. The larger the ratio of beds to population or beds to physicians, the lower their price and/or the greater their availability. This will result in the substitution of care in hospitals for care in the physicians' offices.

Hospital size is widely accepted as a proxy for the quality of medical care available (e.g., Peterson 1973) and may also be viewed as an expression of the community's "tastes" for medical care vis-à-vis other forms of consumption. Hence, larger hospitals in the area are expected to be associated with higher utilization rates in all settings for care.

Occupancy rates is a variable which is difficult to deal with in a cross-sectional analysis. Based on the rationale developed above, high occupancy rates in a prior period (representing a "tight" situation with respect to supply of resources) would be expected to result in an increase in physician visits in the current period (as physicians substitute care in their offices for hospital care) along with a decline in the number of hospital admissions and in length of stay. In a cross-sectional analysis such as this, other things held constant, high occupancy rates will be negatively associated with admission rates and lengths of stay and will result in longer queues awaiting hospitalization as well as increased pressure to discharge patients as soon as possible. But, in addition, the higher the occupancy rate, the fewer the visits to physicians since high occupancy rates represent a situation in which physicians are *currently* substituting care in the hospital for care in their offices and in other settings. Thus, occupancy rates are expected to be negatively associated with all the utilization measures.

The final set of variables in Table 8–3, those measuring the net out-of-pocket cost per occasion of service actually paid by the individual involved, will be negatively associated with utilization of any sort since the higher the price, the lower the quantity of the good or service purchased, other things held constant.

THE RESULTS

Tables 8–4A and 8–4B present the results of the analysis of the effect of availability of resources on the number of visits made by individuals to physicians' offices for both the total population in the study and for only those who actually saw physicians during the year. Findings with respect to the former are relevant to questions of whether or not persons will visit physicians' offices at

Table 8–4A. Impact of Availability of Resources on the Volume of Visits to Physicians' Offices: Regression Results for All Cases

	Mean	Standard deviation	Regression coefficient	t	Elasticity
Dependent variable					
BENOBOFF	2.730	5.415			
Independent variables					
MDPOP	1.224	0.553	0.305	4.996	0.137
PERCGPS	29.415	24.484	0.018	11.156	0.194
BEDSMD	4.102	2.956	−0.022	2.527	−0.033
SIZE	187.397	101.897	0.003	11.008	0.206
OCCUP	75.603	16.403	−0.007	4.865	−0.194
MDOFPRIN	5.922	17.125	0.002	1.590	0.004
R^2 = 0.148					

Table 8-4B.   Impact of Availability of Resources on the Volume of Visits to Physicians' Offices: Regression Results for All Who Saw an MD

	Mean	Standard deviation	Regression coefficient	t	Elasticity
Dependent variable					
BENOBOFF	4.033	6.170			
Independent variables					
MDPOP	1.257	0.563	0.021	0.249	0.006
PERCGPS	28.386	23.860	0.020	9.069	0.141
BEDSMD	4.041	2.968	−0.036	2.869	−0.036
SIZE	191.535	101.392	0.004	9.236	0.190
OCCUP	76.018	15.553	−0.011	4.977	−0.207
MDOFPRIN	8.746	20.209	−0.017	11.404	−0.037
$R^2 = 0.132$					

all, and the latter to the effect of resources upon the volume of visits to physicians' offices for any one individual given the first visit.

In both cases, the measures of the availability of physician resources behave as expected. For both the total sample population and for only those who actually saw a physician, the number of visits to a physician's office are greater the greater the ratio of physicians to population and the larger the fraction of physicians who are general practitioners. Based on the size of the t statistics, we are confident of our inference concerning the direction of these effects in all cases except for the variable representing physician-population ratios. Further, in three of the four cases (again excepting physician-population ratios) the elasticities are relatively large. A 1 percent change in the supply of physicians per 1000 population or in the fraction of physicians who are general practitioners would cause approximately one-fifth as large an increase in the number of physician visits per individual.

The hospital supply variables also perform as expected in both equations, with volume of visits decreased by a larger ratio of beds per physician and higher occupancy rates and increased in association with larger hospital sizes. All of these coefficients are significant at at least the 5 percent level, and the elasticities associated with hospital size and percent occupancy are relatively large (that is, the magnitude of the effect of these variables is relatively large). The net price variable behaves as predicted in the equation representing only those who saw a physician. For the regressions on total sample population net price is relatively meaningless primarily because, while 7099 of the 11,619 individuals in the (unweighted) sample saw a physician during the year and thus may have paid a positive price, the remainder paid nothing and thus had a value of zero for their net price measure.

Table 8–5A. Impact of Availability of Resources on the Volume of Visits to or by a Physician: Regression Results for All Cases

	Mean	Standard deviation	Regression coefficient	t	Elasticity
Dependent variable					
MDTOTVIS	4.004	9.691			
Independent variables					
MDPOP	1.224	0.553	0.623	5.624	0.190
PERCGPS	29.415	24.484	0.021	7.390	0.154
BEDSMD	4.102	2.956	0.003	0.187	0.003
SIZE	187.397	101.897	0.004	6.922	0.187
OCCUP	75.603	16.403	−0.014	5.002	−0.204
MDTOPRIN	7.806	32.765	−0.003	2.296	−0.005
$R^2 = 0.128$					

Table 8–5B. Impact of Availability of Resources on the Volume of Visits to or by a Physician: Regression Results for All Who Saw an MD

	Mean	Standard deviation	Regression coefficient	t	Elasticity
Dependent variable					
MDTOTVIS	5.914	11.287			
Independent variables					
MDPOP	1.257	0.583	0.358	2.324	0.076
PERCGPS	28.386	23.869	0.023	5.423	0.110
BEDSMD	4.041	2.968	0.004	0.184	0.003
SIZE	191.535	101.392	0.004	5.417	0.130
OCCUP	76.018	15.553	−0.029	5.045	−0.373
MDTOPRIN	11.529	39.277	−0.012	8.453	−0.023
$R^2 = 0.115$					

Tables 8–5A and 8–5B present parallel results for all visits to physicians, regardless of site. Once again, after controlling for the demographic, social, belief, family and illness factors influencing demand, one infers from the findings that resources do make a difference in utilization. All of the variables except hospital beds per physician have the expected sign and all except that same variable have "significant" *t* statistics. Based on the elasticities, the resource variables employed, with the exception of hospital occupancy rates, appear to have a greater impact in the regression representing all individuals than in that

representing only those who saw a physician. That is, modificications in the availability of resources are more likely to have an observable effect on the ability of individuals to gain access to sources of care than upon the volume of physicians' services which they receive.

Tables 8–6A and 8–6B present the results of the analysis of the impact of resources on visits to outpatient departments. They are somewhat unsatisfying in the sense that the R^2s achieved are relatively low, indicating that the model chosen was not a particularly good one. Nevertheless, the coefficients estimated

Table 8–6A. Impact of Availability of Resources on the Volume of Visits to Outpatient Departments: Regression Results for All Cases

	Mean	Standard deviation	Regression coefficient	t	Elasticity
Dependent variable					
BENOBOPD	0.232	3.088			
Independent variables					
MDPOP	1.224	0.553	0.505	13.657	2.664
PERCGPS	29.415	24.484	−0.002	2.521	−0.254
BEDSMD	4.102	2.956	0.017	3.179	0.301
SIZE	187.397	101.897	0.000001	–	–
OCCUP	75.603	16.403	−0.007	7.371	−2.221
OPDPRIN	0.306	5.153	0.015	6.105	0.020
$R^2 = 0.035$					

Table 8–6B. Impact of Availability of Resources on the Volume of Visits to Outpatient Departments: Regression Results for All Who Saw an MD

	Mean	Standard deviation	Regression coefficient	t	Elasticity
Dependent variable					
BENOBOPD	0.341	3.374			
Independent variables					
MDPOP	1.257	0.563	0.673	12.702	2.481
PERCGPS	28.386	23.869	0.0005	0.335	0.042
BEDSMD	4.041	2.968	0.028	3.466	0.332
SIZE	191.535	101.392	−0.00001	0.045	−0.006
OCCUP	76.018	15.553	−0.010	7.085	−2.229
OPDPRIN	0.451	6.257	−0.014	4.812	−0.019
$R^2 = 0.035$					

are in the directions expected. In Table 8–6A all except the beds per physician variable have the expected signs and all except size are highly significant. The net price variable has a positive coefficient for the same reasons as those discussed with respect to physicians' office visits above. The elasticities, particularly those between physician-population ratio and occupancy rates and the volume of outpatient visits are quite large.

In the equation estimating the volume of outpatient visits for that segment of the population which actually saw a physician during the year, the beds-physician variable, the variable representing the percent of physicians who are general practitioners and the size variable all have signs opposite from those expected, but only that on the beds-population variable is significant. A possible explanation for the significant (and perverse) findings with regard to the hospital bed ratio in these equations is the fact that, controlling for size of hospitals, the larger the bed-physician ratio, the larger the number of hospitals in the area and, therefore, the greater the *number* of outpatient departments available. If the latter variable had been included in the equation, the results might be quite different.

The remaining three resource availability variables behave as expected and the results on them are significant.

Surprisingly, the average size of hospitals appears to have little effect upon the volume of hospital admissions for causes other than obstetrical care either for the entire population or for those who were, in fact, hospitalized [7]. In Tables 8–7A and 8–7B, the findings on the impact of it and other resource availability variables upon this dependent variable are presented. With the exception of size, however, all of the variables have coefficients with the expected signs. The availability of beds per 1000 population has an important

Table 8–7A. Impact of Availability of Resources on the Volume of Hospital Admissions: Regression Results for All Cases

	Mean	Standard deviation	Regression coefficient	t	Elasticity
Dependent Variable					
OTHHOSP	0.115	0.410			
Independent variables					
MDPOP	1.224	0.553	−0.004	1.172	−0.043
BEDSPOP	4.162	1.749	0.006	6.393	0.217
SIZE	187.397	101.897	−0.00004	2.069	−0.065
OCCUP	75.603	16.403	−0.002	5.945	−0.460
OTHTPRIN	5.831	65.459	0.002	7.120	0.101
$R^2 = 0.204$					

Table 8–7B.   Impact of Availability of Resources on the Volume of Hospital Admissions: Regression Results for All Hospitalizations for Non–OB Illness

	Mean	Standard deviation	Regression coefficient	t	Elasticity
Dependent variable					
OTHHOSP	1.260	0.633			
Independent variables					
MDPOP	1.178	0.545	−0.109	5.472	−0.102
BEDSPOP	4.205	1.874	0.002	0.486	0.007
SIZE	173.311	102.715	0.0003	2.832	0.041
OCCUP	74.162	17.659	−0.001	1.814	−0.059
OTHTPRIN	63.922	208.000	0.0005	5.035	0.025
$R^2 = 0.128$					

effect on the likelihood of hospitalization, but a less marked impact on the number of hospitalizations experienced by an individual; the ratio of physicians to population has a much larger effect on the volume than on the likelihood of hospitalizations.

The net price variable does not perform well, but this is not surprising in light of the fact that fewer than one in ten of the (unweighted) sample population were hospitalized during the year, affecting the distribution of the zero and positive values of that variable.

A 1 percent increase in the supply of physicians will, according to these findings, result in about a one-twentieth of 1 percent *decrease* in the likelihood of an individual being hospitalized, holding constant his sociodemographic attributes, his attitudes and his illness level. A 1 percent increase in the availability of hospital beds will result in a one-fifth of 1 percent increase in admissions and a 1 percent increase in the occupancy levels will result in a nearly one-half of 1 percent decrease in the likelihood of hospital admissions.

Slightly more than 20 percent of the variability in the likelihood of individuals from this sample population being hospitalized is explained by the equation presented in Table 8–7A, but only about 13 percent of the variability in the number of hospitalizations per individual. This should not be surprising in light of the fact that the probability of being hospitalized more than once, given the first hospitalization, is probably much more influenced by individual and physician decisions based on medical findings than on the sort of factors considered in this analysis.

Finally, Tables 8–8A and 8–8B present the results of the regressions estimating the effects of the availability of resources on number of hospital days holding constant other factors influencing demand. Once again, all of the results are in the directions expected (with the exception of bed-population ratio) and all (with the same exception) are significant.

The results reported in Table 8–8A are essentially those reported in Table 8–7A with the dependent variable measure for each individual multiplied by his average length of hospital stay. Since there is significant variability in length of stay by individual, the R^2 for this equation is much lower than it is in the previous results. The results in Table 8–8B, on the other hand, address the question of the impact of the availability of resources on the length of hospital stays of the persons in this sample. Average hospital size and the ratio of physicians to population (and, to a lesser extent occupancy rates) play a very impor-

Table 8–8A. Impact of Availability of Resources on the Volume of Days in the Hospital: Regression Results for All Cases

	Mean	Standard deviation	Regression coefficient	t	Elasticity
Dependent variable					
OTHDAYS	1.276	10.228			
Independent variables					
MDPOP	1.224	0.553	−0.238	2.457	−0.228
BEDSPOP	4.162	1.749	0.010	0.130	0.033
SIZE	187.397	101.897	0.002	4.296	0.294
OCCUP	75.603	16.403	−0.012	4.061	−0.711
OTHDPRIN	0.876	7.540	0.115	9.489	0.079
$R^2 = 0.053$					

Table 8–8B. Impact of Availability of Resources on the Volume of Days in the Hospital: Regression Results for All Hospitalizations for Non–OB Illness

	Mean	Standard deviation	Regression coefficient	t	Elasticity
Dependent variable					
OTHDAYS	13.983	31.132			
Independent variables					
MDPOP	1.178	0.545	−5.942	5.964	−0.501
BEDSPOP	4.205	1.874	−0.285	1.213	−0.086
SIZE	173.311	102.715	0.034	6.107	0.421
OCCUP	74.162	17.659	−0.056	4.044	−0.297
OTHDPRIN	9.606	23.224	−0.075	3.989	−0.052
$R^2 = 0.105$					

tant role in influencing lengths of hospital stay—at least as measured by their elasticities. Net price, though exerting an effect in the expected direction, is somewhat less influential. Slightly more than 10 percent of the variation in the volume of hospital days experienced is explained by this equation.

CONCLUSIONS

Two major sets of conclusions can be drawn from the results reported above. First, the availability of resources does appear to have an impact on the utilization of physician services, both in the office and in total, on outpatient department visits and on both hospital admissions and lengths of stay. These effects are observable even after the demographic, social and illness factors which are thought to influence demand for care have been taken into account. Further, having controlled for both money and time price variables, the residual effects observed appear to result from a shift in the demand curve rather than a movement along the curve. That is, increased availability of resources increases the quantity demanded at any given price rather than increasing the quantity demanded by reducing prices.

Second, the impact is not unidirectional. It is not correct to simply say that more resources result in more utilization. The relationships among the various resource measures employed and between them and the utilization measures are complex and, occasionally, counterintuitive (see Table 8–3 and accompanying discussion). However, it would appear from the findings reported here that modifications in the supply of resources would have an impact upon patterns of utilization. This provides some support for the attitudes of those who advocate regulation or reconfiguration of the system for the purpose of modifying access and patterns of use.

A CAUTION AND A CHALLENGE

The findings reported here should be considered suggestive rather than definitive. Little is known about the "true" structure of the relationships among the variables considered; almost nothing about the interactions among many of them. If anything, the worth of this chapter lies in the elucidation of some of those relationships and structures. It is to be hoped that further research directed at redefining and refining the variables and the models proposed here will provide further insights into the question of the impact of the supply of resources on the levels and patterns of utilization of health services.

NOTES TO CHAPTER EIGHT

1. After controlling for median family income, age distribution of the population, sex, race, births and deaths per thousand, and for the number of medical schools and medical students (which, he argues, affect "in-migration" rates to health resources).

2. In addition to the "resource" variables, May's regressions contained median family income, percent of families below the low income level, percent of population less than five and more than 54 years old, population per housing unit and per square mile, percent of the population female and over 17 years old, race, deaths per thousand, percent with hospitalization insurance and average price of a semiprivate hospital room.

3. This is, in fact, the perspective employed in the studies cited above. It results in an overstatement of the changes in utilization on the part of the members of the local population. On the other hand, the approach employed in this chapter which measures utilization from the perspective of the individuals living in the area will understate (or estimate lower bounds on) the changes in utilization rates in the face of "in-migration."

4. The use of OLS in this situation produces coefficients which are biased and permits "predicted" levels of utilization which are less than zero. However, experimentation with random samples from the study population using tobit analysis techniques provide evidence that the results reported are robust with respect to the technique employed.

5. Elasticity is a measure which facilitates analysis of the *magnitude* (as opposed to the direction) of the effect of a change in the independent variable on the dependent variable. It is computed (in the case of a regression using arithmetic measures of the variables) by multiplying the ratio of the means of the independent and dependent variables by the regression coefficient. Its interpretation is as follows: for a 1 percent change in the independent variable, the resultant change in the dependent variable will be x percent (where x is the elasticity).

6. Full results are, of course, available on request. Also unreported are regression results using unweighted data. There were no major differences in the estimates obtained using the unweighted observations.

7. It was suggested by a reader of this chapter that this finding could result from the inclusion of both bed-population ratios and size in the same equation and the resultant multicolinearity (assuming a high simple correlation between them). In fact, the simple correlation coefficient is small and multicollinearity is therefore not likely to be involved.

Part IV

Need

Chapter Nine

Health Status and Utilization
of Physician Services

John F. Newman, Jr.

It has been argued that an individual's health status is a major determinant of his use of health services. If this is in fact true, then a desired public policy goal would be to insure that appropriate care is received by individuals at a given health level and as a corollary that utilization is directly related to the need for care.

This chapter examines the relative importance of an individual's perceived health status versus clinical evaluation of health status in relation to two measures of physician utilization: contact, and number of visits for persons with one or more visits. Using MCA analysis the results were: (1) both perceived and evaluated measures were important predictors for each of the dependent variables; (2) a perceived measure was the most important predictor of contact; (3) an evaluated measure was the most important predictor of use, given at least one visit.

The author discusses possible strategies of developing and implementing public policy programs in view of the findings in this chapter and the perspectives of other researchers.

INTRODUCTION

It has been argued that an individual's health status or health level is a major determinant of his use of health services (see Andersen and Newman 1973). If this is in fact true, then a desired public policy goal would be to insure that appropriate care is delivered to individuals at a given health level and as a corollary that utilization be directly related to the need for care.

While there are physiological parameters to a person's health status which may be constant over time and are not influenced by medical care contact, the assumption is often made that greater contact and volume of use results in a general increase in health status, all other things being equal. This assumption is challenged by Benham and Benham in Chapter Twelve of this book.

It should also be kept in mind that greater contact may be a result of improved diagnostic procedures which detect previously unknown conditions, which in turn necessitate further utilization. Thus, unless utilization is examined simultaneously with health level—i.e., standardized for need for care—the rationale for policy decisions based on what may be inappropriate data is open to question.

Regardless of the data base, however, another policy goal may very well be improving the quality and appropriateness of medical care so that a person's health status could more accurately guide his utilization.

A pragmatic concern from a policy perspective is whether an individual's perception of his health status is more strongly associated with physician utilization than the clinical evaluation of his health status. If the former (individual perception) is more important, then policy decisions regarding the implementation of educational programs might be an important strategy. In this instance, an overall goal would be to sensitize the population towards either preventive health behavior—i.e., the maintainence of good health—or symptomatic health behavior—i.e., seeking care when symptoms are present. The overall goal, of course, would be to motivate individuals to seek health care on a more or less regular basis depending on their need for care as determined by their perceived health level.

However, if clinical evaluation is a more important predictor of utilization, then a possible strategy would be the implementation of a populationwide health screening and evaluation program resulting in the detection and evaluation of clinical conditions. In this case the organization and financing of such a program would be major issues of legislative debate.

Such screening and evaluation programs would almost surely entail higher costs of implementation and maintainence than the simple identification of perceived need based on an individual's self-reporting of his condition.

In this chapter the purpose is to assess the relative importance of perceived versus clinical evaluation of health status as predictors of physician utilization. In order to accomplish this goal, a brief review of the literature will be presented. The review will be followed by an analysis in which both types of measures are used to distinguish users from nonusers, and the impact of both measures on the number of physician visits will be assessed.

STUDIES ON HEALTH STATUS

Theoretically, most of the utilization literature relating to health status emphasizes social psychological models of health behavior. In the absence of clinical data, the models and/or studies were concerned mainly with the individual's perception of his health level in relation to behavior.

Both Zborowski (1952) and Zola (1966), in studies of persons who have presented themselves for care in hospital based settings, underscore the importance of cultural and ethnic parameters in relation to the individual's perception and reporting of illness and subsequent utilization of medical resources. Suchman (1966), in a similar approach, reported that individuals identified in the social structure as parochial (ethnocentric) as opposed to cosmopolitan (progressive) varied considerably in their orientation to medical care and utilization behavior. The studies cited above emphasized theoretical models developed in relatively limited research settings where the study population was small in total numbers.

However, Rosenstock (1966), borrowing from the work of Kasl and Cobb (1966), Kegeles (1963) and others, developed a generalized model of health behavior in which an individual's actions and responses were important. According to Rosenstock perceived health status, in relation to utilization, is part of a social process whereby decisions to seek or not to seek medical care are made. To summarize, the utilization of health services depends on (1) the individual's perceived susceptibility to the condition, (2) the perceived seriousness of the condition and (3) the perceived benefits of taking health action in relation to potential barriers. Together, these three factors determine an individual's readiness to act. However, in order for an individual to take health related actions, the individual needs to be "cued." That is, exposure to the media or other persons facilitates the seeking (or nonseeking) of care.

Subsequent studies by Goochman (1971; 1972) tend to support the model as proposed by Rosenstock (1966). However, it should be noted that the preceding studies and models were concerned with perceived health status.

Andersen and Newman (1973) reviewed several national household surveys with similar methodologies and conceptual frameworks for analysis. Each survey included perceived measures of health. They conclude that an individual's perceived health status and evaluated measures of health status were the most important variables in predicting utilization of services. The health measures upon which these findings were based included (1) number of disability days, (2) seeing a doctor for symptoms, (3) symptoms reported by the individual and (4) the response to the question, Would you say your health, in general, is excellent, good, fair or poor?

One national study (see Andersen 1968) took the family as the unit of analysis. Two measures of health status—disability days and seeing a doctor for symptoms—emerged as important predictors of physician utilization.

A subsequent analysis of the same data (see Andersen et al. 1970) taking the individual as the unit of analysis was performed. Separate analyses were made for persons under 21 years of age and those 21 or older where the major health status variables were number of symptoms reported and perceived health level.

In predicting use versus nonuse of physicians for persons 21 and older, the number of symptoms reported was clearly the single most important predictor variable while perceived health level was not significant. However, for persons under 21 no health measure was significant. In examining use patterns for those with at least one visit among persons 21 and older, perceived health and symptoms were the two most important variables. Of the two, perceived health was more important. Again, for those under 21 no health measures were significant.

While health status may be the single most important predictor of utilization, some authors have recently focused on the interaction between health status and other predisposing or enabling variables. For example, Antonovsky (1972) suggests that certain nonmedical needs together with the "tendency to define oneself as ill" result in a high frequency of health clinic utilization. Monteiro (1973) in examining the relation of income to physician utilization also included a measure of perceived health—restricted activity days—as well as whether the respondent was on public welfare or not. The analysis in this instance pointed to some of the self-evident and more subtle interactions of health status in relation to utilization. More recently Wan and Soifer (1974) have determined, using a path analysis approach, that the need for care, measured by self-assessments of poor health, response to illness and need for a physician, is the most important dimension in predicting physician utilization at the family level. However, in a summary of their entire analysis they state: "[I] t is also found that the need for care is an intermediate factor through which the enabling and predisposing factors affect the course of health actions" (Ibid., p. 106).

These recent efforts can be viewed as attempts to either synthesize findings or to define other areas of potential research. Both the synthesis and potential research could result in new or different approaches in the delivery of care as other variables are identified as contributing to utilization.

To summarize, a review of relevant literature does suggest that health status is strongly related to the use of health services in general and, by implication, the use of physician services. However, since most of the studies reviewed focused on the individual's perception of health in relation to utilization, it is not clear how the clinical evaluation of an individual's health influences his utilization. In the analysis to follow the relative importance of the health status variables will be assessed.

PROTOCOL FOR ANALYSIS DATA

Health measures from the national survey are classified as either perceived or evaluated. For the purposes of this analysis the perceived health variables are: (1) the number of disability days reported by the individual in 1970; (2) the individual's perceived health status; (3) the amount of worry about his health; and (4) the amount of pain experienced by the individual. The evaluated health measures are: (1) the evaluation of symptoms reported by individuals which were weighted according to relative importance by a panel of 40 physicians; (2) the reported number of lifetime hospitalizations of the individual; and (3) an evaluation by a panel of five physicians of the relative severity of the diagnoses for which the individual saw a physician during the year.

The evaluated symptoms variable is the score obtained by summing weights for the symptoms reported. The number of hospitalizations includes all hospitalizations. Lifetime hospitalizations as used in this chapter is a proxy measure to assess the individual's past health status in terms of the clinical evaluation of conditions requiring hospitalization. In using this measure, we are assuming that persons with low levels of hospital use will, all other things being equal, have low levels of continued physician use. The clinical evaluation of diagnoses is based on the assumption that some diagnoses require mandatory health action on the part of the individual while other diagnoses are less immediate problems and allow elective actions. For a further discussion of this issue the reader is referred to Chapter Ten by Kravits and Schneider.

Analysis Procedure

The analysis will be performed in the following order: (1) a discussion of the intercorrelations among the health status variables, (2) a Multiple Classification Analysis (MCA) of the percent of the population seeing a physician and (3) a MCA analysis of the number of physician visits.

In the analysis on the percent seeing a physician, the first step will be to assess the relative importance of selected perceived health and evaluated health variables taken together, followed by covariance analysis as a second step.

The analysis on number of physician visits will consist of a covariance analysis to answer the question of what is the relative importance of variables, perceived and evaluated, in predicting the number of visits for individuals who have made contact with a physician.

Multiple Classification Analysis is a computer program technique developed by Andrews et al. (1973). It essentially combines features of both regression analysis and analysis of variance to produce: (1) multiple R^2 (the proportion of variance explained), (2) the within class correlation (eta) for each variable, (3) a beta coefficient indicating the relative importance of each variable, adjusted for all of the other variables, (4) unadjusted values (percents or mean visits) for each variable category (these values are based only on the variable in question without considering other variables) and (5) adjusted values (percents or mean visits) for each variable category (these values result when the effect of the other variables—i.e., independent variables only, or independent and covariates together—are taken into account).

The covariance analysis is performed as a feature of the MCA when other variables of experimental interest are used. These variables are in effect control variables—i.e., covariates—which could possibly account for some of the variance between the dependent variables and the health status measures, although the covariates are not of direct interest.

Intercorrelations

Except for perceived health, the correlation between physician seen and the health status variables is higher than the correlation between physician visits and the health variables (Table 9–1).

Table 9—1. Intercorrelations Between Health Status Variables (Gamma) and Number of Physician Visits and Whether a Physician Was Seen or Not

Variable	SEEN	VISITS	DISDAYS	SYMEVAL	PERHEAL	WORRY	PAIN	LIFEHOSP
Physician seen								
Physician visits*								
Disability days	0.472	0.387						
Symptoms evaluated	0.370	0.337	0.364					
Perceived health	0.238	0.268	0.301	0.463				
Worry	-0.465	-0.417	-0.473	-0.534	-0.697			
Pain	-0.377	-0.365	-0.487	-0.601	-0.601	0.749		
Life hospitalizations	0.310	0.350	0.252	0.320	0.319	-0.380	-0.379	

*Gammas are based on crosstabulations where "no visit" was a category.

With respect to the correlation between the two utilization measures and health status variables, disability days and worry over health have the highest correlations followed in descending order by pain, symptoms evaluated, lifetime hospitalizations and perceived health. Each of the health measures is directly related to utilization [1].

As might be expected, the matrix in Table 9–1 reveals a high positive correlation between any two health measures with the following exceptions: (1) disability days has a low but positive correlation with symptoms evaluated, perceived health and lifetime hospitalizations, and (2) lifetime hospitalizations has a low but positive correlation with perceived health and symptoms evaluated.

Percent Seeing a Physician

In the analysis of the percent seeing a physician the independent variables are disability days, symptoms evaluated, perceived health, worry over health and pain level, with age, insurance coverage (present or absent), education of the head of the household and family income as the covariates. Severity of diagnosis is by definition not included as an independent variable since persons with a diagnosis will always have a visit. Lifetime hospitalizations is not included in this analysis because it, strictly speaking, is a proxy variable for need; as such it seems more useful to include it in the subsequent analysis on the number of physician visits where our "strongest" illness variable, severity of diagnosis, is included. Such a strategy should minimize the likelihood of a spurious relation between utilization and hospitalizations.

As shown in Table 9–2, the values for eta with respect to the unadjusted percentages are approximately the same for all variables with the exception of perceived health status, which is slightly lower. When the five measures are taken together, the beta coefficient for the adjusted values reveals that disability days is the most important variable, followed by worry and symptoms evaluated at the same level of importance. Neither perceived health nor pain appear to be important predictors in seeing a physician.

An important issue which is often raised is, What is the effect of an independent variable on the dependent variable when other variables are introduced as statistical controls? Covariance analysis is a technique which permits this question to be answered assuming that the controls (i.e., covariates) are of experimental interest as opposed to assessing their relative importance. Accordingly, as shown under the column headed "adjusted for independents and covariates," each of the health measures was analyzed in relation to the percent seeing a physician with the four covariates mentioned above. This combination of predisposing and enabling variables as covariates were selected because of their presumed overall importance in influencing utilization (see Andersen 1968; Andersen and Newman 1973).

Based on the size of the beta coefficient, disability days remains the most

Table 9–2. Analysis of the Percent of Persons Seeing a Physician With Disability Days, Symptoms Evaluated, Perceived Health Worry and Pain as Independent Variables and Age, Insurance Coverage, Education of Head and Family Income as Covariates

Variable	Percent unadjusted	Eta	Percent adjusted for independents	Beta	Percent adjusted for independents and covariates	Beta
Total population—65 (percent)						
Disability days						
None	52		56		56	
1–2	66		67		66	
3–4	67		66		65	
5–9	78		75		74	
10–19	87		80		80	
20–39	89		79		79	
40–365	94		83		83	
		0.31		0.21		0.20
Symptoms evaluated						
None	51		57		58	
0.0001–0.43	66		65		65	
0.44–0.72	66		67		67	
0.73–1.04	74		71		70	
1.05–1.69	76		71		71	
1.70–2.75	83		74		74	
2.76–11.67	86		83		73	
		0.27		0.14		0.14
Perceived health						
Excellent	58		67		65	
Good	66		65		65	
Fair	76		61		64	
Poor	88		62		67	
		0.15		0.04		0.04

Worry			
Great deal	89	76	66
Some	85	77	68
Hardly any	66	65	65
None	54	59	59
	0.29	0.16	0.16
Pain			
Very often	87	64	64
Fairly often	81	65	65
Occasionally	70	66	66
Not at all	53	64	64
	0.23	0.03	0.03
		Multiple R 0.145	Multiple R 0.164

important variable, followed by worry and symptoms evaluated at the same relative level of importance. Neither pain nor perceived health are important.

The overall effect of the independent variables and covariates, examining unadjusted and adjusted percentages, is twofold: (1) to increase the percentage of persons seeing a physician when individuals are extremely healthy—i.e., no reported disability days, worry, pain or symptoms, and perceived health is viewed as excellent; and (2) to decrease the percentage seeing a physician when individuals report any level of illness.

This finding indicates that variations in the percent seeing a physician can, as expected, be accounted for by differences in the level of both perceived and evaluated health. Differences in contact are as anticipated a function of health level, although neither pain nor perceived health seems to be an important predictor.

Number of Visits (Persons with One or More Visits)

While it is important to be able to assess the relative importance of health measures in predicting either whether a physician was seen or the number of visits, another issue is the relative importance of measures in predicting utilization for those persons with one or more visits. Knowledge of factors related to utilization at this level of analysis helps forecast demand, given contact with the health system.

For this analysis two additional measures are included: the evaluation of diagnoses and the number of lifetime hospitalizations. Diagnoses were obtained only for individuals who had at least one physician visit; lifetime hospitalizations refer to the number of hospitalizations prior to the survey year.

A summary analysis is presented in Table 9—3. In this table disability days, symptoms evaluated, diagnosis severity and hospitalizations were analyzed in addition to perceived health. Table 9—1 shows that perceived health, worry and pain are highly intercorrelated, perhaps indicating that they are measures of the same dimension, i.e., measures of one's perception of his health level [2].

To summarize from Table 9—3: (1) with the exception of hospitalizations which has a lower value, eta is approximately the same for all variables; (2) beta coefficients, adjusted for independent variables only and adjusted for the covariates, are the highest and approximately the same for severity of diagnoses and disability days; (3) beta coefficients, for symptoms evaluated and either perceived health, worry or pain, are next in importance and take on the same approximate values; (4) life hospitalizations has virtually no effect on physician utilization.

As noted in the preceding analysis on the number of physician visits the effect of adjusting the category values is to increase utilization for persons who are relatively healthy and decrease utilization for persons who are not very healthy.

SUMMARY

Based on the correlation matrix (Table 9-1), the relatively high intercorrelations suggest that if attempts to measure health status are made, any one variable may be as good as another, if a single indicator of health is the only consideration. It would seem, then, that each variable is an adequate measure of the underlying dimension, health status.

However, as the subsequent analysis revealed, the impact of these health status variables on the two measures of utilization differs with each dependent variable. For example, in the analysis on the percent seeing a physician a perceived health measure, disability days, was the most important predictor. Worry over health, a perceived measure, and the evaluation of symptoms were the next most important group of predictors.

In the last analysis on the number of visits it was found that severity of diagnosis (an evaluated measure) was the most important predictor followed by disability days. The remaining variables did not appear to differ significantly from one another, although life hospitalizations was the least important variable.

In the light of these findings, what can be said concerning the presumed policy goal of maximizing use of physician services based on need, as measured by these health status variables?

Meeting this goal defies a simplistic approach or solution. As previously noted (see Andersen and Newman 1973), the potential for intervening in the health care system with respect to a group of variables (including health status) depends on: (1) how the variables can be altered to influence the distribution of health services (mutability); (2) the importance of causal relations between the model components and utilization (causation); and (3) the interaction between variables in relation to utilization.

Based on the data in this chapter, the chapter by Andersen (Chapter Two) and studies cited previously (Wan and Soifer 1974; Antonovsky 1972), it is relatively clear that health status measures are causally related to the utilization of physician services. The direction of the causality can be stated in simple terms: health status is directly related to utilization with other predisposing and enabling variables influencing use through health status.

It should be noted in retrospect that the analysis in this chapter also revealed that the covariates had little effect on utilization. The increase in the multiple R between the analysis with health variables only and the analysis with health variables and covariates was quite small.

It is doubtful that the health status variables can be altered easily on a societal basis. Indeed, the mutability of health status variables may be largely academic since in the long run health status may be used to identify appropriate differences in health service use.

From a public policy perspective the most crucial element in developing

Table 9–3. Covariance Analysis for Persons With at Least One Physician Visit by Disability Days, Symptoms Evaluated, Diagnosis Severity, Life Hospitalizations and Perceived Health With Age, Insurance Coverage, Education of Head and Family Income as Covariates

Variable	Unadjusted	Eta	Adjusted for independents	Beta	Adjusted for independents and covariates	Beta
Total population—5.32						
Disability days						
None	4.12		4.69		4.63	
1–2	3.75		4.53		4.49	
3–4	3.89		4.28		4.33	
5–9	5.04		5.07		4.11	
10–19	6.58		6.07		6.14	
20–39	7.78		6.40		6.49	
40–365	11.74		9.17		9.20	
		0.25		0.14		0.15
Symptoms evaluated						
None	3.46		4.61		4.66	
0.0001–0.43	4.45		5.05		5.13	
0.44–0.72	4.54		4.84		4.82	
0.73–1.04	5.02		5.05		5.02	
1.05–1.69	6.24		5.98		5.97	
1.70–2.75	6.32		5.55		5.48	
2.76–11.67	9.59		7.03		6.95	
		0.22		0.09		0.08
Severity of diagnosis						
Elective only	2.64		3.56		3.61	
Elected and mandatory	7.54		6.97		6.95	
Mandatory only	6.12		5.64		5.60	
		0.24		0.16		0.16

Life hospitalizations			
None	4.15	5.17	5.27
1	5.06	5.27	5.28
2	5.54	5.07	4.99
3–4	6.62	5.58	5.46
5 or more	8.28	5.71	5.55
	0.15	0.02	0.02
Perceived health			
Excellent	3.68	4.79	4.77
Good	5.06	5.16	5.17
Fair	7.77	6.13	6.14
Poor	11.28	7.49	7.56
	0.22	0.08	0.08
	Multiple R 0.113	Multiple R 0.113	Multiple R 0.115

programs may be the interaction between two or more variables in the utilization model. Population subgroups, identified as low users relative to other subgroups in terms of disability days, evaluated symptoms or severity of diagnosis, are starting points in the development of program goals. The identification of subgroups should focus simultaneously on other variables in the model of utilization in conjunction with the health status variables which were identified as important predictors of utilization.

Essentially, this position borrows from the conceptual and methodological approach of Aday and Andersen (1975). The general approach seeks to ultimately confront policy issues under the assumption that utilization should be related to the need for care. According to Aday and Andersen, the need for care can be empirically derived by constructing two indexes. The first index is the use-need discrepancy ratio based on physician contact and self-reporting by the individual of his disability days. The second is the symptoms-response ratio based on reported symptoms, weighted for severity, in relation to physician contact. These two measures represent a logical step toward the refinement of health based variables in terms of their impact on utilization. For example, the symptoms response ratio, based on the same symptoms used in this chapter, indicated that children, whites and higher income groups responded to symptoms by seeing a doctor more often than other age, race or income groups. Ideally we want to be able to define target populations like these so that resources can be allocated more efficiently. That is, statements relative to utilization can be made, for example, about age and income taken together with a health status measure.

It seems, therefore, that the first step in the attainment of goals is to develop utilization profiles for combinations of predisposing, enabling and the important health status variables as suggested above. A subsequent step would then be to assess the intervention potential for the various combinations of variables and develop priorities for intervention based on this assessment. Such priority setting might lead, as suggested earlier in this chapter, to either educational or motivational efforts in the case of perceived health measures, or health screening and evaluation programs for evaluated health measures.

The impact of these efforts may initially be less than desired, however, unless a broad perspective toward utilization is formulated. Programs may be less than fully successful because of factors which were not taken into account at the program implementation stage. Goochman (1971) suggests that difficulties in shaping health related behavior may be attributed to a lack of the salience of health on the part of the general population. Berkanovic and Reeder (1974) in a similar vein point out that sociocultural factors are important parameters in utilization behavior. Awareness of such factors may, in the long run, affect the implementation and success of any health intervention program for any target population subgroup.

NOTES TO CHAPTER NINE

1. The coding for worry and pain resulted in a negative coefficient when the true coefficient is, in fact, positive. A negative sign indicates a direct relationship. The coding also accounts for the positive correlation between worry and pain.

2. Only the table with perceived health is included in the chapter; the results with worry and pain in separate tables did not alter any findings with respect to the importance of perceived and evaluated health measures. As was true for perceived health in Table 9–3, worry and pain were of medium importance. Betas for adjusting on the independent variables only were worry, 0.06; pain, 0.08. Betas for adjusting on independents and covariates were worry, 0.06; pain, 0.08.

Chapter Ten

Health Care Need and Actual Use by Age, Race and Income

Joanna Kravits and
John Schneider

Whites are more apt to see a physician and dentist during the year than are blacks and better off individuals more apt to than are individuals with incomes below the near poverty line. These two factors appear to operate independently of one another to some degree so that for some measures of discretionary health care, poor whites are actually more likely to obtain care than are well off blacks. This is particularly true of elective dental care.

When blacks do go to the doctor, they are seen as sicker than whites as judged by a panel of physicians. The same relationship holds independently for income. However, when asked to self-report their own symptoms, blacks consistently report fewer than do whites and also report less serious symptoms on average. Higher income blacks have the greatest discrepancy.

The public policy implications of these findings are twofold:

1. If "equal" access to health care is provided, blacks and low income individuals will use considerably more than the mean amount of care. Under the current system, the reverse is true.

2. The black population appears to see itself as less sick than it actually is as rated by physicians and dentists at the time care is sought. Lower income individuals, however, appear to report their symptoms comparably to individuals with higher incomes. Perhaps blacks, regardless of income, should be singled out by public policy makers for special attention in obtaining health care and in learning to evaluate their symptoms in a more medically appropriate way. Since poor whites do not show the same variance in care obtained, race appears to be a problem independent of income.

How good a determinant of health care use is health care need? The answer to this question may at first seem self-evident, since we assume that people go to the doctor when they are sick and to the hospital when they are very sick. Theoretically, these should be the only considerations, or at least the main ones.

But what is "sick" and what is "very sick?" Attempting to answer these questions, we run into another whole set of speculations, namely that what is "sick" to one group may be "very sick" to another and "not sick at all" to yet a third.

This chapter attempts to face these issues by using medical evaluation of need in examining health care use. The need for health care use is a particularly pertinent question since it is well known that various population groups use health care services differently. The poor, for example, are hospitalized more often but see the doctor less although when they do get into the system, they use about the same number of doctor visits. They see the dentist much less often but have a slightly higher number of visits once they do get into the system. Is it possible that the *reasons* they go to the hospital, the doctor and the dentist are also different?

It has frequently been hypothesized that the poor use health care for more serious conditions than do the nonpoor. Conversely, many feel that provision of medical care without charge to the poor will and does result in their seeking medical care for trivial conditions. Blacks have been singled out as a group for whom both of these hypotheses may hold true. Although they use fewer health care services overall than do whites, their emergency room usage is much higher for nonemergent conditions (Gibson 1971). This chapter attempts to examine these premises using health survey data and to develop a set of objective scales by which health care need can be measured using medical evaluation.

DEVELOPMENT OF DIAGNOSTIC CHARACTERISTICS CODES

Reasons given by those interviewed for hospitalization and for seeing a physician were placed into one of approximately 100 diagnostic classifications which had been modified by the authors from the International Classification of Diseases—Adapted (ICDA) codes so that they could be used for ambulatory care as well as hospitalized illness. The International Classification of Disease index (ICDA 1957) is a detailed listing of several thousand diagnoses which makes possible comparisons across countries as well as within them. This index was originally designed for tabulating causes of death and is still used for this purpose. Later, it was adapted for coding hospital admissions so that medical record librarians could produce statistical summaries of admissions to inpatient facilities. The index is arranged by body systems and by type of cause of illness, but it is sufficiently detailed that comparisons of a given disease (for example, cancer) can be made by summing up all of the subcategories (such as cancer of the lung, leukemia, etc.). Thus, the index can be greatly condensed into a disease index without losing much of its comparative usefulness.

Attempts have been made to apply the ICDA index to physician care outside of the hospital, but without much success. Brown et al. (1971), for example, applied the index to 12,835 patient visits to 15 Massachusetts physicians and found that the system was "grossly inadequate as a means of surveying what problems patients bring to physicians." One-quarter of the diagnoses could not be coded within the ICDA scheme and were assigned to a classification called "nonsickness." Check ups and preventive shots accounted for the majority of visits here. In addition, Brown found the ICDA very poor for classifying functional and psychosomatic problems and visits for trivial illnesses such as colds. Even when these visits were assigned to categories, the results were difficult to use for comparative purposes. Serious illnesses and minor illnesses ended up occupying the same category. The reason for the difficulties was obviously that the index had never been set up to measure nonserious illnesses or social problems which required a visit to the doctor. Brown suggested that any future study of this type utilize a more appropriate coding system which would take these factors into account.

Hurtado and Greenlick (1971) did just this in their attempt to develop a set of codes whereby diagnoses could be obtained and compared for visits to the Kaiser-Permanente hospital and clinic system. They reduced the several thousand ICDA diagnoses to ten and then proceeded to use subcategories of the ten as needed. This system was comprehensive and covered all of the reasons for seeing a physician on an outpatient basis. Hurtado handled the 25 percent of visits mentioned by Brown as not being codable using the ICDA by breaking the tenth category which was "nondisease, refractive error and miscellaneous" into: (1) preventive service; (2) no disease present; (3) other; (4) refractions— (a) refractive error found, (b) no refractive error found. Thus, as early as 1971, attempts were being made to look at reasons for seeing the physician in terms of seriousness or actual need for care. Although an improvement on the ICDA index, the Hurtado-Greenlick index had certain drawbacks. The main one was that both very serious and very trivial illnesses could be accommodated in many of the same categories, making them unsuitable for a single overall severity rating.

At the same time, Richardson (1971) was also approaching the problem. Instead of beginning with the ICDA index, he began with a list of symptoms and diseases that respondents to a social survey in a low income area gave as having caused an episode of illness. He then had an internist classify these episodes of illness in one of two categories: (1) serious—should see a doctor and (2) not serious—doctor care optional or not needed. The classification was done independently of whether the respondent actually *had* seen a doctor for that particular episode of illness. A number of categories proved unclassifiable based on the information provided by the respondent and were given an intermediate code. Richardson examined the reliability of his ratings by having a second internist and a pediatrician rate a sample of the original list of symptoms and diseases. For those which the first internist had been able to classify, there was an 86 percent agreement between the first and second internist and a 90 percent agreement between the first internist and the pediatrician. Richardson's study thus indicated that medical judgments could be made about whether or not the patient needed to see the doctor solely on the basis of reported information.

The approach used here has combined the use of the ICDA codes with the system of rating for severity which was devised by Richardson. The advantage of using diagnostic codes based on ICDA to look at physician use is obvious—standardized codes can facilitate comparisons with other research rather than having each researcher start from scratch with his own set of codes. Furthermore, a physician can rank diagnoses much more easily than vague respondent reported symptoms. On the other hand, Richardson's idea of having a physician decide whether or not the patient needed to see a doctor is a long step in the direction of analyzing utilization in more sophisticated terms than fact and quantity of doctor visits by adding a new variable—relative need for the visit.

Gibson (1971) utilized Richardson's approach but found the two point scale inadequate. He enlarged it to a four point rating system—emergent, urgent, nonurgent and scheduled—to look at emergency room use in the Chicago metropolitan area. Ratings were made by a panel of medical students using the diagnosis of the emergency room physician who first saw the patient. Thus, like Hurtado and Greenlick's sample, Gibson's sample consisted only of those people who actually sought medical care. Besides being more discriminating than Richardson's, Gibson's scale had the advantage of being based on actual medical diagnoses. Each case was considered individually, however—feasible in a small sample but not possible in one involving nearly 12,000 individuals.

What was wanted for the purposes of this study was a scale, which would combine as many of the advantages and as few of the drawbacks as possible of Hurtado and Greenlick's, Richardson's, and Gibson's work and which would still be suitable for a large scale social survey analysis.

The ICDA index was used as a starting point and was summarized into approximately 70 categories which seemed appropriate as reasons for seeing a physician. Ten more categories were added, heeding the advice of Brown et al. (1971), for such items as check ups, birth control advice, and minor social and emotional problems for which doctors other than psychiatrists were seen. These categories were then used to code the first 100 families of the 4,000 which comprise the study. The coding was done by two social science graduate students and a medical student and then by a board certified internist. On the basis of this coding, about ten new categories were added, other categories were rearranged and an agreement was made for the coders to hold all cases for the internist which they could not agree upon among themselves or which they could not locate in a standard physician's diagnostic text (Gordon et al. 1971). About 10 percent of all diagnoses were held for the internist, who became medical consultant to the study. He spent approximately one afternoon a week dealing with the cases and furthering the training of the coders. Thus the study had MD consultation in setting up the diagnostic codes from the beginning.

Although this arrangement worked quite well for the social survey portion of the study, the medical consultant and coders noted improvements which could be made if more medical information were available. Some of the categories originally agreed upon also seemed less satisfactory than had been hoped as coding progressed. For example, "heart trouble" excluded "heart attack" (acute myocardial infarction) and "heart failure," both of which had their own individual codes, but still included a variety of diagnoses ranging from the trivial to serious. In addition, there was a category of uncodable diagnoses which accounted for about 1 percent of all diagnoses given.

Using the information gained by coding the social survey, the medical consultant [1] and staff modified the diagnostic codes before going out into the field with verifications of the data by physicians and hospitals. The codes were enlarged from two digits to three digits so that subcategories could be added to those codes such as "heart trouble" in which medical professionals could be expected to give more accurate diagnoses than the respondents, and several new categories were developed. In analyzing the data, the diagnoses from the verifications always took precedence over the diagnoses from the social survey when the former was available.

Positive verifications were obtained for 58 percent of physician contacts and for 83 percent of hospital stays including new hospital stays and physician contacts which had not been mentioned by the respondent. Negative verifications, which confirmed that the patient had reported care which had *not* occurred in 1970, accounted for an additional 10 percent of physician contacts and 8 percent of hospital stays. This care was eliminated from the analysis of utilization. Adjusting for eliminated care and care new to the verifications, the overall completion rate for which diagnoses were available from the verifications was 93 percent for hospital stays and 68 percent for physician care. In other words, only 7 percent of diagnoses for hospital stays and 32 percent for physician care had to be taken from the respondent reporting of diagnoses in the social survey rather than from the MD or hospital reporting.

While useful for many types of analyses, the diagnostic codes do not by themselves provide an estimate of the medical necessity of the care given. In order to do this, a four part rating scheme was developed:

1 = preventive care *or* care from a physician would make no difference for this condition
2 = symptomatic relief available from physician
3 = should see a doctor
4 = must see a doctor

The rating was performed by a panel of five MDs—two internists, a psychiatrist, a psychiatrist with a secondary specialty in internal medicine and a recent medical school graduate. Using this rating scheme, total agreement on severity was reached on 24 percent of the diagnoses used for the respondents and also on 24 percent of the much more finely divided diagnoses used for physicians and hospitals. A difference in severity ratings of one in either direction was achieved in an additional 75 percent of respondent diagnoses and 66 percent of professional diagnoses.

This procedure left 1 percent of the respondent diagnoses and 10 percent of the professional diagnoses with differences of MD opinion of more than one point on the scaling. One respondent category (blindness) was then eliminated from the analysis and the professional categories with disagreements were given a severity code based upon the respondent's social survey reporting. In all other cases where there was disagreement among the raters the mode or rating given most frequently by the raters was used.

It is obvious from the above discussion that a given individual can have more than one diagnosis and therefore more than one severity code on the one to four point scale. Various means were considered for combining these diagnoses to arrive at a summary of the severity of illness for which the patient sought medical care in 1970. It seemed logical that when a physician was seen for both severe and trivial conditions, this was a different case than either being seen for trivial or preventive care only or for care of a serious illness only. From this conclusion a three point summary scale evolved of all of the severity codes for a given individual's doctor contacts during the year:

A = elective care *only* (all codes are one or two)
B = both elective and mandatory care (codes of one or two *and* three or four)
C = mandatory care *only* (all codes are three or four)

This scaling does have several drawbacks for which the authors have tried to compensate. Obviously, it differentiates best among the two-thirds of the population who consult a physician during the year on an outpatient basis and who have complaints spread over the entire spectrum of illness from trivial to fatal. It works much less well for hospitalized patients, whose illnesses can be assumed to be usually mandatory in the sense of requiring physician care. It does not work at all for the one-third of the population who did not see a doctor during the year; and it does not apply to dental care. These issues will be handled in this chapter by the development of other measures of severity. Use of the diagnostic index is restricted, then, to an analysis of the largest group in the population seeking health care—those who saw a physician on an ambulatory basis.

RELATIONSHIP OF DIAGNOSIS TO ACTUAL USE
OF PHYSICIAN SERVICES

Low income people and blacks are less likely to see a physician in a given period of time than are other population groups (Andersen et al. 1972). Reasons advanced include less financial access to physicians than to hospital care which is more apt to be financed by health insurance and public aid, less opportunity to have a regular source of care, and less inclination to see the physician for elective type appointments. Tables 10–1 through 10–5 indicate how our objective measures of diagnostic severity correlate with physician visits. In general, the measures of diagnostic severity appear to work best with physician visits. It should, of course, be realized that, aside from routine preventive care which is more common among the middle class, a visible minority of people of all classes go to the doctor with very little objective medical reason, but strong psychological reasons for seeking care (Balint 1966).

Table 10–1 shows the percent of the population seeing a physician for elective care only; both elective and mandatory care; and mandatory care only by age, race and income. All categories are based upon a "best estimate" of number of physician visits and diagnoses taking into account the physician verification of respondent information.

It is apparent from Table 10–1 that low income individuals see the physician less often than those of higher income (55 percent versus 67 percent in 1970) and that blacks see the physician less often than whites (53 percent versus 66 percent). Controlling for income, the racial differences remain (higher income whites–68 percent, higher income blacks–60 percent; lower income whites–58 percent, lower income blacks–47 percent) indicating that race has an effect independent of income. The income measure used in this chapter adjusts for family size and allows $5,700 a year for a family of four in 1970. About half of the black population and a fifth of the white population are classified as "below near poverty" using this measure [2].

When age is also controlled for, the differences become more pronounced for individuals under 65 and much less pronounced for those over 65. This latter finding might be expected given the universal coverage provided by Medicare. Even with this coverage, however, there is a substantial difference in use of old people by income (high income–77 percent, lower income–68 percent) although racial differences all but disappear.

Once an individual gets into the system, differences in mean number of visits to a physician or clinic in a year tend to be minimal, below poverty individuals actually having half a visit more than their higher income counterparts (5.7 versus 5.2). This indicates that initial *access* to the health care system is a greater problem than obtaining continuing care once the person is in the system. The main focus of this chapter is not on the *quantity* of use, however, but rather on what might be termed the *quality* of use. That is, granting that the poor, and particularly the black poor, are much less apt to see a physician but do visit him slightly more often in a year if they see him at all, have we said everything there is to say about their physician utilization?

The answer to this question appears to be a resounding "no," at least for the severity of the conditions for which the poor and the black see a physician.

Table 10–1. Distribution of Doctor Visits by Elective Versus Mandatory Diagnosis

Age, race and income	Percent of total seeing a physician	Mean number of physician visits for those with visits	Percent of those seeing a physician with:		
			Elective care only	Both elective and mandatory care	Mandatory care only
Under 65—white					
Above near poverty	67.3	5.1	39.5	32.8	27.8
Below near poverty	54.3	5.0	40.0	27.7	32.3
Total	65.2	5.1	39.6	32.1	28.2
Under 65—black					
Above near poverty	59.5	4.1	45.0	21.1	33.8
Below near poverty	44.8	5.4	38.1	23.8	37.8
Total	51.8	4.5	41.9	22.3	35.6
Under 65—all races[a]					
Above near poverty	66.6	5.0	39.9	32.0	27.8
Below near poverty	51.4	5.1	39.3	26.7	33.9
Total	63.6	5.0	39.8	31.1	28.8
65 and over—white					
Above near poverty	77.3	7.2	15.8	36.3	47.9
Below near poverty	67.4	6.7	15.7	33.3	51.0
Total	72.7	7.0	15.8	35.0	49.3
65 and over—black					
Above near poverty	74.7	7.1	10.7	20.7	68.7
Below near poverty	71.0	10.7	10.4	28.9	60.3
Total	71.7	8.2	10.6	26.8	62.2
65 and over—all races[a]					
Above near poverty	77.2	7.2	15.6	35.7	48.7
Below near poverty	67.7	7.3	15.1	32.5	52.4
Total	72.5	7.2	15.4	34.2	50.4

All ages—white					
Above near poverty	68.0	5.3	37.6	33.0	29.1
Below near poverty	57.6	5.6	32.8	29.3	37.9
Total	66.0	5.4	36.8	32.4	30.6
All ages—black					
Above near poverty	60.1	4.3	43.5	21.0	35.4
Below near poverty	47.7	6.3	33.5	24.6	41.5
Total	53.3	5.3	38.6	22.8	38.4
All races[a]					
Above near poverty	67.3	5.2	38.0	32.3	29.4
Below near poverty	55.0	5.7	32.9	28.2	38.8
Total	64.5	5.3	37.0	31.5	31.3

[a]Includes Orientals and American Indians who are excluded from the white and black categories.

Using the scale previously described, 39 percent of the poor compared with only 29 percent of the nonpoor saw physicians *only* for conditions which our panel of doctors described as mandatory care. This was true for 38 percent of blacks compared with 31 percent of whites and, considering both race and income, for 42 percent of poor blacks compared with 29 percent of nonpoor whites. In other words, the poor, and particularly poor blacks, go to the physician with more serious conditions than the rest of the population.

Oddly enough, the differences for rich and poor, black and white, who go for care described as totally preventive or elective are not nearly so great. These findings suggest that a considerable amount of elective care is being given to the black population. Blacks are much less likely than whites (23 percent versus 32 percent) to use the system for a combination of serious and elective conditions during a year's time. Income does not appear to have much effect here, suggesting that this is mainly a racial difference. The racial differences are particularly pronounced for those blacks 65 and over compared with whites.

In looking at preventive care as represented by physical examinations, blacks are at least as apt as whites to claim that they have had a "check up" within the last year (56.7 percent for blacks versus 54.2 percent for whites). However, about twice as many blacks (10.1 percent) as whites (4.8 percent) claim that they have *never* had a check up. Blacks and whites are also about equally likely to say that they had the check up for preventive reasons rather than for symptoms or as a requirement. This finding lends further support to the hypothesis that while blacks are generally sicker, they do obtain more preventive care and more care for elective reasons from physicians than is generally recognized.

In general, then, Table 10-1 indicates that blacks who see physicians are on average sicker than whites who do so and that poor people are sicker than nonpoor people *using physicians' actual evaluations of the reasons for their care.* This is in direct opposition to the finding that whites and nonpoor people are those most apt to see a physician during the year. These findings suggest that any measure of "equal" utilization of doctors' services must take into account the actual reasons for use and that such a measure would indicate lower use by the poor and blacks than by the rest of the population given the severity of the illness experienced. The importance of this finding is that the measures used in this chapter are based upon *actual* reasons for seeing the physician, as rated by a panel of physicians, rather than upon the respondent's evaluation of his need or his state of health. Thus it is based upon objective professional decisionmaking rather than upon subjective measures, which are known to vary by subgroups in the population (Zborowski 1969).

RELATIONSHIP OF DIAGNOSIS TO HOSPITAL CARE USE

Low income people have higher hospital admission rates (Andersen et al. 1972) and longer lengths of stay (NCHS 1971: series 10, no. 64) than do higher income people. This relationship appears to be less clear for blacks than for the rest of the population. Age is an important variable which must be controlled for here, since the black population is younger than the white. Older people have, of course, more hospital admissions.

The difference in use rates may be due to a sicker low income population which is more in need of treatment than the rest of the population [3], but no one to our knowledge has correlated severity of illness with actual health care use. This is because in general the very fact of being in the hospital denotes severity. An exception is elective surgery where the availability of specialized services rather than severity appears to be the major factor in hospitalization. Most surgery is performed in the hospital because the hospital has the facilities for it, but recently outpatient surgery centers have been set up for a variety of procedures previously requiring hospitalization.

In addition to surgical procedures, nonsurgical admissions may sometimes be considered discretionary. Certain diagnostic procedures are performed on hospitalized patients because of convenience and the availability of machinery. In addition, hospitalization may be for the convenience of the patient who would otherwise have to commute from his home to receive care, or for the physician because of the greater ease of access to diagnostic procedures and consultation. This means that in addition to a severity code, a scale with emphasis on whether the diagnosis required a surgical procedure; a delivery; special diagnostic or therapeutic modalities; or convenience is necessary to fully explain hospital use.

A good discussion of this whole issue is contained in Anderson (1967) in which it is argued that physicians consider the vast majority of admissions mandatory so that considerations other than actual need of the hospital facility itself must enter into any discussion of discretionary hospital care. Specifically Anderson found that, according to the admitting physician, 74 percent of the surgical procedures were impossible except in the hospital, while an additional 15 percent would have been extremely difficult except in the hospital, leaving only 11 percent discretionary admissions once surgery had been decided upon. Discretionary medical admissions totaled 17 percent and diagnostic admissions 23 percent, but even in these categories most of the discretionary admissions fell into a "possible but less satisfactory outside of the hospital" group.

Bunker (1970) noted that the United States has a surgical procedure rate approximately twice as high as that of England and Wales and that the main differences appear to be in elective surgery. Vayda (1973) makes the same point comparing Canada with England and Wales, with Canada having about 1.7 times as much surgery performed. The conclusion is that the U.S. population experiences a relatively large amount of elective surgery compared with other countries. A reasonable hypothesis would be that, under a fee-for-service system, more affluent individuals experience more elective surgery, assuming that free care is more difficult to obtain for elective surgery.

This hypothesis is looked at in Table 10–2 on elective versus non elective surgical procedures. The elective procedures chosen were tonsillectomy, hemorrhoidectomy, hernioraphy and eye muscle adjustments. Normal deliveries were not considered surgery and are excluded from the analysis.

As might be expected, higher income people have surgery in general more often than do low income people [4] and in particular have elective surgery more often. The surprise in Table 10–2 is that, even controlling for income, whites have surgery, and particularly elective surgery, more often than blacks. In other words, race contributes to the difference as well as income. Certainly this table bears out the hypothesis mentioned at the beginning of this chapter that the poor and the black use hospitals for more serious conditions than do the nonpoor and white. We are not able to explain why the black group above the near poverty level has the least elective surgery of any group, having even less surgery than the poor black group. It should be pointed out, however, that this group has only 63 surgical procedures, allowing for considerable sampling error.

In addition to sampling error, other reasons why this group might be particularly low include: (1) the *mean* income of the black above poverty income group is not as high as their white counterparts, $11,148 compared with $13,227 for the whites [5]. In other words, the black group may contain a disproportionate number of individuals barely above the near poverty line who behave more like the below poverty group than like the group they are assigned to. This point

Table 10–2. Distribution of Elective Surgery by Race and Income

| | | | Of all surgical procedures: | |
| | | | Proportion elective surgery | Proportion nonelective surgery |
Race and income	Unweighted number of surgical procedures	Surgical procedures per 100 persons per year	percent	
White				
Above near poverty	346	6.6	21.2	78.8
Below near poverty	147	5.8	16.3	83.7
Total	493	6.3	20.4	79.6
Black				
Above near poverty	63	5.6	7.2	92.8
Below near poverty	119	4.0	14.1	85.9
Total	182	5.0	10.5	89.5
All races[a]				
Above near poverty	410	6.2	20.4	79.6
Below near poverty	266	5.0	15.8	84.2
Total population	676	6.1	19.5	80.5

[a]Includes Orientals and American Indians who are excluded from the white and black categories.

might explain why blacks as a group have lower surgical rates than whites, but could not explain the lower elective surgical rates compared to poor blacks; (2) the below poverty black group is heavily covered for hospitalization and surgery by welfare, Medicaid and other free care programs; the above poverty black group is not and may well lack the resources, particularly good hospital insurance coverage, to take advantage of elective surgery. This is an appealing hypothesis which is borne out to some extent by the finding that 89 percent of the white population above the near poverty level has health insurance coverage compared with only 73 percent of the black population.

RELATIONSHIP OF SEVERITY TO DENTAL CARE USE

It was not possible to develop measures of diagnostic severity for dental care use since the questions on dental care use were phrased in terms of services received, not diagnoses. It is, however, possible to develop a proxy measure of severity by dividing the services into mandatory versus discretionary care with the aid of a dental consultant. This was done as follows:

1 = teeth cleaned, X-rays, check ups, orthodontia, fluoride treatments, gum treatments
2 = crowns or capping
3 = dentures or teeth filled, inlays or bridgework
4 = teeth extracted

Discretionary care is considered to be items one and two; mandatory care, three and four. Gum treatment is highly elective and usually performed only on rather well off individuals. The inexpensive treatment for gum disease is full extraction and dentures. Bridgework may be a more expensive means of avoiding dentures and should therefore be considered discretionary. Unfortunately, it is not possible to separate out partial dentures and bridgework from full dentures in this study so they are all considered as mandatory. The same is true of inlays and fillings which are lumped together and also considered mandatory. If a person had seen a dentist for care in more than one category, he was considered to have gone for the most serious care shown.

The poor and the black see dentists much less frequently than the rest of the population. Our hypothesis is that even when they *do* see a dentist, it is for more serious reasons, making the disparity even greater.

This hypothesis is dramatically borne out by Table 10–3 which shows the sharpest racial differences for any kind of health care discussed in this chapter. Only 23 percent of blacks compared with 47 percent of whites saw a dentist at all in 1970. Below poverty whites were actually more likely than above poverty blacks to see a dentist, indicating that racial differences remain even after

Table 10–3.   Distribution of Discretionary and Mandatory Dental Care by Race and Income

Race and income	Percent of group with dental care in 1970	Mean number of visits for those who had care	Percent with dental care in 1970				
			Mandatory care		Preventive care		
			Teeth pulled	Fillings inlays dentures	Crowns or capping	Preventive care only	
White							
Above near poverty level	51.5	3.3	18.1	48.9	1.4	31.6	
Below near poverty level	30.0	2.8	29.9	45.0	0.6	24.6	
Total	47.4	3.2	19.5	48.4	1.3	30.7	
Black							
Above near poverty level	26.8	3.6	47.2	41.1	0.2	11.4	
Below near poverty level	19.5	3.5	61.5	22.3	0.7	15.5	
Total	22.8	3.5	53.8	32.4	0.4	13.3	
All races[a]							
Above near poverty level	49.8	3.3	19.1	48.5	1.4	31.0	
Below near poverty level	27.2	2.9	36.0	40.7	0.6	22.7	
Total population	44.6	3.2	21.5	47.4	1.3	29.8	

[a]Includes Orientals and American Indians who are excluded from white and black categories.

income is controlled for. Although the mean number of visits once in the system is quite similar—blacks actually have slightly more—the reasons for going are sharply different. Fully 54 percent of blacks who went to the dentist had teeth extracted as part of the dental work done compared with only 20 percent of whites. Although the differences are substantial by income level regardless of race (36 percent poor versus 19 percent nonpoor), income is clearly not the overriding factor. For example, 47 percent of *higher* income blacks versus 30 percent of *lower* income whites who went to the dentist had teeth extracted.

The findings for routine preventive care only also differ significantly by race and by income (13 percent of blacks versus 31 percent of whites who went to the dentist had preventive care only) but these differences are not as striking as those for inadequate use of dental care—having a tooth extracted. In this connection, Table 10–4 looks at the entire population who had a toothache in 1970, whether or not they went to a dentist for it. About three-quarters of the population who had a toothache did consult the dentist, with the variation apparently being due to both income and race acting independently.

A deviation from this pattern not found in any of the other tables, however, is that lower income whites behaved almost exactly like blacks in their actions. More than a third of lower income whites, higher income blacks and lower income blacks did not consult a dentist even though they had a toothache, compared with only 20 percent of higher income whites. For the black population, income appeared to make virtually no difference, in reactions to a toothache; while for the white population it made a decided difference.

The conclusion, then is inescapable that blacks and whites, regardless of income, go to the dentist for very different reasons and types of treatment and that blacks go for much more serious care, less often for purely preventive care, and less often when they have a toothache. Income also has an effect independent of race on these three types of behavior. Neither race nor income influence the number of dental visits in a year once the person is in the system. As with physician care, then, we have seen that measures based upon utilization alone heavily understate the actual differences between income and racial groups and that, in order for utilization to be "equitable" (Chapter Two), the poor and the black would receive considerably more dental care than the nonpoor and the white.

SYMPTOMS AND SEEING THE DOCTOR

Approximately one-third of the sample, or 4,137 individuals, did not see a doctor during 1970 and therefore are not included in the analysis of reasons for going to the physician. Since the study upon which this chapter is based is primarily one of health care utilization, these individuals were not asked about any specific *diagnoses* of conditions they suffered from for which they did not consult a physician. As a proxy for this omission, however, there is available a

Table 10–4. Distribution of Population Having a Toothache and Not Seeing a Dentist by Race and Income

Race and income	Percent of population with a toothache in 1970	Percent seeing a dentist	Percent not seeing a dentist
White			
Above near poverty level	9.6	80.1	19.9
Below near poverty level	11.8	62.0	38.0
Total	10.0	76.1	23.9
Black			
Above near poverty level	15.8	63.4	36.6
Below near poverty level	15.9	61.4	38.6
Total	15.8	62.3	37.7
All races[a]			
Above near poverty level	10.0	78.4	21.6
Below near poverty level	13.0	61.8	38.2
Total population	10.7	73.7	26.3

[a]Includes Orientals and American Indians who are excluded from the white and black categories.

set of *symptoms* which these individuals might have suffered from but may not have seen a physician for in 1970. One example taken from this set of symptoms was the distribution of the population who did not consult a dentist for a toothache by race and income.

Table 10–5 looks at 20 symptoms of a medical nature reported as experienced by the population and at whether or not a physician was seen for at least one of them. These symptoms are, of course, not exhaustive of all symptoms which could have been experienced by the population during the year, but they are representative of many of the more common symptoms for a variety of body systems. Slightly over one-third of the population reported that they had experienced one or more symptoms, and, contrary to previous tables, the black population and to a lesser extent the low income population reported *fewer* symptoms than did the white and higher income populations.

Controlling for age, the 20 symptoms were ranked in severity by a panel of 40 physicians—mostly internists, pediatricians and obstetricians-gynecologists—as to the percent of individuals with a given symptom who should have gone to the doctor. These weights were then applied to those individuals in each of the age groups reporting symptoms to give an overall severity score of the symptoms reported. The weights were additive so that the more symptoms, and the greater their severity, the higher the score [6].

Of the 20 symptoms which respondents were asked about, unexpected bleeding from any part of the body not caused by accident or injury and unexplained

Table 10–5. Percent of Population Experiencing One or More Symptoms, Mean Severity of Symptoms for Those Who Experienced Them, Whether or Not a Doctor Was Seen, and Mean Number of Doctor Visits by Race and Income

Race and income	Percent of population reporting one or more symptoms	Total severity weighting of symptoms for those who had symptoms	Percent of individuals with one or more visits to a physician for any symptom experienced	Mean number of visits for those individuals who saw a physician for any symptom[b]
White				
Above near poverty	37.3	3.0	60.8	2.3
Below near poverty	35.7	3.9	57.6	3.0
Total	37.0	3.3	60.2	2.4
Black				
Above near poverty	24.7	1.7	49.7	2.5
Below near poverty	29.1	3.2	59.0	3.4
Total	27.1	2.4	54.7	3.0
All races[a]				
Above near poverty	36.4	2.9	60.2	2.3
Below near poverty	33.8	3.7	57.8	3.0
Total population	36.0	3.2	59.7	2.5

[a]Includes Orientals and American Indians who are excluded from the black and white categories.

[b]This figure does *not* represent visits to the doctor for any reason and thus cannot be compared with the means in Table 10–1. Rather, each time a physician was said to have been seen for a symptom in 1970, the individual was credited with a visit in a simple additive fashion.

loss of over ten pounds in weight were considered the most serious by the panel of physicians. It was the consensus of the panel that 81 percent of the individuals with bleeding and 76 percent of those with weight loss should have seen a doctor. At the other end of the spectrum, only 29 percent of those with nose stopped up or sneezing for two weeks or more and 39 percent of those with sore throats should have seen a doctor according to the panel. When these weights were applied to all of the individuals experiencing symptoms, the lower income respondents appeared to have more serious symptoms, but the black respondents had less serious symptoms than their white counterparts. Much of this difference is accounted for by the higher income blacks whose reported symptoms are not only least in number but, on an objective medical scale, are judged to be the least serious. Blacks are slightly less apt to have seen a physician than are whites for the symptoms they do experience but once in the system repeat the by now familiar finding of having a higher average number of visits for these symptoms.

Table 10–5 appears to contradict some of the previous findings of this chapter. Up until now, we have seen that blacks appear to be considerably sicker than whites when they use either medical or dental care and low income people sicker than higher income individuals. Several interpretations of this table are possible: (1) that the black population actually does have fewer symptoms and that these symptoms are less severe, and (2) that there is considerable under-reporting going on, particularly of more serious symptoms. This second hypothesis is strengthened slightly by the finding that, once in the system, blacks and low income individuals with symptoms have more visits than their apparently (judging by symptoms reported) sicker white counterparts.

CONCLUSIONS

By all the objective measures of severity of illness used in this chapter, blacks and low income individuals who see physicians and dentists suffer from more serious illnesses than do whites and higher income individuals. Race and income appear to operate independently in this. The conclusion is that, if "equal" access to care is provided, blacks and low income individuals will use considerably more than the mean amount of care. Under the current system, the reverse is true. On the other hand, if a subjective measure such as the number of symptoms a person suffers from and what those symptoms are is used, the income differences are not nearly as pronounced and, in fact, the black population appears to be in better physical condition than the remainder of the population, even when physicians objectively rate the reported symptoms. This contradiction indicates that blacks do not consider themselves as sick as utilization rates indicate they are once physician contact is made. They may try to minimize symptoms when reporting, or perhaps think some symptoms not worth mentioning. Koos (1954) found this was true for lower social class and income groups two decades ago. Lower income individuals now appear to be reporting their symptoms about as frequently as higher income persons. Perhaps blacks, regardless of income, are the group least in the mainstream of the United States health care system in the early 1970s.

NOTES TO CHAPTER TEN

1. Lloyd Ferguson, MD, the original medical consultant on the study, designed the social survey coding system and helped to modify it for verification use.

2. The income cutoff was updated from a 1969 Bureau of Labor Statistics measure which was designed to approximate eligibility for Medicaid. Although Medicaid had not been implemented in all 50 states in 1970 with income standards higher than those set for welfare recipients, this measure guarantees that virtually all welfare recipients and almost all Medicaid recipients fall into the "below near poverty" categories. The exceptions are in high income states such as New York and California which, in 1970, had income requirements for Medicaid eligibility substantially higher than those used here. Some Medicaid recipients in these states, and a few recipients with unusually high medical expenses, will therefore fall into the "above near poverty" category.

3. For example, Bruce Flashner, MD, has analyzed data from the Hospital Admission and Surveillance Program (HASP) in Illinois which indicates that recipients of welfare and of Medicaid are admitted for very different diagnoses than the general population and that these diagnoses tend to be much less elective in nature (Flashner 1973).

4. This is true when family size is controlled using the above versus below near poverty measure because many old people with relatively modest incomes live alone or with a spouse only and fall into the above near poverty category. Older people have more surgery. Using a regular measure of family income as was done in Andersen et al. (1972) gives an inverse rather than a direct relationship between income and surgery.

5. This difference is further increased by the somewhat larger black family size above the near poverty level, 4.4 individuals per family compared with 4.1 for whites. White families above the near poverty level have a per capita income more than 20 percent higher than their black counterparts ($3,226 compared with $2,534 for blacks).

6. See Aday and Andersen (1975:87–92) for a discussion of this rating process.

Part V

Medical Care Patterns and Effects

Chapter Eleven

The Effects of Patterns of Medical Care on Utilization and Continuity of Services*

Stephen M. Shortell

This chapter examines the relative importance of a particular subset of enabling characteristics (for example, type of regular source, type of most amount source, means of referral) in explaining differences in volume of visits among individuals experiencing a "major illness" during the survey year. Primary source of payment and type of most amount source are the most important predictors of volume of visits. Patient characteristics such as age, sex, race and family income were the least important predictors. The results suggest that changes in third party insurance coverage along with changes in sources of care are likely to have the greatest impact in altering existing ambulatory utilization rates and patterns. Change in sources of care implies a basic restructuring of patient-provider relationships.

The results also suggest that the more "disadvantaged" groups in society (those below the near poverty line, those with Medicaid type coverage, those who have to pay out-of-pocket for most of their care and those with less education) are more likely to receive most of their care from a provider who is their usual source. Whether this is "desirable" or "undesirable" cannot be answered in the absence of data on quality of care received. Using an episode of illness framework, future research which links the variables associated with access, continuity and quality of care is suggested.

INTRODUCTION

General Background
What is the relative effect of patient and provider variables in influencing the utilization of medical care services? How are these variables related to the

*The comments of Ronald Andersen, Joanna Kravits and Odin Anderson on earlier drafts of this chapter were most helpful. Appreciation is expressed to Ken Laitinen for computer programming associated with this chapter.

continuity of services received? Important public policy issues pertaining to access to medical care services are inherent in an examination of these questions. The issues center on the interaction of the patient and provider of care. How do patients with certain age, sex, race, income, third party payers and related characteristics differ in their sources of care? In turn, what is the effect of such differences on total volume of visits received? For a given condition, why do some people have more sources of care than others? What is the effect of additional sources of care on total volume of visits received? The economist primarily views these issues in terms of demand and supply; the sociologist sees them in terms of social organization; and to the public at large, the major issue is one of consumer satisfaction and social equity. The data examined in this chapter provide some beginning answers to the above questions. In the process, suggestions for further avenues of inquiry and public policy implications will be discussed.

Selective Literature Review and Current Approach

It is well established that persons with a regular source of care are more likely to make at least one physician visit during a given year (Andersen and Anderson 1967; Andersen et al. 1972; Bice et al. 1973; Richardson 1971). Those with a regular source of care also appear to experience a greater total amount of care (Andersen 1968:33). There is also some evidence to suggest that the particular type of regular source (clinic, solo practitioner, group practitioner, etc.) makes a difference. For example, Richardson (1971:98) found that for serious conditions only 62 percent of patients who saw general practitioners had revisits versus 75 percent for those who saw a group practitioner and 76 percent of those reporting a clinic as a regular source. Roghmann et al. (1970) found that over 90 percent of children covered by Blue Cross plans saw a private practitioner as a regular source of care and experienced 5.4 medical contacts per year while only 46 percent of children covered by Medicaid saw a private practitioner. These children experienced only 3.7 contacts per year.

In general, the physician's important decisionmaking role as an allocator of medical resources is well accepted in the literature (Feldstein 1966; Kaitaranta and Purola 1972). But an understanding of its effects on overall utilization and continuity of services received is less well documented. The basic thesis to be examined is that provider and "pattern" variables such as type of regular source, type of most amount source and means of referral assume greater importance as predictors of utilization for people who have made contact with the medical care system than for those with little or no contact with medical services. In other words, the decision whether to make contact with the medical care system is primarily a function of individual predisposing, enabling and need variables, but provider variables become more important in explaining differences in utilization after contact has been made. Donabedian (1972:111) makes this distinction in terms of initiation of services versus continuation of services and believes that different factors influence each although any one factor may influence both.

A major advantage of the 1970 national study is the availability of particular characteristics of providers of care (e.g., specialty, board certification status and means of referral to the provider) in conjunction with the predisposing, enabling and need variables examined in earlier chapters. This provides the opportunity to analyze "patterns of medical care"—a person's regular source of care, a person's most amount source of care, characteristics of the most amount source of care, means by which the person came into contact with the most amount source of care and travel time—as these variables relate to the total number of visits and sources of care within specific illness episodes.

The group analyzed here is respondents who experienced an illness episode requiring either five or more physician visits or $100 in expenditures during the survey year, but not requiring hospitalization (unweighted $N = 1697$) [1]. This group is referred to as "major illness respondents." A great number of different types of illness conditions were experienced by this group but eight conditions accounted for 45 percent of all conditions reported. These were hypertension, diabetes, heart trouble, allergies, arthritis and rheumatism, sprains and strains, chronic sinusitis and bronchitis, and acute musculoskeletal disorders (muscle spasm, slipped disc, sciatica, etc.).

The basic approach in the ensuing sections is to first show the simple relationships between such variables as age, race, income, third party payment source and selected pattern of medical care variables (for example, type of regular source of care, type of most amount source of care). Then both sets of variables will be used to explain differences in total number of ambulatory visits received. In this way, the relative importance of the pattern of care variables can be assessed. In the process, some simple relationships between the above variables and continuity of care will be examined.

MAJOR ILLNESS RESPONDENTS

Background and Variable Description

Solon et al. define an episode of illness as ". . . a block of one or more medical services received by an individual during a period of relatively continuous contact with one or more providers of service in relation to a particular medical problem or situation" (1967:403). This approach is used in the current analysis. For each condition (injury/illness) experienced by a respondent a separate major illness supplement form was completed listing visits, cost and related data.

The dependent variable of interest is the total number of ambulatory visits received by major illness respondents. The independent variables in the analysis are indicated in Table 11–1. The ways in which they are measured or categorized differently from earlier chapters are also indicated in the table.

Table 11-1.   Independent Variables and Their Measurement for Major Illness Episode Respondents

Variable	*Measurement categories*
Patient age	0–17 years 18–54 years 55 years and over
Sex	Male Female
Race	White Nonwhite
Income[a]	Above near poverty Below near poverty
Primary third party payment source[b]	Voluntary insurance, Medicare and other non-free expenditures[c] Medicaid, welfare and free care Self-pay
Type of regular source of care	General practitioner Specialist Clinic, other,[d] none
Type of most amount source of care[e]	General practitioner Internist Other specialist Clinic, other, none[f]
Board certified status of most amount source	Board certified specialist Non–board certified specialist[g] General practitioner,[h] clinic, other
Means of referral to most amount source	Most amount source is usual source, referred by usual source or referred by another doctor Picked by self, family, friends, relatives, ambulance or institutional referral
Residence	Rural farm and rural nonfarm SMSA inner city SMSA non–inner city and other urban
Residential mobility	< 1 year in this community 1 to < 5 years in this community 5 years and beyond in this community
Travel time to regular source	≤ 30 minutes 31 minutes and over
Personal health evaluation	Excellent, good Fair, poor

Table 11-1.   continued

Variable	Measurement categories
Disability days for 1970	None 1–7 8–14 15 and over
Physician rated severity of illness[i]	Preventive and symptomatic Should see a doctor Must see a doctor

[a]This is family income adjusted for family size.

[b]Primary third party payment source is defined as that source which paid the highest percentage of the costs incurred.

[c]Includes CHAMPUS—insurance provided for the armed forces dependents of members; and accident and liability insurance carried by some member of the patient's family.

[d]"Other" sources included osteopaths, chiropractors, podiatrists, etc. Of the total category "clinic, other, none" 60 percent (212) reported a clinic as their regular source; 25 percent (88) an osteopath, chiropractor, podiatrist, etc.; and 15 percent (53) reported no regular source.

[e]Respondents were asked for the name of the doctor or place which provided the most care for the condition. For respondents with more than one source, the most amount source information was verified by comparing it with cost and visit data for each source. It was almost always the case that both visits and costs were highest for the doctor or place named as the most amount source. Where there was a discrepancy, the provider associated with the most costs was chosen as the most amount source except where the number of visits to another source was over twice as many as to the source with the most costs and there was only a $25 or less difference in costs.

[f]Of the "clinic, other, none" category 91 percent (326) are clinics, 2 percent (8) are other practitioners such as osteopaths and 8 percent (31) are respondents reporting no source of care.

[g]Physicians who claimed they were a specialist but who according to the American Medical Association Directory were not board certified.

[h]Up to 1970, general practitioners (family practitioners) did not have a board and are, therefore, grouped with clinic and other.

[i]Where there were multiple diagnoses for a given illness episode, the most serious diagnosis was selected.

Basic Relationships

From a policy viewpoint, the initial issue is one of determining how the pattern of medical care variables are related to important predisposing and other enabling variables. Do nonwhites have different types of sources of care than whites? Do they differ in the ways in which they make contact with the various sources? Similar questions can be asked in terms of age, income and third party payment source. The results are shown in Tables 11-2 through 11-9 [2].

A summary review of the tables reveals that older patients (especially those 55 and over) were more likely to have a general practitioner as both a regular source and most amount source than younger patients and less likely to have a

Table 11–2. Type of Regular Source for Major Illness Episodes by Respondent Age, Race, Income and Third Party Payment Source[a]

Variable	*Type of regular source*[b] General practitioner	Specialist	Clinic, other, none[c]	Total[d]
	percent			
Patient age				
0–17 years	39.4	40.6	20.0	100
18–54 years	48.4	35.5	16.1	100
55 years and over	53.4	35.0	11.6	100
Race				
White	50.1	36.7	13.1	100
Nonwhite	40.3	30.3	29.4	100
Income				
Above near poverty	49.3	37.5	13.1	100
Below near poverty	48.1	31.3	20.6	100
Primary third party payment source				
Voluntary insurance, Medicare and other nonfree expenditures	42.6	45.2	12.2	100
Medicaid, welfare and free care	48.4	21.5	30.2	100
Self-pay	53.5	34.2	12.3	100
All respondents	49.1	36.1	14.8	100

[a]The percentages are based on the weighted cases (weighted N = 8939). In none of the cells was the unweighted N less than 25.

[b]This is the response to the question: "Is there a particular medical person or clinic (person) usually goes to when sick, or for advice about health?" This source may or may not have been involved in the care for this particular illness condition.

[c]See footnote d, Table 11–1.

[d]The percentages may not exactly equal 100 due to rounding error.

clinic as either a regular or most amount source; were more likely to have a source which is their usual source; and were more likely to have had just one source of care than younger patients.

Nonwhites were more likely to have a clinic as both a regular and major source of care than whites; and were somewhat more likely to have a most amount source which is their usual source than whites.

Those below the poverty line were more likely to have a clinic as a regular source and less likely to have a specialist than those above the poverty line; were somewhat more likely to have a general practitioner or clinic as a most amount source; were more likely to have a most amount source who is a usual source

Table 11-3. Type of Most Amount Source for Major Illness Episodes by
Respondent Age, Race, Income and Third Party Payment Source[a]

Variable	General practitioner	Internist	Other specialists	Clinic, other, none[c]	Total
			percent		
Patient age					
0–17 years	33.8	—[d]	39.1	22.4	100
18–54 years	39.1	14.7	26.8	19.5	100
55 years and over	45.5	22.3	17.5	14.7	100
Race					
White	41.0	16.8	25.1	17.0	100
Nonwhite	39.6	11.9	22.5	26.1	100
Income					
Above near poverty	39.3	16.6	27.1	16.9	100
Below near poverty	46.0	15.2	17.3	21.6	100
Primary third party payment source					
Voluntary insurance, Medicare and other nonfree expenditures	32.2	19.1	32.5	16.2	100
Medicaid, welfare and free care	39.8	—[d]	19.2	35.3	100
Self-pay	46.8	17.5	21.4	14.4	100
All respondents	40.9	16.3	24.8	18.0	100

Top of table: *Type of most amount source[b]*

[a]See general explanatory footnotes for Table 11–2.
[b]See footnote e, Table 11–1.
[c]See footnote f, Table 11–1.
[d]Less than 25 respondents (unweighted).

rather than being referred; and have more visits than those above the poverty line. Those whose primary source of payment was Medicaid or some other welfare type program were more likely to have a clinic as both a regular source and most amount source than those with a private third party payment source or those who self-paid, and those who self-paid were more likely to have a general practitioner as both a regular source and most amount source. Among those reporting a specialist as a most amount source, 61 percent of those with a private third party payment source received care from a board certified specialist versus only 47 percent of those with Medicaid type coverage and 47 percent of those who self-paid [3]. Those with Medicaid type coverage or who self-paid were somewhat more likely to have a most amount source as their usual source than those with a private third party payment source; and those who self-paid were

Table 11–4. Board Certification Status of Most Amount Source for Major
Illness Episodes by Respondent Age, Race, Income and Third Party Payment
Source[a]

	Board certification status of most amount source			
	Specialists		General practitioner,[b] clinic, other, none	Total
Variable	Board certified	Not certified		
	percent			
Patient age				
0–17 years	21.0	23.0	55.9	100
18–54 years	23.9	18.1	58.0	100
55 years and over	21.0	19.5	59.5	100
Race				
White	22.9	19.5	57.5	100
Nonwhite	17.1	18.0	64.9	100
Income				
Above near poverty	25.0	19.2	55.7	100
Below near poverty	13.2	19.8	67.0	100
Primary third party payment source				
Voluntary insurance, Medicare and other nonfree expenditures	31.5	20.1	48.4	100
Medicaid, welfare and free care	11.5	13.3	75.2	100
Self-pay	18.3	20.6	61.1	100
All respondents	22.3	19.4	58.3	100

[a]See general explanatory footnotes for Table 11–2.
[b]General practitioners did not have a board in 1970 and thus are grouped with clinic, other and none.

much more likely to have only one source of care and received markedly fewer visits than those with a private third party payment source or Medicaid type coverage; while those with Medicaid type coverage had the highest number of visits [4].

Although not shown in the tables, differences by level of education were also found. For example, those with 13 or more years of education were more likely to have a specialist as both a regular source and most amount source and less likely to have a general practitioner than those with less education. In addition, among those reporting a specialist as a most amount source, 64 percent of those with 13 or more years of education saw a board certified specialist, versus 49 percent of those with less education. Finally, persons with 13 or more years of

Table 11–5. Means of Referral to Most Amount Source for Major Illness Episodes by Respondent Age, Race, Income and Third Party Payment Source[a]

	Means of referral to most amount source			
Variable	Most amount source is usual source	Referred by usual source or another doctor	Picked by patient, family, relatives, friends, other [b]	Total
	percent			
Patient age				
0–17 years	53.0	25.0	21.9	100
18–54 years	48.8	15.0	36.1	100
55 years and over	65.0	10.7	24.2	100
Race				
White	55.2	15.0	29.8	100
Nonwhite	61.2	12.8	26.1	100
Income				
Above near poverty	52.9	16.0	31.1	100
Below near poverty	65.8	10.6	23.7	100
Primary third party payment source				
Voluntary insurance, Medicare and other nonfree expenditures	50.7	17.4	31.8	100
Medicaid, welfare and free care	56.0	9.7	34.3	100
Self-pay	59.1	14.4	26.5	100
All respondents	55.9	14.7	29.4	100

[a]See general explanatory footnotes for Table 11–2.

[b]"Other" means of referral include ambulance, employer and miscellaneous institutional referrals. This group also includes the 31 respondents who reported no source of care.

education were less likely to have a most amount source who was their usual source than those with less education.

Table 11–8 indicates a considerable degree of congruence between *type* of regular source and *type* of most amount source: 74 percent for those seeing general practitioners, 89 percent for those seeing specialists and 69 percent for those involved with clinics. In addition, 94 percent of those reporting a general practitioner as both most amount source and regular source actually saw the same general practitioner. The respective figures for specialists and clinics were 69.5 percent and 78.9 percent. Altogether, 31.6 percent of respondents reporting a general practitioner as a regular source of care actually saw a different *physician* as a most amount source while 41 percent of those reporting a specialist as a regular source actually saw a different *physician* as a most amount source [5].

Many of the above patterns are not surprising. Nonwhites, those below the poverty line and those with primarily Medicaid type coverage receive relatively more of their care from clinics. And those with primarily Medicaid type coverage who did not receive care from clinics or general practitioners were more likely to receive it from a non–board certified specialist. Among those with Medicaid type coverage the difference between those selecting clinics as their most amount source and those selecting general practitioners is relatively small (35 percent versus 40 percent) while among those who self-pay, general practitioners

Table 11–6.   Total Sources of Care for Major Illness Episodes by Respondent Age, Race, Income, Third Party Payment Source, Regular Source of Care and Most Amount Source of Care[a]

	Total sources of care[b]		
Variable	One	Two or more	Total
		percent	
Patient age			
0–17 years	63.1	36.8	100
18–54 years	71.2	28.8	100
55 years and over	81.7	18.3	100
Race			
White	74.5	25.5	100
Nonwhite	71.5	28.5	100
Income			
Above near poverty	73.2	26.8	100
Below near poverty	77.3	22.7	100
Primary third party payment source			
Voluntary insurance, Medicare and other nonfree expenditures	68.7	31.3	100
Medicaid, welfare and free care	65.8	34.2	100
Self-pay	80.1	19.9	100
Regular source of care			
General practitioner	78.7	21.3	100
Specialist	70.8	29.2	100
Clinic and other	67.9	32.1	100
Most amount source of care			
General practitioner	79.9	20.1	100
Internist	71.3	28.7	100
Other specialists	71.2	28.8	100
Clinic and other	67.0	33.0	100
All respondents	74.2	25.8	100

[a]See general explanatory footnotes for Table 11–2.

[b]The 31 respondents with no source of care are excluded from the table.

Table 11-7.   Total Ambulatory Care Visits for Major Illness Episodes by Patient Age, Race, Income, Third Party Payment Source, Total Sources of Care and Means of Referral to Most Amount Source of Care

	Total ambulatory care visits	
Variable	*Mean[a]* *(standard deviation)*	*Unweighted N*
Patient age		
0–17 years	11.1 (11.5)	203
18–54 years	10.2 (11.3)	689
55 years and over	11.1 (11.8)	805
Race		
White	10.6 (11.8)	1280
Nonwhite	11.0 (9.4)	417
Income		
Above near poverty	10.4 (11.7)	1029
Below near poverty	11.5 (10.9)	668
Primary third party payment source		
Voluntary insurance, Medicare and other nonfree expenditures	11.7 (12.6)	511
Medicaid, welfare and free care	14.1 (17.0)	373
Self-pay	9.0 (8.2)	813
Total sources of care[b]		
One	10.2 (10.4)	1268
Two or more	12.9 (14.8)	398
Means of referral to most amount source		
Most amount source is usual source	11.3 (11.4)	1030
Referred by usual source or another doctor	9.0 (8.4)	196
Picked by patient, family, relatives or friends, and other miscellaneous means[c]	10.2 (11.3)	471
All respondents	10.7 (11.6)	1697

[a]The means and standard deviations are based on the weighted sample.

[b]The 31 respondents with no source of care are deleted.

[c]See footnote b, Table 11–5.

Table 11-8.   Type of Most Amount Source of Care for Major Illness Respondents by Regular Source of Care[a]

	Type of most amount source of care[b]				
Variable	*General practitioner*	*Internist*	*Other specialists*	*Clinic, other, none*[c]	*Total*
	percent				
Regular source of care					
General practitioner	74.4	_[d]	11.3	11.3	100
Specialist	5.0	39.8	49.2	5.9	100
Clinic, other, none	16.9	_[d]	10.4	69.4	100
All respondents	40.9	16.3	24.8	18.0	100

[a]See general explanatory footnotes for Table 11-2.
[b]See footnote e, Table 11-1.
[c]See footnote f, Table 11-1.
[d]Less than 25 respondents (unweighted).

predominated over clinic users (47 percent versus 14 percent). The effect of Medicaid type coverage is also demonstrated by the fact that these respondents received the highest number of visits while those who self-paid received the fewest.

Some of the findings are particularly interesting, however, in relation to the continuity of services received. For a given illness, continuity can be conceived as the extent to which health care and/or medical care services are received as an uninterrupted succession of events. How one defines or measures an "interruption" is, of course, a difficult issue. The approach used here is to assume that for a given condition, care received from a single source is more continuous than care received from two or more sources. The underlying assumption is not that care received from two or more sources is *always* likely to be less continuous than care received from one source but, rather, that it is *more likely* to be less continuous in terms of transfer of knowledge about the patient's condition from one source to another, a possible change in the site at which care is rendered, the beginning of a new provider-patient relationship and related issues of coordination between the various providers (Shortell 1972). For example, Becker et al. (1974:212) have found that children suffering from otitis media who receive all their care from the same physician have an increased probability that followup visits will be kept, that appropriate medicines will be taken and that mothers of the children will know the current number of times the medicine should be given.

In brief, it is assumed that the probability of a delay or interruption in the sequence of receiving care is greater when two or more sources are involved than when one source is involved. A similar approach to this problem has been taken by Mindlen and Densen (1969:1294).

The above is essentially an episode of illness approach to continuity. A different dimension concerns the extent to which individuals seek care from the same provider for *different* episodes of illness. In the context of the current study this can be examined indirectly by looking at the percentage of respondents who received most of their care from a provider who is their regular source of care. Thus continuity is examined both in terms of number of sources seen for a given condition and the extent to which the primary source is a provider with whom the patient is already familiar.

It should be emphasized that the relationship between continuity of care as measured here and quality of care is not known. For example, for a given condition such as diabetes mellitus, quality norms may dictate that two sources of care ought to be seen. A visit should be made to a primary care physician for initial diagnosis and a thorough exam, followed by a referral to a specialist in diabetic conditions for treatment. In this instance a person who had only one source of care may be considered to have received "inappropriate" care from a quality viewpoint. Thus, a minimum number of sources necessary for quality care to be rendered would need to be defined for given conditions. Only if this minimum number was exceeded might one begin to question the continuity of services received as measured by the number of different sources seen.

Simply put, it is not clear that continuity of care and quality of care are positively related. The current state of knowledge does not permit inferences concerning whether more sources of care are "better" or "worse" than fewer sources of care. In any event, the distinction between continuity and quality needs to be kept in mind in interpreting the following findings.

Table 11−5 shows that those below the near poverty line and those covered by Medicaid or who self-paid are more likely to have received most of their care from a provider who is their usual source of care [6]. Although the difference is small, nonwhites are somewhat more likely than whites to have received most of their care from a usual source. These data do not support the proposition that when less advantaged groups in society experience an illness episode they do not have established sources of care [7]. And, with the exception of those who self-paid, Table 11−7 reveals that the less advantaged individuals have approximately as many and, in some cases, more visits than the more advantaged groups. Thus, treating visits as an outcome measure of access, the differences between the less advantaged and more advantaged are small. This, of course, says nothing about those who never come into contact with the delivery system.

Individuals 55 and over are much more likely to have received most of their care from a provider who is their usual source than the younger age groups. This may be due to the chronic nature of many of the illnesses which affect the elderly requiring them to see the same practitioner over time (Mott et al. 1973). Similar results have been found by Wessen (1974).

Table 11-6 reveals essentially no differences in number of sources of care by race or income. But those 55 and over are much more likely to have received all of their care from a single source than the younger age groups. Also, those who primarily had to pay for their own care [8] were much more likely to have received care from only one source than those with private insurance, Medicare or Medicaid type coverage. In this case, it seems reasonable to suggest that lack of a third party payment source may be acting as a deterrent to referral to a second source in cases where such a referral may be clinically indicated. The finding that those who had to self-pay were more likely to have only one source was true for all categories of physician rated severity of illness—"preventive and symptomatic," "should see a doctor" and "must see a doctor." This adds support to the deterrent argument.

The financial deterrent argument is further supported by recalling the data from Table 11-7 showing that those who had to primarily pay for their own care averaged only nine visits compared to nearly 12 for those with private insurance, Medicare and other nonfree payment sources and 14 visits for those with Medicaid type coverage. It might be argued that this comparison is artifactual in that the self-paid groups are "self-paid" because they haven't had enough medical care visits for their insurance policies to take over most of the payment. In essence, the deductible limits had not yet been met. But if this were true, then the self-pay group should be in better health than the other groups. As discussed earlier, a greater percentage of the self-paid groups reported themselves to be in "good" or "excellent" health than those with Medicaid type coverage (58 percent versus 46 percent), but there was virtually no difference between the self-paid and those with private insurance, Medicare or other nonfree payment sources (58 percent versus 56 percent).

Further, controlling for perceived health status revealed that among those with "fair" or "poor" health, those with Medicaid type coverage averaged 17 visits, those with private insurance and related coverage averaged 14 visits, while the self-paid group averaged only 10 visits. For those in "good" or "excellent" health the respective figures were 10.5 visits, 10 visits and eight visits. These data support the suggestion that lack of a third party payment source may indeed be acting as a deterrent to medical care for the self-paid group.

Table 11-6 also reveals that those with a general practitioner as a regular source or most amount source are more likely to have had just one source of care than those seeing specialists and clinics.

These results simply document that different patterns of receiving care do exist for people with varying socioeconomic characteristics. The data examined are of a structural or, at best, process nature and the relationship between them and outcomes of medical care in terms of technical quality and patient satisfaction is largely not established in the literature. From a quality of care viewpoint, the issue of whether it is "better" or "worse" to receive care from a clinic than a personal physician or to receive care from a board certified physician than a noncertified physician cannot be addressed here. What can be examined is the relationship between the pattern of care, predisposing, enabling and need variables as they affect the number of visits received. Further implications of the continuity findings will also be discussed.

TOTAL AMBULATORY VISITS AMONG MAJOR ILLNESS RESPONDENTS

The Model

Since the distribution of ambulatory care visits was strongly skewed, the data were transformed by natural logs to provide a more normal distribution and better fit [9]. Multiple classification analysis (Andrews et al. 1973) was used to examine the effects of the variables in explaining total ambulatory visits among major illness respondents [10]. Multiple Classification Analysis (MCA) is similar to dummy variable regression with the major exception being that coefficients are expressed for each category of the predictor variable as a deviation from the grand mean of the dependent variable, while in dummy variable regression they are expressed in terms of the deviation of the one category of the predictor variable from the omitted category. Since for present purposes the interest is in assessing the effect of the entire variable (that is, all of the subclasses) the results given by MCA are more useful than those of dummy variable regression. In addition, MCA shares the same advantages of dummy variable regression in that the relationships among the variables need not be linear and, of course, the data need not be expressed in interval form.

There are five types of output statistics most meaningful for interpretation of the results shown in Table 11-9. These are defined and discussed below:

1. *Unadjusted mean*—is simply the mean value of the dependent variable for a particular category of the predictor variable; it is the "raw" mean.
2. *Coefficient*—is the deviation of the category mean of a predictor variable from the grand mean after adjusting for the effects of other predictors in the model—that is, after all other predictors have been "held constant."
3. *Adjusted mean*—is simply the grand mean plus the coefficient defined above. It indicates what the mean would have been if the group had been exactly like the total population with respect to its distribution over all the other predictor classifications.
4. *Eta²*—is the correlation ratio and indicates the proportion of the total sum of squares explainable by each predictor individually without taking into account other predictors.
5. *Beta²*—is analogous to eta² but is based on the adjusted mean rather than the raw mean. It measures the *relative* ability of a predictor to explain variation in the dependent variable after adjusting for the effects of all other predictors [11].

Table 11–9. Natural Logarithm Multiple Classification Results for Total Ambulatory Care Visits for Major Illness Episodes; Grand Mean = 7.6[a]

Variable	N (unweighted)	Unadjusted mean	Coefficient	Adjusted mean	Eta²	Beta²
1. Primary third party payment source					0.032	0.036
Private insurance, Medicare, etc.	511	8.3	0.90	8.5		
Medicaid, welfare, etc.	373	9.9	2.20	9.8		
Self-pay	813	6.8	-1.00	6.6		
2. Most amount source					0.009	0.033
General practitioner	709	8.2	1.00	8.6		
Internist	239	7.8	0.20	7.8		
Other specialists	384	7.5	-0.10	7.5		
Clinics, other, none	365	6.6	-1.90	5.7		
3. Regular source of care					0.006	0.025
General practitioner	795	7.4	-0.60	7.0		
Specialist	549	7.5	0.00	7.6		
Clinic, other, none	353	8.8	2.40	10.1		
4. Physician rated severity of illness					0.011	0.017
Preventive and symptomatic	240	9.2	2.00	9.6		
Should see a doctor	751	7.5	-0.10	7.5		
Must see a doctor	706	7.2	-0.50	7.1		
5. Personal health status					0.023	0.015
Good, excellent	793	6.8	-0.60	7.0		
Fair, poor	904	8.8	0.90	8.5		
6. Residential mobility					0.009	0.010
<1 year in this community	128	9.8	2.30	9.9		
1 to <5 years in this community	473	7.9	0.30	7.9		
5 years and beyond in this community	1096	7.3	-0.30	7.3		

	N					
7. Disability days					0.018	0.007
None	570	7.0	−0.50	7.1		
1–7	359	7.8	0.40	8.0		
8–14	206	6.6	−0.70	6.9		
15 and over	562	8.8	0.60	8.2		
8. Travel time					0.0007	0.005
≤ 30 minutes	1309	7.7	0.20	7.8		
31 minutes or more	388	7.3	−0.90	6.7		
9. Means of referral					0.008	0.005
Usual source, referred by usual source or by another doctor	1226	8.0	0.30	7.9		
Self, family, relatives, friends, institutional referrals	471	6.8	−0.60	7.0		
10. Board certification of most amount source					0.005	0.004
Board certified specialist	316	7.0	−0.40	7.2		
Non–board certified specialist	307	8.4	0.80	8.4		
General practitioner, other, no source	1074	7.6	−0.10	7.5		
11. Residence					0.001	0.003
Rural farm and rural nonfarm	550	8.0	0.60	8.2		
SMSA inner city	755	7.5	−0.40	7.2		
SMSA non–inner city and other urban	392	7.5	0.00	7.6		
12. Patient age					0.002	0.006
0–17 years	203	8.1	0.20	7.8		
18–54 years	689	7.4	−0.20	7.4		
55 years and over	805	7.8	0.20	7.8		
13. Race					0.002	0.00009
White	1280	7.5	0.00	7.6		
Nonwhite	417	8.5	0.20	7.8		

Table 11–9. continued

Variable	N (unweighted)	Unadjusted mean	Coefficient	Adjusted mean	Eta^2	$Beta^2$
14. Sex					0.0001	0.00005
Male	715	7.5	0.00	7.6		
Female	982	7.7	0.10	7.7		
15. Family income					0.006	0.00000
Above near poverty	1029	7.4	0.00	7.6		
Below near poverty	668	8.6	0.00	7.6		

R^2 (adjusted) = .12

[a]The means expressed are the geometric means reconverted from the natural logarithm transformation. The geometric mean is always less than the arithmetic mean. As with previous analyses, these results are based on the weighted sample but the unweighted N's are provided.

An Example

Before examining Table 11—9, overall, it is useful to select a variable for detailed analysis to assure clear interpretation of the statistics. Using personal health status as an example, Table 11—9 shows that those who evaluated their health as good or excellent averaged 6.8 visits [12] versus 8.8 for those evaluating their health status as fair or poor. These are the unadjusted means. The mean for all major illness respondents was 7.6 visits. The coefficients indicate that after taking into account the effects of all the other predictors those in good or excellent health had nearly six-tenths of a visit less than all major illness respondents while those in fair or poor health experienced nine-tenths of a visit more. The adjusted means show that if those in good or excellent health had been exactly like the total sample of major illness respondents with respect to their distribution over all the other variable classifications they would have had 7.0 visits while those in fair or poor health, under similar conditions, would have had 8.5 visits. The eta^2 indicates that *without* taking into account other variables, personal health status evaluation explains 2.3 percent of the total sum of squares, while the beta^2 indicates that when all the other variables are taken into account this is reduced to 1.6 percent. The variables in Table 11—9 are listed in the order of their betas^2—that is, according to their relative importance as a predictor [13].

Results

Table 11—9 shows that primary third party payment source [14] is the most important predictor of total number of ambulatory visits. However, type of most amount source of care and regular source of care also figure prominently [15].

Those actually receiving most of their care from clinics tended to experience the fewest number of visits [16], although those listing a clinic as a regular source experienced the highest number of visits. Other pattern of care variables such as travel time, means of referral and board certification of most amount source are less important predictors.

In regard to means of referral, those who received most of their care from their usual source or were referred by their usual source or another doctor (physician referral system) received more visits than those getting to their most amount source themselves or through family members, relatives, friends or institutional referrals. Thus, having a usual source or at least some contact with a physician may expedite the process of receiving care resulting in more visits, in contrast to those who have to pick a source themselves or rely on others. The latter process may entail initial delay resulting in a fewer number of total visits. In this case one would expect that for a given illness the amount of time a physician would spend with a patient for the first visit would be longer for those who delayed than those who did not. Such data are not available from the current study but are an example of the type of information which needs to be collected in order to examine more closely the relationship between means of referral, delay, initial contact and subsequent utilization in terms of the tradeoff between number and duration of visits.

Respondents receiving most of their care from physicians claiming a specialty but who are not board certified experienced a greater number of visits than those seeing board certified specialists. For those specialties which have a board, board certification is felt by many to be at least a gross measure of physician competence. An interesting question to ask is in what way do the practice habits of non–board certified specialists differ from those who are board certified? Is it really a function of differences in ability to diagnose or treat which accounts for the greater number of visits by patients seeing non–board certified specialists or is it a function of other factors such as level of technology used, number and types of allied health manpower employed, or organization of practice? [17]

As a person experiences symptoms of illness or an illness condition it is expected that medical need variables will begin to play an important role in influencing utilization. This is seen clearly in Table 11–9 where physician rated severity of illness, personal health status and disability days are relatively important predictors. The finding that those respondents with conditions rated by physicians as "preventive or symptomatic" have *more* visits than those with conditions rated as "should see a doctor" or "must see a doctor" requires explanation. Detailed analysis of the particular diagnostic conditions revealed that allergies, nonallergic acute skin diseases, bursitis and related conditions, and minor psychiatric problems comprised over 50 percent of the preventive and symptomatic category. These are conditions requiring a large number of visits. In contrast, a majority of the conditions rated as "should or must see a doctor" are chronic conditions (diabetes, heart disease, cancer, etc.) which, although more serious, do not require as many ambulatory visits over the course of a year as some of the less serious but more acute conditions.

As expected, those respondents rating their health as fair or poor experience more visits than those in good or excellent health and those with 15 or more disability days have somewhat more visits than those with fewer disability days.

The predisposing variables of residence, age, sex and race and the enabling variable of family income are least important as predictors of utilization for people experiencing acute or chronic ambulatory conditions [18].

The effects of the variables were also examined separately for respondents with a condition evaluated as "should see a doctor" (unweighted $N = 751$) and those evaluated as "must see a doctor" (unweighted $N = 706$). It was felt that the medical need variables would have a stronger impact on those with conditions judged as "must see a doctor" than on those judged only as "should see a doctor." This was confirmed for both personal health status and disability days. For personal health status the $beta^2$ increased from 0.013 for the "should see a doctor" group to 0.023 for the "must see a doctor group," and for disability days from 0.006 to 0.015. It was also expected that the specialty of the most amount source would increase in importance with increasing severity. This was also confirmed with an increase in the beta^2 from 0.012 to 0.059. It was expected that there would be little difference in the effect of third party payment source between the two groups or, if anything, that the effect would be attenuated on the grounds that the more serious the illness condition, the less lack of a third party payment source would act as a barrier to utilization. Contrary to expectation, the beta^2 of third party payment source increased from 0.025 to 0.050. Examination of the adjusted means revealed an even larger differential between number of visits received by those with Medicaid or welfare as a payment source and those with private third party payment source or no third party source for the group judged as "must see a doctor" than for those judged only as "should see a doctor." Thus, not only did Medicaid and similar types of coverage have an overall positive impact on number of visits received by its recipients but the effect was stronger the more serious the illness condition involved.

Overall the model explained 12 percent of the variance in total number of ambulatory visits. Among the major illness respondents with a condition evaluated as "should see a doctor" the adjusted R^2 was 13 percent and for those judged as "must see a doctor" the adjusted R^2 was 16 percent.

These data indicate that type of third party payment source clearly is an important variable in determining utilization of ambulatory care services. Those who have to self-pay, holding other factors constant, do not receive nearly as many visits as those with some third party payment source. And those with Medicaid type coverage receive even a greater number of visits, holding other factors constant, than either those with private insurance, Medicare or other nonfree coverage. The implications in terms of the elasticity of demand for ambulatory care, the effects of deductibles, coinsurance and related issues are discussed in more detail in Chapter Seven.

But in terms of various programs for the reorganization of the American health services system, the above findings indicate that source of care variables are nearly as important as third party payment coverage. This presents a somewhat more difficult policy issue because sources of care are less susceptible to change through the political process—at least in terms of changing the composition of various types of physicians graduated by influencing changes in medical education and the processes of specialization. There has been some attempt to deal with this problem through the development of a specialty board in family practice, a growing number of medical schools adopting family practice programs, earlier exposure of the medical student to patient care and related developments (Carnegie Commission on Higher Education 1970).

A more direct approach has been to alter the organizational settings in which physicians practice, especially through the provision of development money for health maintenance organizations. A major consideration in terms of current findings is exactly what form the HMO concept takes in particular practice settings in regard to the number and composition of practitioners, development of stable doctor-patient relationships, whether the HMO is based in one building or practitioners are dispersed throughout an area, how the physicians themselves are paid, patterns of referral and consultation, and related issues. These factors, of course, will also affect the continuity of services received.

CONCLUSIONS AND IMPLICATIONS

The focus of the current chapter has been on the relationship between provider and patient variables in terms of utilization and continuity of care examined within an episode of illness approach. From a public policy viewpoint the most important results of the preceding analysis are as follows:

1. Source of payment is the single most important determinant of number of ambulatory visits received by people experiencing "major illness" condition not requiring hospitalization. Those who primarily have to pay for their own care do not receive nearly as many visits as those whose primary payment source is a third party. Those covered by Medicaid or related welfare programs receive the highest number of visits.
2. The type of provider who delivers most of the care is nearly as important as third party payment coverage in determining number of visits received. Those receiving most of their care from clinics tend to receive fewer visits than those receiving most of their care from general practitioners, internists and other specialists.
3. As a group, the provider or pattern of medical care variables (type of most amount source, type of regular source, means of referral, etc.) are more important determinants of volume of visits than such predisposing and enabling variables as patient's residence, age, race, sex and family income.
4. The more "disadvantaged" groups (those below the near poverty line, and those on Medicaid or welfare or who self-pay) are more likely to receive most of their care from a provider who is their usual source of care than the more "advantaged" groups.
5. Those who primarily have to pay for their care are much more likely to have received care from only one source than those whose care was primarily paid for by a third party.

The direct implications of the above have been discussed in the preceding sections. It is useful, however, to place them within the specific context of current national health insurance proposals and other strategies for reorganization of the health services system.

Previous experience with Medicare and Medicaid as well as current findings indicate that expansion of third party coverage for medical care services is likely to result in increased demand for those services (see Chapter Seven). Policy issues then arise in terms of the supply and organization of services. Increased demand without a concomitant increase in supply or productivity of services suggests not only longer waiting times but the possibility of harmful effects on the continuity and quality of services delivered.

The present findings also suggest that the types of providers seen, indeed, play an important role in determining the overall volume and pattern of utilization [19]. Thus, the issue is not simply one of removing financial barriers to care but of actually structuring or restructuring patient-provider relationships. The latter is a much more complex issue requiring additional study building upon current findings. The likely effects of new types of health maintenance organizations and related proposals, for example, require careful scrutiny especially given the great variety of forms which they may take.

The findings pertaining to continuity of care are extremely preliminary and suggestive particularly in the absence of outcome data on the quality of care received. For example, is it really "good" that the more "disadvantaged" groups are more likely to receive care from their usual source than those better off? In such circumstances, are they receiving care from the "most appropriate" source in terms of level and quality of services required? Certainly, the finding that those who primarily have to pay for their own care are much more likely to have only a single source of care regardless of illness severity suggests that financial barriers as perceived by *both* the physician and patient may be acting as a deterrent to necessary referral. But in the absence of quality data no firm inferences can be made.

Rogers (1973:1379) states: "The uneven availability of continuing medical care of respectable quality is one of the most growing and unacceptable problems that we face in our democracy today." Outside of the issue of cost which is widely recognized by everyone, this statement emphasizes the three major issues of accessibility (expressed in terms of availability of services although other factors are clearly involved), continuity and quality of care in an interrelated fashion. Future research which operationalizes these *interrelationships* within a theoretical or at least conceptual model of the medical care delivery process seems necessary. More needs to be known about the relationships between initial access into the system; patient-provider interaction in terms of "appropriate" number of visits, referrals and continuity of care; and outcome of care in terms of the effect on health status, patient satisfaction and provider satisfaction. Starfield (1973:135) presents a similar approach emphasizing that relatively little is known about the relationship between individual physician-patient encounters and the health care system as a whole. The work by Falk et al. (1967) and Schoenfeld et al. (1968) is a step in this direction. It would appear to be difficult to make enlightened policy decisions in the area of health services delivery without a greater understanding of these processes.

NOTES TO CHAPTER ELEVEN

1. The focus is on person-illness episodes. A few respondents had more than one major illness during the survey year. Of the 1591 respondents, 1492 had only one, 92 had two and seven had three episodes yielding a total of 1697 illness episodes. Maternity care is excluded from the analysis.

2. Two respondents who reported a large number of visits are deleted from the analysis based on verification data. One respondent reported four hospital outpatient department visits per week during the year for a total of 208 visits. Followup with the hospital revealed no record of such visits. The second respondent claimed a doctor visited him at home three times a week during the year for a total of 156 visits. The doctor involved claimed he did not treat the respondent at all, but had seen other members of the household.

3. These percentages are derived by deleting the third column of Table 11–4 and recalculating on the basis of the first two columns.

4. This difference is, in part, a function of perceived health status. Fifty-four percent of those whose primary payment source was a Medicaid type program rated their health as "fair" or "poor" versus 42 percent of those who self-paid. On the other hand, only 44 percent of those whose primary payment source was private insurance, Medicare or some other type of nonfree source rated their health as "fair" or "poor," suggesting that the lower number of visits experienced by the "self-pay" group is not solely a function of health status but may also be due to financial barriers to care. This point will be developed further in the text.

5. Interpretation of the data for "clinic, other, none" is not straightforward because the specific general practitioner, internist or other specialist reported as most amount source may have actually been located at clinics which the respondent reported as being his regular source. Simply put, the respondent may have mentioned the clinic's name when asked for regular source and a specific doctor at the clinic when asked for most amount source.

6. These are the same groups which if they have a specialist as their most amount source are more likely to have a non–board certified specialist. This cannot be seen directly from Table 11–4 but is derived from a recalculation of Table 11–4 based on the first two columns only. Thus, to the extent that board certification is a measure of quality of care, the possibility of a tradeoff between continuity and quality is at least suggested.

7. It should be kept in mind that, as shown in Tables 11–3 and 11–4, the nonwhites are somewhat more likely to report a clinic as their regular source and most amount source. The extent to which continuity of care exists for these people may depend on whether or not they usually see a particular doctor at the clinic. For all respondents in the national study, the low income and the nonwhite were less likely to see a particular doctor at the clinic than were the higher income and white (Andersen et al. 1972:7). Thus, for these people it can be argued that receiving most of their care from an established source does not have the same continuity implications as it does for those receiving care from particular physicians.

8. It should be noted that this is largely a different group than those 55 and over. In other words, those who primarily self-pay are not the same as those 55 and over.

9. Before the transformation the skewness on the dependent variable was 4.6 and kurtosis 34.7. After the natural log transformation, skewness was reduced to 0.012 and kurtosis to 1.02.

10. The variables were first screened for interaction effects using AID (Automatic Interaction Detection program; Sonquist and Morgan 1964; Sonquist, Baker and Morgan 1973). A MCA run incorporating various interaction terms proved to be no better a predictor than the direct additive model.

11. This must *not* be interpreted in terms of percent of variance explained. Beta^2 is the sum of squares due to the predictor (after holding other predictors constant) relative to the total sum of squares. This could be interpreted as percent of variance explained only in the case where all predictors are uncorrelated. The sum of squares based on adjusted deviations when summed across all predictors may add to either more or less than the explained sum of squares and might even exceed the total sum of squares. Thus, the sum of betas^2 across all predictors could be more or less than the square of the multiple correlation coefficient (R^2) and could be even greater than 1.00. It is most useful to think of beta as being analogous to the standardized regression coefficient which measures the number of standard deviation units a dependent variable moves when the explanatory variable changes by one standard deviation.

12. The visits are expressed as geometric means reconverted from the natural logarithm transformation. The geometric mean is always less than the arithmetic mean.

13. Waiting time, mode of transportation, family size and age of the physician who was the patient's most amount source were excluded because preliminary analysis revealed little association with number of ambulatory visits.

14. It should be noted that this variable is somewhat different from the insurance coverage variable used in the overview findings presented in Chapter Two.

15. In the overview findings presented in Chapter Two, source of care was found to be of little consequence in explaining volume of physician visits for the total sample. The findings reported here, however, suggest that for those people experiencing "major illness" episodes source of care is of some consequence in explaining differences in total volume of physician visits.

16. It will be recalled from Table 11−3 that 35 percent of those with a Medicaid type payment source used clinics as their most amount source, while Table 11−7 revealed that the Medicaid group as a whole averaged the highest number of visits (14.1). The current finding that those with clinics as their most amount source received the *fewest* number of visits is in large part explained by the fact that the Medicaid recipients using clinics averaged only 10.7 visits while those seeing general practitioners averaged 13.3 visits and those seeing "other specialists" 22.9 visits. Thus, the high number of visits received by those with Medicaid type coverage is due to those seeing general practitioners and other specialists and not those visiting clinics. It should also be noted that for clinic

and "other" users the adjusted and unadjusted means are biased downward somewhat because of inclusion of the "none" category—that is, those with no most amount source of care. Additional analysis deleting these 31 (unweighted) individuals did not substantially change the nature of these relationships.

17. It should be noted that patient characteristics and severity of illness variables are already taken into account in the model.

18. The number of physicians per 1000 population in the respondent's primary sampling unit was also included in several analyses. The effect of this variable was as expected in that those respondents living in areas with a higher doctor-to-population ratio (1.13/1000 or above) had somewhat more visits than those living in areas with a lower ratio (< 1.13/1000). However, the doctor-to-population variable did not figure prominently as a predictor in any of the multiple classification analyses. The effect of this resource variable on total physician visits for all nonmaternity respondents in the sample is examined by May in Chapter Eight; see especially Tables 8–6A and 8–6B.

19. The question might be raised as to whether it's really the provider exerting the influence or a characteristic of the patient selecting the provider. It should be noted that the MCA results are net of the influence of other variables. Thus, the coefficients and adjusted means for type of most amount source, for example, are net of the effects of patient's race, age, sex, income and related variables. Since MCA assumes an additive model the next question is whether or not there are important interactions between patient characteristics and provider characteristics. The preliminary AID analyses revealed essentially no interactions between patient characteristics and provider characteristics. Thus, given the current sample, it appears that type of provider seen exerts an important independent effect on utilization of services.

Chapter Twelve

The Impact of Incremental Medical Services on Health Status, 1963–1970

Lee Benham and
Alexandra Benham

Will higher levels of medical care utilization lead to improved health status in the U.S.? To investigate this, we examine the net health benefits of increments in utilization of physician and hospital services by comparing changes in health status of 28 education-age cohorts with changes in medical care utilization between 1963 and 1970. During this period, government support for medical services increased rapidly, inducing changes in costs, access and utilization.

A simple model is constructed and tested which relates health status to prior health status and to changes in demographic characteristics and medical care utilization. Three health indicators are used: individuals' self-evaluation of health status, number of self-reported medical symptoms and number of disability days during previous year.

The statistical results are all consistent with the view that increased medical utilization by adult education-age cohorts over this period was not associated with improvements in these health indicators. These results suggest that alternatives to increases in traditional medical care should be explored in the programs seeking to improve the health of the population.

Underlying many current proposals for expanded government support for medical services is an assumption that increasing such medical services will improve the health of the population. This chapter investigates the validity of this assumption.

Obviously health benefits are derived from medical services. If all hospital and physician services were eliminated, the health status of the population almost certainly would decline substantially. The existence of these overall benefits of medical care, however, does not tell us about the benefits associated with somewhat more or somewhat fewer services. The incremental impact can be negligible or negative even though total benefits are large. Failure to distinguish between total and incremental (marginal) effects has led to confusion in some previous discussions of this question. Many have argued that since health benefits are derived from the existing level of medical services, providing more services will improve health even more. This need not follow.

Incremental medical services can clearly make a positive contribution to some individuals' health; a little more medical intervention can on occasion be life-saving. However, there may be no net health benefits from these increments, and, in fact, adverse consequences may be associated with them. Complications resulting from elective surgery, infections resulting from hospital stays and blood transfusions, adverse reaction to drugs, and emotional trauma associated with false positives of diagnostic tests are examples of such adverse effects. To examine only the beneficial consequences of medical care would obviously over-state the improvements in health status resulting from providing more medical services.

The objective here is to study the net impact on health of increments in medical services for population groups, starting with the 1963 level of medical services within the United States. The approach is described in the next section.

THE APPROACH

For various reasons it is difficult to draw inferences concerning the effects of medical care on health status from cross-sectional observation of individuals' health and medical care utilization.

First, individuals whose health is poor are likely to use more medical services than those whose health is good. This applies both to persons whose lifetime level of health is poor and who thus tend to utilize more services throughout, and to persons who are temporarily in poor health and therefore increase their current level of utilization. This impact of health status on utilization confounds measurement of the relationship running in the opposite direction, namely, the impact of utilization on health status.

Second, the full effects of medical care received during a given period are likely to appear only after an interval of time, perhaps a lengthy one, has passed. Thus, to the extent that individuals' current utilization differs from their past utilization, data showing current utilization and current health status do not include these lagged effects.

One way to surmount these difficulties is to examine a situation in which medical care utilization changes for reasons independent of individuals' health status and then to compare their health status at some later time with their health status prior to the change in utilization. One possibility would be to undertake an experiment over a period of time during which one group is pro-vided with increased medical services while a control group is not, and to com-pare changes in the subsequent health status and death rates of the two groups. Such experimental data are not available. However, the available data can be used to approximate such an experiment.

The data used in this study are taken from comparable national surveys conducted by the Center for Health Administration Studies covering medical care experiences of the population for the calendar years 1963 and 1970 (Chapter One). Between 1963 and 1970 government support for medical services increased rapidly, inducing changes in costs, access and utilization. These changes provide an opportunity to estimate the impact of medical care utilization on health under three assumptions: first, that these government medical programs had a substantial effect on changes in the level of medical utilization across groups over this period; second, that these programs were not influenced by any relative change over the period in the health status of the groups examined [1]; third, that death rates across groups were unaffected by these programs [2].

Given these assumptions, changes in medical utilization across population groups can be related to changes in health status of those groups. If increments in medical services lead to improvements in health, groups receiving larger increments over this period should have a greater improvement (or smaller decline) in health status [3].

For this analysis, it seems desirable to compare groups defined in terms of criteria related to economic status because (1) persons of lower economic status tend to be less healthy and (2) many of the government programs of the period were directed toward the poor and elderly. Individual earnings are not satisfactory as a classificatory variable here because earnings tend to be partly a function of health status, and for this analysis the groups must be defined in such a way that representation within each group is independent of changes in individuals' health status. Education is a more satisfactory classificatory variable; it is a good proxy for permanent income, and in the case of adults who have completed their education is unaffected by changes in health. (Most schooling was already completed by individuals in the age range used in this study, which begins at age 23.) Education is therefore used as one basis of group classification. Age is also included as a classificatory variable because health tends to decline with age.

For 1963 and 1970, the surveyed individuals between the ages of 23 and 71 are sorted into four education categories (0–8, 9–11, 12 and 13+ years of schooling completed) and seven, seven year age categories (23–29, 30–36, 37–43, 44–50, 51–57, 58–64 and 65–71 years of age). This provides 28 education-age cells for each survey year. Within each cell, the means of the following individual characteristics are then estimated: reported health status, number of symptoms reported, disability days during previous year, nonobstetric visits to physicians during previous year and nonobstetric hospital days during previous year. The means obtained for the education-age groups are taken as representative of those for corresponding education-age groups in the whole United States population for the survey years [4].

The means of two other variables are also calculated for the cells—marital status and family size. Married individuals are generally in better health than unmarried individuals. To the extent that this better health is due to marital status itself rather than simply to self-selection, then as the relative proportion of married individuals in a group declines, the health of that group should also decline. Changes in mean family size are also likely to affect the mean health status of groups, although the sign of the effect is less clear. The critical factor here is the relationship between family size and the physical, financial and emotional support afforded to family members.

A simple model is then constructed to obtain estimates of the relationship between medical utilization and health status. In this model, the mean health status of a given education-age group in 1970 is a function of the mean health status of the comparable education-age group in 1963, the changes in mean medical utilization from the 1963 to the 1970 group, and the changes in mean marital status and mean family size from the 1963 to the 1970 group.   (12.1)

$$HS^{i,j}_{k,1970} = \beta_0 + \beta_1(MC^{i,j}_{m,1970} - MC^{i,j}_{m,1963}) + \beta_2\ HS^{i,j}_{k,1963} + \beta_3\ (FAMSIZ^{i,j}_{1970}$$

$$- FAMSIZ^{i,j}_{1963}) + \beta_4\ (MARRY^{i,j}_{1970} - MARRY^{i,j}_{1963}) + \mu^{i,j}$$

where the superscripts i, j denote the education and age categories, respectively, for the given cell; $k = 1,2,3,4$; $m = 1,2$; the variables for the cell are the means of the variables for the individuals in the cell; and

HS_1 = 2 if individual reported own health as excellent
        = 3 if individual reported own health as good
        = 4 if individual reported own health as fair
        = 5 if individual reported own health as poor
HS_2 = 0 if individual reported own health as good or excellent
        = 1 if individual reported own health as poor or fair
HS_3 = number of symptoms (from a list of 20) individual reported experiencing in previous year [5]
HS_4 = disability days individual had during previous year
MC_1 = number of nonobstetric visits to physicians individual made during previous year
MC_2 = number of days of nonobstetric hospitalization individual had during previous year
$FAMSIZ$ = family size
$MARRY$ = 1 if individual is married [6]
           = 0 otherwise

The coefficient of primary interest here is β_1, which provides an estimate of the relationship between mean health status of groups in 1970 and changes in group medical utilization from 1963 to 1970. Under the set of assumptions discussed above, β_1 is an estimate of the impact of changes in medical care utilization on health status. If increases in medical care utilization improve health status, then β_1 should be negative [7].

THE FINDINGS

Table 12–1 shows the estimates with medical services measured as the number of nonobstetric visits to physicians. Column one shows the β_1 coefficient estimates for the four health status measures examined. The estimate is positive in each case. These results indicate that education-age groups with larger increases in physician visits between 1963 and 1970 had larger declines in mean health status relative to other groups over this period.

In Table 12–2, the same equations are reestimated with medical services measured as the number of nonobstetric hospital days. The results are similar. The β_1 coefficient is positive in all cases, a strong indication that increases in hospital utilization between 1963 and 1970 were not associated with an improvement in health status for age-education groups.

The estimates in Tables 12–1 and 12–2 are computed taking only two other group characteristics into account—mean family size and mean marital status in 1963 and 1970. If other group characteristics affecting group health status changed for these groups between 1963 and 1970, and if these changes were systematically associated with changes in medical care utilization, the estimates above are biased. There is a wide variety of such possible changes. One particular class of changes which can be examined with the existing data is that of changes associated with age cohorts' life experiences. These might include long term changes in average diet and physical activity, effects of increased urbanization, the impact of wars and so forth. Such factors might result in differences in the impact of medical care on health status for, say, 23–29 year olds in 1963 as compared with 23–29 year olds in 1970 [8]. We can examine this to some degree by using groups matched for education but in the next higher age category in 1970 than in 1963. To the extent that education is completed by age 23, we are thus comparing samples at two points in time from a set of individuals of specified educational attainment who were born during a specified (seven year) period.

The modified specification of the model is as follows: (12.2)

$$HS^{i,j}_{k,1970} = \beta_0 + \beta_1 (MC^{i,j}_{m,1970} - MC^{i,j-1}_{m,1963}) + \beta_2 HS^{i,j-1}_{k,1963} + \beta_3 (FAMSIZ^{i,j}_{1970}$$

$$- FAMSIZ^{i,j-1}_{1963}) + \beta_4 (MARRY^{i,j}_{1970} - MARRY^{i,j-1}_{1963}) + \mu^{i,j}$$

The coefficient of principal interest is again β_1. If increases in medical utilization for education cohorts result in better health, β_1 should be negative.

Table 12–1. Estimates of the Effect of Changes in Number of Visits to Physicians on Health Status for 28 Age-Education Groups Between 1963 and 1970 *(t statistic in parentheses)*

Dependent variable: health status in 1970	Change in number of non-OB physician visits	Health status in 1963[a]	Change in family size	Change in marital status	Constant	R^2	N
Mean reported health status HS_1	0.0265 (1.7)	0.8299 (9.5)	-0.0560 (-0.9)	-0.1595 (-0.3)	0.5682	0.85	28
Mean reported health status HS_2	0.0112 (2.0)	0.7262 (8.9)	0.0168 (0.8)	-0.0072 (-2.7)	0.1540	0.91	28
Mean number of symptoms HS_3	0.0574 (0.9)	0.3993 (1.8)	-0.3639 (-1.5)	-0.0460 (-1.6)	1.889	0.51	28
Mean number of disability days HS_4	1.5008 (2.5)	0.4454 (2.3)	-3.4010 (-1.5)	-19.3224 (-8.4)	9.1464	0.56	28

[a] In each equation the health status variable $HS_{k,\ 1963}$ used as independent variable corresponds to the health status variable $HS_{k,\ 1970}$ used as dependent variable.

Table 12–2. Estimates of the Effect of Changes in Number of Hospital Days on Health Status for 28 Age-Education Groups Between 1963 and 1970 *(t statistic in parentheses)*

Dependent variable: health status in 1970	*Change in number of non-OB hospital days*	*Health status in 1963[a]*	*Change in family size*	*Change in marital status*	*Constant*	R^2	*N*
Mean reported health status HS_1	0.0256 (1.5)	0.9056 (10.7)	−0.0694 (1.1)	0.2105 (0.4)	0.3374	0.85	28
Mean reported health status HS_2	0.0051 (0.7)	0.9415 (11.3)	0.0011 (0.04)	0.1091 (0.5)	0.0244	0.86	28
Mean number of symptoms HS_3	0.0214 (0.3)	0.7097 (3.1)	−0.4430 (1.7)	0.8679 (0.4)	0.7244	0.41	28
Mean number of disability days HS_4	1.4095 (2.2)	0.7970 (4.3)	−4.2877 (1.8)	4.2284 (0.2)	5.0078	0.54	28

[a]See note, Table 12–1.

The results shown in Tables 12–3 and 12–4 are similar to those in Tables 12–1 and 12–2. The β_1 estimate is in one case negative but not significantly different from zero. In all other cases, the β_1 estimates are positive. Taken literally, these estimates are not consistent with the view that increased utilization of medical services was associated with improved health status from 1963 to 1970. Before further discussion of the implications of these results, several statistical and conceptual problems will be considered.

PROBLEMS

One serious problem associated with these estimates is the question of the independence of changes in medical care utilization from changes in health status. It was assumed that groups' changes over time in medical care utilization were not a function of changes in groups' health status, but were primarily due to the increased level of government support. This assumption is not investigated empirically here and the magnitude of any existing bias is unknown. It is worth noting, however, that most coefficients of the medical care utilization variables are positive, some significantly so. In order to conclude that incremental medical services improved health, one would have to assert that the bias is so large it has reversed the signs of these coefficients.

Another set of criticisms has to do with the measures of health status used. It can be argued that the indexes examined here measure only a part of health status and neglect some very important components. This is obvious. It is often further asserted that the unmeasured components would show improvement with increments in medical care. This is not so obvious. The available evidence is limited, but that which does exist—studies using mortality measures of health status as cited in footnote two—shows relationships consistent with the results of this chapter. Furthermore, many critics of current medical policy are willing to accept the indexes used here for measuring the "need" for medical services. It might then also seem appropriate to accept these indexes for measuring the benefits.

One component of health status which is frequently mentioned as having been omitted here is level of anxiety and worry concerning one's health. It is often asserted that medical services benefit individuals by reducing such worry and anxiety, and that the results here are therefore severely biased. However, provision of medical services may reduce individuals' perceptions of their own level of health status, either because their expectations are increased and hence satisfaction with their current health declines, or because they become more aware of their health problems. This may be accompanied by increase in anxiety and worry. Even then, this can be worthwhile if individuals perceive their "objective" health status more accurately, take appropriate medical and non-medical precautions, and improve their health over the long run. Early diagnosis of treatable cancer would be an extreme example. If, on the other hand, there

Table 12–3. Estimates of the Effect of Changes in Number of Visits to Physicians on Health Status for 24 Age-Education Cohort Groups Between 1963 and 1970 *(t statistic in parentheses)*

Dependent variable: health status in 1970	*Change in number of non-OB physician visits*	*Health status in 1963[a]*	*Change in family size*	*Change in marital status*	*Constant*	*R^2*	*N*
Mean reported health status HS_1	0.0651 (3.8)	0.5440 (4.8)	-0.1294 (-2.1)	0.0970 (0.3)	1.4271	0.87	24
Mean reported health status HS_2	0.0287 (3.8)	0.6483 (5.5)	-0.0651 (-2.5)	0.1497 (5.8)	0.1083	0.88	24
Mean number of symptoms HS_3	-0.0223 (-0.4)	0.8281 (3.5)	-0.0876 (-0.4)	-0.9912 (-0.8)	0.5106	0.58	24
Mean number of disability days HS_4	2.1442 (4.2)	0.5145 (2.4)	-1.543 (-0.8)	-8.1531 (-0.7)	8.7921	0.73	24

[a]See note, Table 12–1.

Table 12-4. Estimates of the Effect of Changes in Number of Hospital Days on Health Status for 24 Age-Education Cohort Groups Between 1963 and 1970 (t statistic in parentheses)

Dependent variable: health status in 1970	Change in number of non-OB hospital days	Health status in 1963[a]	Change in family size	Change in marital status	Constant	R^2	N
Mean reported health status HS_1	0.0178 (0.9)	0.8012 (6.0)	-0.1007 (-1.3)	0.4345 (1.2)	0.6996	0.77	24
Mean reported health status HS_2	0.0073 (0.83)	0.9092 (6.6)	-0.0548 (-1.6)	0.2997 (1.8)	0.0585	0.79	24
Mean number of symptoms HS_3	0.2066 (3.7)	0.3742 (1.7)	-0.0470 (-0.3)	-1.9071 (-2.1)	1.439	0.75	24
Mean number of disability days HS_4	1.1232 (1.6)	1.0203 (3.5)	-2.0856 (-0.8)	11.7042 (0.8)	4.0398	0.55	24

[a] See note, Table 12-1.

are no commensurate benefits associated with this medically generated tendency to rate oneself in less good health, the anxiety generated is an uncompensated cost of increments in medical services. The whole issue is therefore quite complex and it is not clear what the magnitude or the direction of the bias may be.

In sum, there are sufficient problems with these results to suggest caution during interpretation. While it is very difficult to determine the net bias introduced by these problems, the effects would have to be both systematic and substantial before the conclusions drawn here were changed.

CONCLUSION

A simple model was developed above to examine the impact of increments in physician and hospital services on alternative measures of health status. The results are consistent with the view that positive increments in nonobstetric medical services for adult population groups from 1963 to 1970 did not lead to improvements in health status. While further evidence could obviously overturn the conclusions drawn here, it is noteworthy that earlier studies on this topic using mortality indexes as measures of health status obtained qualitatively similar results.

These results should tend to shift the burden of evidence more to those who argue, either explicitly or implicitly, that providing more medical services will raise health levels. Increasing ease of access to medical services by adults will perhaps satisfy some concerns about equity of access, but these results suggest that improvements in the level or distribution of health status will not follow. Increased expenditures by government on medical services can be further counterproductive in that they draw resources away from other more effective programs. Indeed, if the objective is to improve the health of the population, increased search for such alternative programs should be undertaken. A potentially fruitful area is suggested by the strong observed relationship between educational attainment and health status (Grossman 1975). More highly educated individuals tend to be healthier. If it can be established that more education leads to improved health, this has obvious policy implications for future investments to improve health.

NOTES TO CHAPTER TWELVE

1. This assumption precludes the possibility that the programs were implemented merely to keep the health of the poor, elderly, etc. from declining relatively. The targets of these programs could, and probably did, have lower *levels* of health.

2. If death rates did in fact fall as a consequence of the provision of more medical services, then it would be inappropriate to compare the health status of those alive before the change in services with those alive afterwards. However, several studies examining the relationship between mortality rates and utilization

of physician and hospital services across states or counties have found in general no association. (Fuchs 1965; Auster et al. 1969; Glazer 1971; Stewart 1971).

3. Differences in 1963 and 1970 utilization levels by groups are likely to represent reasonably smooth trends over time and we should be observing some lagged effects of utilization.

4. The sample sizes are small for the procedure followed. The overall sample size is large in both 1963 and 1970, but the analysis here reduces the data into 28 education-age cells. For each cell the sampling error is obviously larger than for the sample as a whole. As a consequence, the confidence which can be placed in the characteristic estimates for any particular cell is lower than for the whole sample.

5. The specific symptoms are listed in Aday and Andersen (1975:84–85).

6. The cell mean is the proportion of individuals who are married.

7. For all measures of health status (HS) used here, the poorer the health, the larger the value of HS.

8. For example, the level of educational attainment was increased over this period. A smaller proportion of individuals in 1970 had eight years of education or less. Consequently, this group is likely to constitute a more adverse selection of individuals on the basis of health in 1970 than in 1963.

Chapter Thirteen

The Effect of Measurement Error
on Differences in the Use of Health
Services*

Ronald Andersen

Much of this book deals with comparisons of health utilization among groups defined according to age, income, residence and racial characteristics. The purpose of this chapter is to provide a framework for assessing the extent to which the differences between these groups might be affected by social survey measurement error. The resulting analysis suggested few changes in the utilization differences between subgroups which would have important policy implications, with the exception that measurement bias seemed to reduce the magnitude of the difference in number of physician visits between the races and between the poor and the nonpoor. Suggestions for further exploration of the influence of measurement error are made.

Much of this volume has been devoted to analysis of differences in utilization according to demographic, social and economic characteristics. Both the magnitudes of the differences and reasons why they exist have been explored. The policy implications drawn from these analyses, though, should be tempered by consideration of measurement issues which might cause the differences to be either larger or smaller than they appear. The purpose of this chapter is to investigate such possibilities.

Two aspects of the study facilitate such an investigation. One is a special computer program developed to calculate the sampling errors of estimates made from data in this study. Sampling errors show variations that may occur by chance because only a portion of the population is surveyed. The computation of sampling errors for estimates based on the present sample is especially complex because of the weighting scheme, because families in this sample were geographically clustered and because stratification was used in the selection of the unit of analysis. The method used to estimate sampling errors tends to

*The author wishes to thank Martin Frankel for comments on an earlier draft of this chapter.

slightly overestimate their magnitude because of the impossibility of taking into account the full range of stratification used in the sample design [1]. But this method still allows us to examine the relative error for different subgroups in the population and assess the statistical significance of differences found between them.

The second feature facilitating this analysis of error is more unique to this particular study. An attempt was made to verify all hospital admissions and physician contacts reported by families in the social survey. Hospitals were contacted where an admission was reported to have taken place, as were physicians or clinics where a visit reportedly occurred and third party payers who received claims for these services. The dual purpose of this procedure was to determine if the reported care was, in fact, given during the calendar year 1970 and to get more precise information than the families were likely to give on diagnoses, cost, kinds of treatment and sources of payment for the services. Unfortunately, verifying information was not obtained on all hospital and physician services reported in the social survey. Approximately 10 percent of the families in the social survey refused to sign the permission forms which were needed to obtain information from doctors and hospitals. Further, not enough information was obtained to contact some providers, and others did not cooperate with the study. Still, verifying data were obtained for over 90 percent of the hospital admissions and for two-thirds of the physician visits. These data are used in the following analysis to test the accuracy of utilization estimates for various subgroups in the population.

The measures of utilization which will be examined include hospital admissions, mean number of days in the hospital, percent of the population seeing a physician and mean number of physician visits per year. These utilization measures will be compared according to age of oldest family member, family income level, race and type of residence. Response rates for each of these items are shown in Table 13-1. Estimates made exclusively from survey data as well as estimates which incorporate the verification information will be analyzed. The latter are referred to as "best estimates." In general, the verifying information was selected for inclusion in the "best estimate" data over what the family reported, although in isolated instances where the respondent had documenting records or the provider reports were particularly suspect, the respondent data was selected. When no information was obtained from the provider, the respondent data was automatically selected. The best estimate, then, is an amalgam of what we judge to be the best data available for each family.

A MODEL OF MEASUREMENT ERROR

To assess the relative impact of measurement error on each of the subgroups some scheme is needed which defines the various sources of error and suggests how they might be measured. The general model which will be used here is that

Table 13-1. Estimated Response and Nonresponse by Selected Population Characteristics

	Response (1-p)	Nonresponse (p)	Total
Family characteristics		*percent*	
Age of oldest person in family			
Under 65	81.7	18.3	100.0
65 and over	84.5	15.5	100.0
Family income			
Above near poverty	83.0	17.0	100.0
Below near poverty	81.6	18.4	100.0
Race			
White	82.0	18.0	100.0
Nonwhite	81.5	18.5	100.0
Residence			
SMSA central city	78.1	21.9	100.0
SMSA other urban	81.6	18.4	100.0
Urban non-SMSA	82.9	17.1	100.0
Rural nonfarm	84.4	15.6	100.0
Rural farm	89.7	10.3	100.0
Total	82.0	18.0	100.0

described by Leslie Kish (1965:509–527). This perspective, which is diagrammed in Figure 13–1, divides total error into variable error and bias. Variable error is thought to be the result of some random process. It usually is described in terms of a probability statement which says the true population estimate is within an interval around the estimate given. Bias is a constant error which causes a given estimate to be larger or smaller than the true number.

Variable error includes both sampling and nonsampling errors. The multistage stratification and weighting aspects of the sample will be taken into consideration when measuring sampling errors. Nonsampling errors can be represented in a manner similar to sampling errors. Figure 13–1 allows for random field and processing error as components of nonsampling errors. While nonresponse errors could be included here, they tend to affect biases more than variable error.

Biases can also be divided into sampling and nonsampling sources. Included under sampling bias are biases from the sampling frame and consistent statistical bias. Frame biases result from using inappropriate selecting procedures to choose a sample from the universe. Consistent biases for any given sample have a constant effect on the estimator but decrease with increasing sample size. Using the variance of a sample to estimate the variance in the population is one example.

Nonsampling biases are important and often undefined sources of error in surveys. Kish divides them into biases of observation and nonobservation.

Figure 13–1.   Classification of Sources of Survey Error

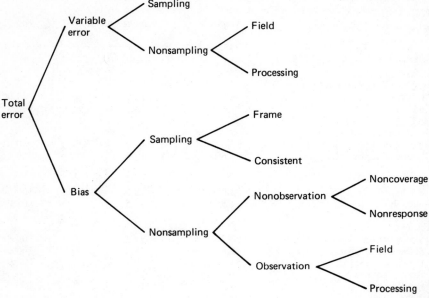

"Biases of observation are caused by obtaining and recording observations incorrectly" (Ibid., p. 520). These again may be divided into two classes. Field biases arise in the collection of observations and include interviewing, enumerating, counting or measuring problems. Processing biases occur during the office process and in coding, tabulating and computing the estimates.

Nonsampling biases of nonobservation can also be split into noncoverage and nonresponse. Nonresponse refers to failure to obtain observations on some subjects selected and designated for the sample. It may be due to refusals, not at homes, lost questionnaires, etc. In contrast, noncoverage denotes failure to include some units or entire sections of the defined survey population in the actual operational sampling frame. Because these units have a zero probability of selection, they are in effect excluded from the survey result.

Kish assumes "for practical purposes, we may often resort to a simple model for the deviation of a sampling mean from its true value" (Ibid., p. 24). In the relationship below, $\overline{Y}$ = the mean of the sample distribution; $\overline{y}$ = the sample mean and $\overline{Y}_{true}$ = the population mean:

$$(\overline{y} - \overline{Y}_{true}) = (\overline{y} - \overline{Y}) + (\overline{Y} - \overline{Y}_{true}). \tag{13.1}$$

The first term incorporates all variable errors, both sampling and nonsampling; the second term contains all nonsampling biases. This model assumes that the sample design reduces the sample biases to negligible proportions.

The following analysis will attempt to measure various components of this model. The standard error program is designed to measure the variable error from sampling and also a portion of the variable nonsampling error. It is, of course, not possible to measure all sources of nonsampling bias; no measurement of noncoverage is available, for instance. However, aspects of the other three sources of nonsampling bias (nonresponse, field and processing biases) will be measured. While these measurements do not take into account all possible types of error related to the three types of bias, they do treat problems which may have important effects on the apparent utilization differences among population subgroups.

VARIABLE ERROR AND BIAS MEASUREMENTS

In addition to the standard error measurement, the three specific nonsampling biases we will attempt to assess include: (1) nonresponse bias resulting from differences between families interviewed and other families in the sample who refused to participate or were not interviewed for some other reason; (2) a field bias resulting from families who were interviewed giving incorrect or incomplete information about their utilization experience; and (3) a processing bias caused by differences between estimates of units of service received by families who gave no indication of quantities of services used and the actual units of service received by those families.

Standard Errors
The standard error terms shown in Tables 13–2 through 13–5 were produced using a technique described by Kish (Ibid., pp. 282–293) for multistage area probability samples of the type employed in this study. These errors provide an interval around the sample mean with a two-thirds probability that the actual population mean falls within that interval [1].

Nonresponse Biases
The nonresponse biases shown in Tables 13–2 through 13–5 are calculated according to the formula:

$$NB = R \, (1 - p) + NR \, (p) - R \qquad (13.2)$$

where NB = nonresponse bias; R = use rate for responders; $1-p$ = proportion of sample responding; NR = use rate of nonrespondents; and p = proportion of sample who are nonresponders.

The response rates for the various subgroups in the population were derived from a number of different sources. The sample design for the study included a special screening for families with persons 66 years of age and older in order to oversample the elderly. The experience of this screened sample was used to

Table 13–2.   Error Components in Estimates of Hospital Admissions Per 100 Person-Years for Selected Population Characteristics

Family characteristics	Admissions per 100 person-years	Standard error	Nonresponse bias	Field bias	Processing bias
			Social survey		
Age of oldest family member					
Under 65	12.9	0.7	-0.1	-0.3	*
65 or over	18.7	1.5	-0.1	-1.0	*
Family income					
Above near poverty	13.2	0.7	-0.1	-0.2	*
Below near poverty	15.4	1.0	-0.1	-0.7	*
Race					
White	14.0	0.7	-0.1	-0.3	*
Nonwhite	11.1	0.8	-0.1	-0.7	*
Residence					
SMSA central city	12.1	0.7	-0.1	-0.5	*
SMSA other urban	13.8	1.6	-0.1	-0.2	*
Urban non-SMSA	15.4	2.3	-0.1	-0.8	*
Rural nonfarm	14.5	1.2	-0.1	**	*
Rural farm	14.0	1.3	-0.1	-1.0	*
Total	13.7	0.6	-0.1	-0.4	*

			Best estimate		
Age of oldest family member					
Under 65	12.7	0.7	-0.1	**	*
65 or over	18.0	1.4	-0.1	-0.1	*
Family income					
Above near poverty	12.9	0.7	-0.1	**	*
Below near poverty	14.8	1.0	-0.1	**	*
Race					
White	13.7	0.7	-0.1	**	*
Nonwhite	10.5	0.8	-0.1	-0.1	*
Residence					
SMSA central city	11.7	0.7	-0.1	-0.1	*
SMSA other urban	13.6	1.6	-0.1	**	*
Urban non-SMSA	14.9	2.1	-0.1	**	*
Rural nonfarm	14.4	1.1	-0.1	**	*
Rural farm	13.0	1.2	-0.1	-0.1	
Total	13.3	0.6	-0.1	**	*

*Indicates no estimating was done.

**Indicates a bias of less than 0.05; numbers were rounded to the nearest tenth.

Table 13–3.   Error Components in Estimates of Hospital Days Per 100 Person-Years for Selected Population Characteristics

Family characteristics	Hospital days per 100 person-years	Standard error	Nonresponse bias	Field bias	Processing bias
			Social survey		
Age of oldest family member					
Under 65	107	8.1	2.7	−17.9	**
65 or over	264	26.5	5.7	−29.3	**
Family income					
Above near poverty	118	9.5	3.0	−18.1	0.1
Below near poverty	159	16.5	3.8	−22.5	−0.4
Race					
White	130	9.2	3.2	−19.1	0.1
Nonwhite	110	11.6	2.8	−19.2	**
Residence					
SMSA central city	110	12.3	3.3	−12.3	**
SMSA other urban	130†	22.4	4.0	−13.0†	−0.2
Urban non-SMSA	105	14.2	2.5	−10.7	**
Rural nonfarm	128	12.4	2.8	−17.9	0.5
Rural farm	130	20.5	1.9	−13.0	**
Total	128	8.6	3.2	−19.2	0.1

Best estimate

			Best estimate		
Age of oldest family member					
Under 65	88	6.6	2.3	− 0.8	* *
65 or over	235	23.6	5.1	− 3.0	* .
Family income					
Above near poverty	99	8.0	2.5	− 0.9	* *
Below near poverty	136	14.1	3.2	− 1.6	* *
Race					
White	109	7.7	2.8	− 1.0	* *
Nonwhite	90	9.5	2.3	− 1.8	* *
Residence					
SMSA central city	98	11.0	3.0	− 0.9	* *
SMSA other urban	124	17.8	3.2	− 1.6	* *
Urban non-SMSA	92	12.5	2.2	− 0.3	* *
Rural nonfarm	106	10.3	2.3	− 1.6	* *
Rural farm	112	17.6	1.6	− 0.2	*
Total	107	7.2	2.7	− 1.1	*

*Indicates no estimating was done.

**Indicates a bias of less than 0.05; numbers were rounded to the nearest tenth.

†Excludes one patient on kidney dialysis who was estimated to have 180 unweighted hospital days. On the basis of the verification, these services were changed to outpatient care. The initial estimate of hospital days per 100 person-years is 156 including this observation; the field bias becomes 33.0.

Table 13–4.   Error Components in Estimates of Percent of Population Seeing a Physician for Selected Population Characteristics

Family characteristics	Percent of population seeing a physician	Standard error	Nonresponse bias	Field bias	Processing bias
			Social survey (percent)		
Age of oldest family member					
Under 65	68	1.1	-0.5	-5.7	*
65 or over	71	1.3	-1.3	-3.2	*
Family income					
Above near poverty	72	1.0	-1.1	-5.3	*
Below near poverty	59	1.5	-0.9	-5.3	*
Race					
White	70	1.1	-1.3	-5.0	*
Nonwhite	59	2.2	1.7	-8.8	*
Residence					
SMSA central city	66	1.7	-1.3	-5.2	*
SMSA other urban	73	2.5	-1.2	-5.1	*
Urban non-SMSA	71	4.4	**	-4.5	*
Rural nonfarm	69	1.5	-1.6	-5.7	*
Rural farm	62	1.6	-0.9	-6.9	*
Total	67	1.0	-0.8	-5.3	*

			Best estimate (percent)			
Age of oldest family member						
Under 65	64	1.1	-0.5	-2.0	*	*
65 or over	67	1.3	-1.2	-0.8	*	*
Family income						
Above near poverty	68	1.0	-1.1	-1.8	*	*
Below near poverty	55	1.5	-0.9	-1.7	*	*
Race						
White	66	1.1	-1.2	-1.6	*	*
Nonwhite	53	2.3	1.6	-3.3	*	*
Residence						
SMSA central city	62	1.7	-1.2	-2.0	*	*
SMSA other urban	69	2.6	-1.2	-1.9	*	*
Urban non-SMSA	66	4.6	0.4	-1.2	*	*
Rural nonfarm	64	1.6	-1.5	-1.7	*	*
Rural farm	56	1.7	-0.8	-1.9	*	*
Total	65	1.1	-0.7	-1.8	*	

*Indicates no estimating was done.

**Indicates a bias of less than 0.05; numbers were rounded to the nearest tenth.

Table 13–5.   Error Components in Estimates of Mean Number of Physician Visits for Selected Population Characteristics

Family characteristics	Mean number of physician visits	Standard error	Nonresponse bias	Field bias	Processing bias
			Social survey		
Age of oldest family member					
Under 65	3.8	0.2	**	−0.7	**
65 or over	5.6	0.2	−0.1	−0.9	**
Family income					
Above near poverty	4.0	0.2	**	−0.7	**
Below near poverty	4.0	0.3	**	−1.0	**
Race					
White	4.1	0.2	**	−0.7	**
Nonwhite	3.6	0.3	−0.2	−1.6	**
Residence					
SMSA central city	4.2	0.3	**	−1.0	**
SMSA other urban	4.1	0.2	**	−0.7	**
Urban non-SMSA	4.4	0.3	−0.1	−1.2	−1.7
Rural nonfarm	3.7	0.2	**	−0.6	**
Rural farm	3.3	0.4	**	−0.3	**
Total	4.0	0.1	**	−0.8	**

			Best estimate		
Age of oldest family member					
Under 65	3.3	0.1	**	-0.2	**
65 or over	4.6	0.2	**	-0.3	**
Family income					
Above near poverty	3.5	0.1	**	-0.2	**
Below near poverty	3.2	0.2	**	-0.3	**
Race					
White	3.5	0.1	**	-0.2	**
Nonwhite	2.8	0.3	-0.1	-0.6	**
Residence					
SMSA central city	3.4	0.3	**	-0.3	**
SMSA other urban	3.9	0.2	**	-0.2	**
Urban non-SMSA	3.4	0.2	-0.1	-0.3	-0.2
Rural nonfarm	3.3	0.2	**	-0.2	**
Rural farm	3.1	0.4	**	-0.1	**
Total	3.5	0.1	**	-0.3	**

*Indicates no estimating was done.
**Indicates a bias of less than 0.05; numbers were rounded to the nearest tenth.

estimate the overall response rate of younger families compared to those with at least one member 66 and over.

Low income families were also oversampled for special analyses. This was done by using a higher selection rate in 73 urban segments of the NORC master sample which, according to 1960 census data, contained a higher proportion of low income urban families. In addition, the part of the overall sample which was screened for elderly persons was also screened for low income families. The response rate of the families in low income segments and those low income families discovered in the screening process were used to estimate the response rate for families below the near poverty level. The response of families not in the special low income segments and families who were found to be above the near poverty level in the screening process was used to estimate the response rate for families above the near poverty level.

No information was collected on any nonrespondents concerning race. However, information on factors correlated with race was collected on both non-respondents and respondents. Using the respondents, an estimating equation was developed by regressing race on measures of residence, region, type of dwelling and income level. The regression weights from this equation were then used to estimate the proportion of nonwhites among the nonresponders. Response rates for whites and nonwhites could then be estimated.

Residential information was collected on both respondents and nonres-pondents from interviewers' observations. This information was then used to estimate response rates for the analytical residence categories in Tables 13–2 through 13–5 as follows:

Analytic Category	*Residential Information Group Used to Estimate Response Rate*
1. SMSA central city	1. "Inside largest city in the primary unit."
2. SMSA other urban	2. "In a suburb of the largest city in primary sampling unit."
3. Urban, non-SMSA	3. Weighted mean response of "2" plus residences described as "In the out-skirts (including nearby small towns of the primary sampling units)."
4. Rural nonfarm	4. "In the outskirts," as in "3."
5. Rural farm	5. "Located on farm."

The estimated response and nonresponse rates for each of the population groups using the above calculations are shown in Table 13–1.

In addition to estimated response rates for each group, utilization rates for both respondents and nonrespondents must be calculated in order to determine the nonresponse bias. While utilization rates for responders are, of course, available from the study data, estimates of these rates for the nonresponders must be calculated from other sources for each service being examined: hospital admissions, hospital days, percent seeing a physician and mean number of physician visits.

Hospital Admissions.   The estimated admission rate for the noninterviewed population was based on a probability selection of 1589 persons with one or more discharges from 21 short term hospitals as determined from hospital records in 1958–1959 (NCHS 1965: series 2, no. 6). Respondents or proxies for them were asked about hospitalizations for the 12 month period prior to the interview. Five percent of the patients did not respond and they were assumed to represent the universe of hospitalizations not reported in health interview surveys (Ibid., p. 95). The universe of all nonrespondents (both those hospitalized and those not) for the same time period was estimated from the National Health Survey study of hospital discharges from short stay hospitals for the U.S. from 1958–1960 (NCHS 1962: series B, no. 32). The rate of nonrespondents was then adjusted upward for increases in hospital utilization between 1958 and 1970. For subgroup calculations, the ratio of the utilization of the nonresponders to the utilization of the responders was assumed to be the same as that for the total population.

Hospital Days.   Estimating hospital days per 100 persons per year for nonrespondents is possible using the estimated admission rates calculated in the previous section plus some estimate of average length of stay. The mean length of stay for the nonresponders in the study of 21 short term hospitals (NCHS 1965: series 2, no. 6, p. 59) was 8.8 days compared to 7.4 days for the responders. The estimate for nonresponders for 1970 was then adjusted to take into account changes in length of stay between 1958–1959 and 1970. The days per 100 persons per year for nonresponders were then calculated by multiplying the average length of stay by the admissions rate. For each subgroup, the ratio of the utilization rates of the nonresponders to the responders was assumed to be the same as that for the total population.

Percent of Population Seeing a Physician.   Some evidence concerning the physician utilization experience of families who do not cooperate with health interview surveys is available from a study done of a housing estate just outside of London with a population of 17,000 (Cartwright 1959). Eighty-six percent of the people on the estate were registered with six general practitioners who recorded details of each of their consultations for one calendar year. Interviews were attempted with a sample of three-sixteenths of the families concerning their health and medical care utilization. The nonresponse rate was 14.5 percent. The proportion of nonresponders who saw a physician according to the GPs' records, adjusted by the differences between the proportion of people seeing a physician on the estate and the proportion seeing an MD in the U.S. in 1970, was used as the estimate for nonresponders in the U.S.

No studies were found which examined the use of physicians by people who refused to cooperate with a health *interview* for the subgroups considered in this study. However, physician utilization experience for persons who refused to participate in a health *examination* survey according to age, income, race and residence is available (NCHS 1969: series 2, no. 36). In 1960–1962 a nationwide probability sample of the noninstitutionalized population ages 18 to 79 was drawn. Of the total sample of 7710 persons, 86.5 percent were examined and tested. Prior interviews showed that the unexamined people were less likely to have seen a physician in the last year than those examined. The experiences of the examined and unexamined people corresponding most closely to the sub-population groups examined in this chapter were used to adjust the estimate of percent seeing a physician among all nonresponders for each subgroup (NCHS Ibid., pp. 34, 44).

Mean Number of Physician Visits. While the London study showed nonrespondents less likely to see a physician than respondents, the mean number of visits for those seeing the physician was slightly greater for the nonrespondents than the respondents (Cartwright 1959: 359). The ratio of visits of responders to nonresponders was assumed to be the same in the U.S. as in the London study. Since the U.S. response rate is known, the mean number of visits for nonresponders could be calculated. The estimated mean number of visits for nonresponders in each subgroup was adjusted for the difference in proportion seeing an MD between that subgroup and the total population.

Field Bias

The field bias we will attempt to measure is operationally defined as the difference between the utilization of sample persons recorded in the social survey and that recorded in the verification studies of hospitals and physicians who provided care. While there are biases included in both sources, the verification data will be accepted as the "true" population value in this analysis.

The verification studies picked up some unreported utilization, particularly for people who reported contact with a physician or hospital, but underreported the number of visits or admissions. However, they are not optimally designed to identify respondents who incorrectly reported no visits to physicians or no hospital admissions since verification was not attempted on these "false negatives." Care not mentioned by the respondent was discovered only if a source that was mentioned reported it. For example, an insurance company identified by the respondent might report a claim for a hospitalization not reported by the respondent or a hospital confirming a reported hospitalization may indicate that surgery was performed by a physician not reported as having provided care by the respondent. The impact of the verification on the overall study estimates can be seen in the generally lower values of the best estimates compared to estimates from the social survey in Tables 13–2 through 13–5.

The problem of underreporting increases with length of recall period (NCHS 1969: series 2, no. 6; Cannell and Fowler 1963). Since the respondent was asked to report on medical care received over a calendar year, recall might be a particular problem in this study. However, certain procedures used in the study were expected to reduce the bias. These included asking utilization questions for each episode of illness and each provider within an episode separately. The importance of checking records before reporting medical experience was emphasized and crucial questions concerning hospitalizations and insurance coverage were followed up with the patient himself if the family respondent was unable to provide detailed information [3].

Some indication of the success of these procedures in reducing the overall recall bias can be noted by comparing the estimates from this study with those from other studies which used shorter recall periods or record rather than respondent sources. For calendar year 1970 the mean number of physician visits per person (excluding telephone calls) as estimated by the National Center for Health Statistics (NCHS) using a two week recall period was 4.1 visits compared to the CHAS social survey estimate of 4.0 visits [4]. NCHS estimates of a sample of short stay hospitals in the U.S. show a discharge rate for the U.S. of 14.6 and 117 days of care per 100 people per year for 1970 (NCHS 1973: series 13, no. 14, p. 20). The comparable estimates for the CHAS social survey are 13.7 and 128—slightly lower on the admission rate but actually higher on the days. These comparisons suggest that recall bias has been considerably reduced in the CHAS study.

The general formula used to calculate the field or reporting bias for the social survey estimates is:

$$F_{SS} = d - r \qquad (13.3)$$

where

$$F_{SS} = \text{field bias}$$

d = rate of use of services not reported in the social survey but discovered in the verification

r = rate of use of services reported in the social survey but rejected through the verification

The assumption made in the above formula is that the field bias for persons for whom verifying information is not obtained is the same as that discovered for the verified group.

The field bias for the best estimates is calculated according to the formula:

$$F_{BE} = (d - r)p \qquad (13.4)$$

where

p = proportion of the sample for which no verifying information was obtained *p* includes utilization of people who refused to sign permission forms allowing hospitals and physicians to release medical information, services for which insufficient information was available to a contact provider and services for which verification was attempted, but the provider refused or failed to cooperate. Thus, field bias is restricted to that proportion of the sample for which no verifying information was obtained.

Processing Bias

When the length of a hospital stay or the number of times a physician was seen were not known by the respondent, they were estimated by the office staff using rules based on diagnoses, type of facility, cost, age of patient, etc. An evaluation of this processing bias indicates whether the estimating rules used would over- or underestimate actual utilization and whether any discovered bias would affect some subgroups more than others.

In order to calculate the processing bias *(P)* two items of information are necessary. One is the proportion of all hospital days and physician visits that were estimated by the office staff *(e)*. The other is the percentage difference between the results using estimating techniques and those that would have been obtained from information from hospitals and physicians *(d)*. *d* can be calculated using all admissions and doctors seen for which hospital days or visits were estimated by the staff *(U_e)* and for which days and visits were *also* reported by the provider *(U_r)*. According to the formula

$$d = \frac{\Sigma U_r}{\Sigma U_e} - 1 \tag{13.5}$$

The processing bias is then calculated as follows where U_T = the overall use rate including the office estimates:

$$P = U_T(e)(d) \tag{13.6}$$

A basic assumption in this calculation is that the relationship between office estimated values and those obtained in verification would also hold for the office estimated values where no verification was obtained.

FINDINGS

Hospital Admissions

Table 13-2 shows estimates for hospital admission rates among various subgroups in the population and the effect of variable error and bias on these apparent differences. The variable errors (standard error) are generally larger than the sum of the biases measured (nonresponse, field and processing). The nonresponse bias appears consistent, negative and relatively negligible for all population groups. It suggests that nonresponders have fewer admissions than those who respond and thus would reduce the total population rates if taken into account.

The field bias is also negative, but is not consistent among subgroups in the population. People in older families, the poor, nonwhites and the rural farm population were more likely to report admissions later rejected in the verification. These field biases are virtually eliminated in the "best estimates" where the verification is taken into account.

Hospital Days

Biases are of greater magnitude relative to standard errors for hospital days than for admissions, particularly for the social survey estimate. The nonresponse bias in Table 13-3 suggests that nonresponders spend more days in the hospital, even though they experience fewer admissions than respondents. The bias is greatest for the groups with the highest use of hospitals.

The field biases are of greater magnitude than the nonresponse biases and go in the opposite direction. They suggest that people report longer lengths of stay than are shown on hospital records. The field bias does not appear to be associated with particular subgroups, except for a somewhat higher level for persons in older families. This type of bias is substantially reduced in the best estimates.

The processing bias has little impact on the estimates. This reflects the small amount of estimating in the office and the relatively high correspondence between the estimates made and subsequent verifying information.

Percent Seeing an MD

The sums of the biases are generally greater than the standard errors for percent of population seeing an MD (Table 13-4). The nonresponse bias indicates that, overall, the nonrespondents are less likely to see a doctor than respondents. However, there may be certain exceptions, in particular the nonwhite population.

The field bias implies that more people report seeing an MD than can be verified through third party sources. It should be remembered that we were unable to check on many people who did not report seeing a physician, but may actually have done so. The field bias appears to be highest for the nonwhite population. As with field biases for other utilization measures, the best estimate has a considerably lower field bias than the social survey estimate.

Mean Number of Physician Visits

Again, the biases tend to be larger than the standard errors for estimates of number of physician visits. The nonresponse bias tends to be negligible, but there is considerable field bias. The number of visits reported is generally higher than the number verified and the bias is particularly large for nonwhites. The processing bias appears negligible except for the urban non–SMSA group [5].

Differences Among Subgroups

The main purpose of this exercise is to examine the effect of biases and variable errors on the apparent differences among major subgroups in their utilization of health services. Tables 13–6 and 13–7 show this effect. The differences shown (unadjusted and adjusted error) result from subtracting subsequent categories of each variable from the first category. For example, the first unadjusted difference reported in Table 13–6 is admissions for persons in families with no member over 65 (12.9 per 100 persons per year) minus the rate for persons in families including members 65 and over (18.7) which equals −5.8. The adjusted difference follows the same procedure but uses scores corrected for nonresponse, field and processing biases. This calculation for the above example is

$$(12.9-0.1-0.3)-(18.7-0.1-1.0) = -5.1. \tag{13.7}$$

Thus, the adjusted difference between age groups is less than the difference not considering biases. The standard error *(SE)* of the difference tests the statistical significance of the unadjusted and adjusted differences. It is calculated by the formula [6]

$$SE_{\text{diff}} = \sqrt{\left(\frac{SE \text{ of}}{\text{mean}_x}\right)^2 + \left(\frac{SE \text{ of}}{\text{mean}_y}\right)^2} \tag{13.8}$$

For the example above:

$$SE_{\text{diff}} = \sqrt{(.7)^2 + (1.5)^2} = 1.7 \tag{13.9}$$

Note that for residence, "SMSA other urban" is the comparison group for each of the other types of residences.

Age Differences

The unadjusted differences in utilization from the social survey showed that families with older members have considerably more hospital admissions, days spent in the hospital and physician visits. Adjustment for biases tended to reduce the differences slightly, but the differences remained significant. The unadjusted difference in percent seeing a physician was less pronounced than for the other utilization measures. It was, in fact, less than twice the standard error of the difference although the adjusted difference exceeded twice the standard error. In sum, the error analysis had little impact on conclusions about utilization differences between older and younger families with the exception of percent seeing a doctor. In the latter case, the error analysis suggests that the difference in seeing a physician may be of greater magnitude than the original estimates would indicate.

Income Differences

The unadjusted differences in utilization from the social survey indicated the poor use more hospital services, those above poverty are more likely to see a physician and there is no difference in mean number of physician visits by income level. The differences in hospital utilization were reduced slightly by adjusting for biases in the social survey but remained unaffected in the best estimate. Adjusting for biases also slightly reduced the differences by income level in percent seeing a physician. The only service for which the adjustment resulted in a significant change in the difference, however, was for mean number of visits. While no difference was originally shown, the adjustments suggest a higher mean number of visits for the above poverty group (in fact, the adjusted difference in the best estimate—0.4 visits—is greater than twice the standard error of the difference).

Race Differences

Whites showed higher rates of health service utilization than nonwhites by all of the measures used according to the unadjusted social survey differences. The bias adjustment had little impact on the magnitude of these differences for hospital utilization or percent seeing a physician. However, the adjustment increased considerably the difference in mean number of physician visits. This result suggests that the effect of measurement bias may be to underestimate the higher utilization of the white population compared to that of nonwhites.

Residence Differences

All of the residence differences compare the utilization rates of people living in Standard Metropolitan Statistical Areas but not in the central city with other residence groups. The unadjusted differences computed from social survey data suggest few significant differences with respect to hospital utilization, although the suburban residents tend to spend more days in the hospital than other residents. However, significant differences are noted for percent seeing an MD as central city and rural farm residents are less likely to see the doctor than suburban residents. The unadjusted differences from the social survey data also show rural residents have fewer physician visits. The best estimates suggest greater differences in number of hospital days and number of physician visits between suburban residents and the other residential groups than was shown by the social survey alone. The adjustment for biases further increases the differences shown for number of physician visits using best estimate data. In sum, the error analysis suggests that suburban residents spend relatively more days in the hospital and see physicians more often than do people living in other urban or rural areas.

CONCLUSION

The purpose of this exercise has been to examine the impact of survey error on conclusions which might be drawn about differences in the utilization of health

Table 13–6.   Differences Between Subgroups for Hospital Admissions and Hospital Days Per 100 Person-Years

| | Social survey | | | | | |
| | Admissions per 100 person-years | | | Hospital days per 100 person-years | | |
Family group characteristics	Unadjusted difference	Adjusted difference	Standard error of difference	Unadjusted difference	Adjusted difference	Standard error of difference
Age						
Young versus old	-5.8**	-5.1**	1.7	-157.0**	-148.6**	27.7
Family income						
Above poverty versus below poverty	-2.2*	-1.7*	1.2	-41.0**	-37.4*	19.0
Race						
White versus nonwhite	2.9**	3.3**	1.1	20.0*	20.5*	14.8
Residence						
SMSA other urban versus:						
SMSA central city	1.7*	2.0*	1.7	20.0	20.0	25.6
Urban non-SMSA	-1.6	-1.0	2.8	25.0	24.2	26.5
Rural nonfarm	-0.7	-0.9	2.0	2.0	8.1	25.6
Rural farm	-0.2	0.6	2.0	0.0	2.1	30.4

				Best estimate		
Age						
Young versus old	−5.3**	−5.2**	1.6	−147.0**	−147.6**	24.5
Family income						
Above poverty versus below poverty	−1.9*	−1.9*	1.2	− 37.0**	− 37.0**	16.2
Race						
White versus nonwhite	3.2**	3.3**	1.1	19.0*	20.3*	12.2
Residence						
SMSA other urban versus:						
SMSA central city	1.9*	2.0*	1.7	26.0*	25.5*	20.9
Urban non-SMSA	−1.3	−1.3	2.6	32.0*	31.7*	21.8
Rural nonfarm	−0.8	−0.8	1.9	18.0	18.9	20.6
Rural farm	0.6	0.7	2.0	12.0	12.2	25.0

*Greater than one standard error.
**Greater than two standard errors.

Table 13–7. Differences Between Subgroups for Percent of Population Seeing a Physician and Mean Number of Physician Visits

	Social survey					
	Percent of population seeing a physician			Mean number of physician visits		
Family group characteristics	*Unadjusted difference*	*Adjusted difference*	*Standard error of difference*	*Unadjusted difference*	*Adjusted difference*	*Standard error of difference*
Age						
Young versus old	−3.0*	−4.7**	1.7	−1.8**	−1.5**	0.3
Family income						
Above poverty versus below poverty	13.0**	12.8**	1.8	0.0	0.3	0.4
Race						
White versus nonwhite	11.0**	11.8**	2.4	0.5*	1.6**	0.4
Residence						
SMSA other urban versus:						
SMSA central city	7.0**	7.1**	3.0	−0.1	0.2	0.4
Urban non-SMSA	2.0	1.8	5.1	−0.3	−0.7*	0.4
Rural nonfarm	4.0*	5.0**	2.9	0.4*	0.3*	0.3
Rural farm	11.0**	12.5**	3.0	0.8**	0.4*	0.4

			Best estimate			
Age						
Young versus old	−3.0*	−3.5**	1.7	−1.3**	−1.2**	0.2
Family income						
Above poverty versus below poverty	13.0**	12.7**	1.8	0.3**	0.4**	0.2
Race						
White versus nonwhite	13.0**	11.9**	2.5	0.7**	1.2**	0.3
Residence						
SMSA other urban versus:						
SMSA central city	7.0**	7.1**	3.1	0.5*	0.6*	0.4
Urban non-SMSA	3.0	0.7	5.3	0.5*	0.9**	0.3
Rural nonfarm	5.0*	5.1*	3.1	0.6**	0.6**	0.3
Rural farm	13.0**	12.6**	3.1	0.8*	0.7*	0.4

*Greater than one standard error.
**Greater than two standard errors.

services among various subgroups in the U.S. population. A number of different sources of survey error were identified and attempts were made to measure some of those in the national social survey of health services utilization which has been the basic data source for this volume.

The error analysis suggested few changes in the utilization differences between subgroups which would have important policy implications. Comparing the unadjusted social survey estimates with the adjusted best estimates using verification sources, the following changes appear most salient: (1) a significantly higher mean number of physician visits for persons in families above the near poverty level compared to those in families with lower incomes, rather than no difference between them, and (2) an increase in the difference in mean number of visits by race, with whites being the highest utilizers.

While this analysis suggested relatively few major difficulties in estimating differences in utilization according to age, race, income and residence, it must be considered preliminary and exploratory. That is, there are problems not explored here which might cause important changes in some estimates. These problems are of two types: those concerning the validity of assumptions made for this analysis; and potential sources of error which were not measured at all in this study.

Among the most crucial assumptions were: (1) that the utilization of nonrespondents was accurately estimated by secondary data sources and by procedures discussed in the text for calculating the nonresponse bias, and (2) that the field bias for persons for whom we were unable to collect verifying information would be the same as that for persons with both social survey and verification data available. Among potential sources of error not measured in this study were sampling biases and nonsampling noncoverage biases. The latter might be a special problem for certain subgroups such as young male blacks and migrant workers. Further, sources of field and processing biases which would be common to both social survey and verification studies, including various interviewing, coding and data processing techniques, have not been examined. Additional work on these issues would prove useful not only in improving our understanding of the importance of measurement error in health survey analyses, but also for assessing the validity of policy implications based on such analyses.

NOTES TO CHAPTER THIRTEEN

1. This results because it is necessary to use the "collapsed strata" technique of variance computation (see Kish 1965:282–293).

2. This is a Bayesian credible interval interpretation. Due to the costs of the computations, not all of the errors were computed directly. The following procedures were used: (1) For hospital services, only best estimate errors were computed directly. Social survey errors were based on the error for the best estimate for the same service and population group adjusted for differences in the unweighted Ns and magnitudes of the estimate. (2) For physician services,

only social survey errors were computed directly. Best estimate errors on physician services were calculated in the same way as social survey errors for hospital services. (3) Errors for hospital days were calculated using the coefficient of variation for hospital expenditure estimates for the same population group. (4) In certain instances when the subgroups for which the errors were computed did not correspond exactly to the subgroups used in this chapter the computed errors were adjusted for differences in the unweighted *N*s.

3. Effects of these procedures are examined in the following publications of the National Center for Health Statistics—series 2, no. 7 (1965), no. 8 (1965), no. 48 (1972).

4. The NCHS estimate was reduced by 10 percent to adjust for telephone calls which are not included in the CHAS estimate (NCHS 1972: series 10, no. 72, p. 3).

5. Two cases are responsible for the high estimating error in the social survey in Table 13–5. In both, respondents indicated a high number of physician visits in answer to the question "How many visits were there during the past year at doctor's office or private clinic, home, hospital outpatient department" and other locations. Their responses were vague ("no idea how many times") and estimates were made on the basis of information from the respondent about cost of visits. In one case 77 visits were estimated and only five verified (one of the physicians mentioned claimed not to have seen the patient during the survey year) while 40 were estimated in the other case and only one visit was verified. Excluding these two cases not only reduces the estimating bias but results in a sign change for the social survey, from −1.7 to +0.1. The −0.2 in the best estimate is reduced to less than one-tenth.

6. This calculation assumes the means are calculated from independent samples. In fact, these estimates are not independent because of clustering the sample design. However, violation leads to a conservative bias and the results should be considered upper limits of the SE of the differences.

Part VI

Conclusions

Chapter Fourteen

A Summary of Findings

Joanna Kravits

This book has addressed the issue of health care use from a range of perspectives, using a wide variety of professional and technical skills and producing varied findings. Although all chapters were based on the same set of data, each author selected and combined data in ways which were most compatible with his own analysis so that some of the variables are unique to a chapter and not comparable. What are comparable, however, are the basic variables of the model, representing the predisposing, enabling and need components of health care utilization which are set forth in Chapter One. Chapter Two, which presents this model, will be used in this chapter as a comparative base from which findings of later chapters will be discussed.

PREDISPOSING VARIABLES

In general, none of the predisposing variables, including a history of past hospitalizations, had any predictive value as far as who would be admitted to the hospital. Age, however, was the second best predictor of length of stay in the hospital because of the tendency of the elderly to have longer lengths of stay even controlling for the severity of the diagnosis (Chapter Two). Andersen found in the same chapter that older people are also more likely to see a physician and have more visits than other age groups; most of this difference, however, was attributable to higher illness levels among the old. So, although older people go to the physician much more frequently in the course of a year, these differences, unlike those for length of stay, can be explained almost entirely by other variables—severity of diagnosis, disability days and symptoms being the most important. Newman (Chapter Three) produced essentially similar findings while addressing the issue of how the effect of age on physician use was modified by other variables, as did Phelps (Chapter Seven) in his investigation of the effects of insurance on demand for care.

After dental symptoms and education of the head, age makes a modest contribution to explaining the variance in dental care use. Age explains only about 2 percent of the variance for both contact and use, but less variance is explained for dental care volume by the key variables (10 percent) than for any other type of utilization. Age is, of course, related to dental care use in a U shaped curve, with teenagers and adults receiving the most care. Andersen's analysis indicates, and Newman's analysis confirms, the finding that younger people receive more dental care, independent of variables such as presence of a toothache which might be expected to be age related.

To summarize the findings on age: it is related to length of hospital stay and to fact of seeing a dentist and number of dental visits *independent of factors which are age related.* Age is not related to use of physician care or to fact of hospitalization when factors which are age related are controlled for. It can, of course, be argued in the discussion of this variable and of all other variables in this chapter, that physician care was emphasized more than hospital and dental services in developing variables related to severity of care.

If similarly refined measures had been developed for hospital care and dental care, age might no longer be directly related to utilization of these two services. Our best guess, however, would suggest that this argument is only partially supported (scaling hospitalized illnesses on the severity scale indicates that almost all hospital care is mandatory) and that age is still related to these variables. It is, however, not as powerful a determinant of *any* type of health care use when considered independently from its connecting links with illness level. Sex has virtually no impact on any of the three services under consideration.

In contrast to sex, race appears to have a marked impact on health care utilization, even considered separately from the variables most closely associated with it—income, education of head and residence. Race does not explain much of the overall variance in health care use, since 90 percent of the United States population is white. Andersen's findings (Chapter Two) show that race does, however, have a profound effect on the levels of physician care and dental care of the 10 percent of the population which is nonwhite. Utilization of both physician and dental care is lower for nonwhites than what would be expected *even when adjusting for income and residence.*

Other authors also addressed themselves to the effects of race. Newman (Chapter Three) considered education as a variable and found strong differences in the percent of the population seeing a dentist by race and education. For families with heads who had not completed high school, in the age range most likely to have seen a dentist (6—54), 44 percent of whites, but only 24 percent of blacks had been to the dentist during the year. For families whose heads had had some college education, 57 percent of whites, but only 27 percent of blacks had been to the dentist during the year.

Kravits and Schneider (Chapter Ten) considered the interaction of race and income related to the use of discretionary physician and dental services. Race was shown to have an effect on discretionary physician use independent of income, with high income blacks less likely to go to the physician for this type of care than high income whites. As Newman indicated in Chapter Three, however, the most striking differences were found for dental care. Chapter Ten showed low income whites were actually *more* likely to have seen a dentist during the year than were high income blacks. Further, among individuals who went to the dentist at all, 47 percent of *higher* income blacks had teeth extracted (an indication that preventive dental care has been put off) compared with 30 percent of *lower* income whites. One unexpected interaction between race and income appeared in response to presence of a toothache—high income whites were apt to go to a dentist for this symptom but low income whites, and blacks regardless of income, were much less apt to go. These findings taken together clearly indicate that race operates independently of income and education in influencing health care use, especially dental care use which is the most discretionary of the types of health care considered here.

Attitudes and beliefs have consistently been shown to bear very little relationship to health care use—that is, individuals with negative feelings toward the value of health care tend to use about as much of it as those with positive feelings. Andersen (Chapter Two) found that beliefs influenced only two types of utilization—how long individuals stayed in the hospital and how many dental visits they had. For dental visits, beliefs explained more variance than any other predictor, partly because of the extremely discretionary nature of dental care use referred to earlier. Newman, however, did not find a relationship between attitudes and beliefs and dental care (Chapter Three); perhaps because he defined volume of visits to include persons with no visits to a dentist, while Andersen examined only persons with at least one contact.

Kravits (Chapter Five) looked at attitudes and beliefs from the standpoint of whether they could be used to distinguish patterns of discretionary physician and dental care use when race and income were controlled for. She found that attitudes and beliefs had virtually no predictive power except for dental care, bearing out Andersen's findings, and that, for dental care rated by a dentist as discretionary, high income blacks were the one group where favorable attitudes led to increased dental care use. All authors agreed that for the population as a whole, attitudes and beliefs appeared to have little or no effect upon health care utilization. This is unfortunate for health educators, providers of care and public policy makers since attitudes are the one predisposing variable that is somewhat amenable to change.

In Chapter Two, Andersen suggests persons in large families have fewer physician visits than persons in small families. Investigating the effects of family size further, Kasper (Chapter Four) found the effects of family size on both physician contacts and visits were negligible for adults. For children, however, family size influenced whether a physician was seen and to a lesser degree mean number of visits even when need variables and regular source of care were controlled. The interactions of family size with income, residence, age and race showed that physician use by children in large families became even less likely in the presence of low income, rural or inner city residence and increasing age. Children in small families on the other hand, became even higher utilizers of physician care if they were young, high income or other urban (interactions with race were less impressive).

ENABLING VARIABLES

Andersen (Chapter Two) found in his analysis of all variables explaining differences in health care use that presence of a regular source of care influenced the fact of seeing a physician (although it may be argued that the act of seeing a physician then enables an individual to designate him as a source of regular care so that cause and effect cannot be separated). Income, independent of education, explained some of the variance in the amount of dental care received, but was not otherwise an important variable. Benham and Benham (Chapter Six) addressed themselves entirely to the subject of the effect of income and third party coverage such as Medicare and Medicaid upon physician use. They found that income was an important determinant of physician use in 1963, before the introduction of Medicare and Medicaid and the expansion of major medical insurance coverage to a majority of the population, but that by 1970 income explained very little physician utilization.

In his overall analysis, Andersen found that the presence of insurance coverage explained little of the variance in any type of health care use. However, he considered only private insurance coverage and Medicare, both of which have deductibles and coinsurance for outpatient physician visits and which do not normally cover dental care at all. Phelps (Chapter Seven) used demand equations to estimate the effect of various deductibles and coinsurance. His conclusion was that as extent of comprehensiveness of third party coverage increases, physician utilization will increase much more rapidly than will hospital utilization which is already heavily covered by first dollar reimbursement. Shortell's analysis (Chapter Eleven) of individuals with major illness episodes also suggests that the more comprehensive the coverage the greater the volume of physician visits.

Andersen found that the hospital bed ratio in a community explained some of the variance in length of stay and that MD ratio in a community explained some of the variance in volume of dental (but not physician) visits. MD ratios and dentist ratios, which were not used, are highly correlated, so the inference is that the former acts as proxy for the latter. (Once again, controlling for more sensitive dental illness measures might have nullified this finding.) May (Chapter

Eight) considered these findings in much more detail for hospital and physician use and found that number of physician visits are directly related to MD-population ratios in the area and inversely related to hospital bed–population ratios in an area, suggesting that a substitution takes place between inpatient and outpatient care, depending upon which is more readily available. Phelps (Chapter Seven) reported a reduction in demand for physician visits with longer delays in waiting time for appointments.

Using physician visits for care defined as a major illness only, Shortell (Chapter Eleven) examined the effect of having a regular source of care in combination with a number of variables not looked at by other authors. He agreed with Andersen that having a regular source of care made more visits to a physician likely, but the nature of the third party payment source was actually the most important determinant of the number of physician visits. Differences were also found by type of most amount source seen. The enabling variables along with the need variables were more important determinants of physician utilization for this subsample than any of the predisposing variables, a finding consistent with the results reported throughout this book.

Shortell also explored some proxy measures of continuity of care finding that the elderly, the poor, and those on Medicaid, welfare or who self-pay were more likely to receive most of their care from a provider who is their usual source. The elderly and primarily self-pay were also more likely to receive all of their care from a single source. But, as noted, in the absence of data on quality of care, these findings are only suggestive and additional research on the relationship between use, continuity and quality is needed.

NEED VARIABLES

Andersen found in his analysis of all variables purporting to explain health care use that need was by far the most important. Disability days and worry about health were the best predictors of hospital care, the severity of the diagnosis the best predictor of the volume of physician visits and dental symptoms the best predictor of dentist contact. Two other authors did further work on the interrelationships of the need variables.

Newman (Chapter Nine) found that for fact of seeing a physician, number of disability days was the most important predictor followed by amount of worry and evaluation of symptoms. Kravits and Schneider (Chapter Ten) found that when blacks go to the physician, they are seen for more serious diagnoses than are whites. When asked to self-report their symptoms, however, blacks consistently report fewer symptoms than do whites and also report less serious symptoms on the average. Higher income blacks exhibit the greatest discrepancy in this regard. The implications of these findings are that need as measured by the conventional self-assessment techniques may understate blacks' needs for medical care and that more variance in use of physician services could be explained with more sensitive measures. Andersen's and Newman's finding that actual severity of the diagnosis for which individuals were seen as evaluated by the physician is the best predictor of number of physician visits is another indication of this.

Recognizing the central importance of health status (need) in any examination of reasons for health care utilization, Benham and Benham (Chapter Twelve) used three measures of health status—disability days, symptoms and perceived health—to investigate whether health status improved with increments in utilization of health care. Their analysis found that from 1963 to 1970, when utilization increased greatly for some groups because of changes in enabling factors such as availability of third party coverage, health status for these groups did not improve according to these measures. This is a sobering finding, since the implicit assumption in equalizing access to health care is that, in fact, increments in health care for groups will improve the groups' health status. There are two alternative explanations to that which suggests increments in care are ineffectual. One is that health levels actually have improved per se but that the public's expectations have also risen over this seven year period so that subjective reporting measures pick up discomforts that would not have been classified as illnesses earlier. The other is that health indexes are still very crude measuring devices and given the current state of the art, these indexes are relatively insensitive to the impact of medical care on the health status of the population.

CONCLUSIONS

In general, although the authors of this book discussed the above issues from a variety of perspectives and disciplines, their conclusions were consistent with the findings using the basic model of determinants of health care use presented in Chapter Two. Many of the interrelationships of key variables in the model were explored for the first time. In addition, some of the less important variables in explaining variance in health care use were examined in detail for possible relationships to portions of the population where they might have more explanatory power.

One area this chapter has not touched upon is the public policy implications of the findings from this analysis. The concluding chapter of this book addresses these public policy implications by building upon the factual findings which are summarized here.

Chapter Fifteen

Public Policy Implications

Odin W. Anderson

There are several implicit and explicit objectives in the range of legislative proposals for national health insurance which should be differentiated. Each objective has implications for the methods of financing and organizing personal health services, even independent of national health insurance, which is usually a financing mechanism. Depending on the basic objectives sought, national health insurance can range from a comprehensive, highly structured and centrally directed and financed health service to one mainly designed to protect families from high cost or "catastrophic" medical episodes. One approach can be called the "provision of services;" the other can be called "indemnification" for medical care contingencies above certain cost magnitudes. Both approaches, however, are basically concerned with equity related to access and cost sharing, the former with the deployment of services, regardless of income level and residence; the latter with a graduated method of indemnifying for medical care episodes relative to income on the assumption that services will appear where there is effective demand.

The overriding current objective of national health insurance is to assure access to services regardless of family income and residence. The dominant concept is to reduce, if not eliminate, direct costs to the family for medical care episodes. It is demonstrable that amount of payment at time of service results in lessened demand for services and, presumably, greater unmet need.

A longer range assumption implicit in a comprehensive and highly structured type of national health insurance proposal is that the level of health of a population, and subgroups within it, is dependent in large part on access to health services.

An index of access can be developed by determining the volume and nature of access to types of services by family income and place of residence and assuming that equal use of physician services across income groups means equitable access. The extent to which indicators of health levels can be related to

265

access is at the present time very limited, except for more or less easily targeted indicators such as infant mortality rates, say, above 25 per 1000 live births, and hypertension.

A perverse index of equity would be one in which all income groups experience the same rates and variety of morbidity (corrected, of course, for age and sex composition of the population segments) and die of the same causes in equal rates and variety. For the time being, however, our concern is mainly with equity of access with the hope that such access will narrow morbidity and mortality rates between income groups. The foregoing chapters have devoted themselves to these problems. My aim is to synthesize them.

Contrary to what might be expected, given the individual incidents of difficult or no access to health services reported in the media and in "everybody knows" informal conversations, it is worth noting that in general there has been a persistent trend toward the equalization of access regardless of income. Voluntary health insurance, Medicare and Medicaid have all been factors behind this trend. During the period between 1963 and 1970 Chapter Five suggests that Medicare and Medicaid had an appreciable impact. The use of hospital services clearly indicates that use related to family income now favors the low income groups. The trend in physician services shows a convergence by income groups although a gap remains. When morbidity levels as measured by disability days are related to use, then indications are that the low income group may indeed still not be getting the services they should if such a measure of need and its fulfillment is accepted as a valid one.

I point out these basic trends to reveal that there are profound influences in the social and health service systems which are seemingly independent of a well formulated and implemented national health policy. It is commonly assumed that only by a deliberate national policy as expressed in targeted objectives can we influence mortality and morbidity rates and assure increasingly equitable access to health services. I am inclined to believe that a deliberate national health policy will legitimize trends already in motion. I would also suggest that it seems to be much easier to accelerate trends already present by deliberate public policy implementation than to reverse trends in the opposite direction of policy. This observation is based on my view—with a fair amount of evidence outside of the foregoing chapters—that social policy must build on trends already present. The best that can be done with an undesirable trend is to slow it.

As illustrated in this book, some aspects of human behavior and social systems are more amenable to modification than others. Making health services free or almost free at time of demand is in essence a problem of policy and mechanics. It is also essential for assuring access to services, as has been demonstrated abundantly. Still, inequities remain because of peoples' perceptions of their symptoms and disabilities leading to seeking services and to systems' difficulties in distributing services so that access is relatively convenient even when there is no direct cost to the individual.

It should be almost a truism that illness as perceived by the public should be the prime determinant in seeking services once the financial barriers are lowered. Then we find that perception of illness varies among income groups and other defined segments of the population. To achieve pure equity it follows that the level of perception of illness and its triggering to seek services should also be randomly distributed throughout the population. This concept is, of course, utopian, but it at least provides a point of reference.

In addition to the reduction of the financial barrier it is evident that there are some structural features which, if present, will facilitate access. It was found, in Chapter Ten for example, that the manner in which an individual member of the population is connected with the delivery system is nearly as important as insurance coverage in determining the number of visits to physicians. Those who said they had a "regular" source of care had more services.

Another consideration that seems a truism, but is not regarded as such until after it is discovered, is that resources make a difference in demand (Chapter Seven). The ratio of physicians to population has a much larger effect on the volume of physician services than on the likelihood of hospitalization. There were indicators, e.g., that an increase in the supply of physicians will result in a decrease in the likelihood of an individual being hospitalized holding constant sociodemographic attributes, attitudes and illness levels. On the other hand, an increase in hospital beds will result in an increase in admissions and an increase in the occupancy levels will result in a decrease in admissions. Differential provider resources of physicians and hospital beds will affect the mix of use of provider components. Availability of resources, then, does appear to have an impact on use of physician services and referrals from them. This observation has important implications for the ratio between physicians and hospital beds in health services delivery systems.

It is perverse that the most expensive health service component is also the one component where use has achieved a high degree of equity. Attempts to reduce the availability and use of hospital services must result in more access to physicians. There need to be methods to assure that physicians are located in areas of great need.

So far, I have considered only the problem of equity of access as an end in itself, regardless of the presumed impact of that access on health levels of the population. In Chapter Twelve it is demonstrated that the increase in the use of physician and hospital services between 1963 and 1970—with a proportionately greater increase for the low income and the aged—had no impact on health indicators as measured by disability days. It is often argued from results like these that a comprehensive national health insurance scheme would be a misallocation of resources in the public sector if the objective is to improve health levels. Rather, it is argued, it would be a wiser policy to allocate fewer resources to a comprehensive curing system and more to programs designed to inculcate healthful life styles.

Life styles do not lend themselves easily to manipulated change, at least in the short haul. Public opinion will dictate that the health services delivery system will have to cope with the deleterious effects of prevailing life styles somehow. I do not believe there will ever be a puritanic majority who are so healthy and ascetic that they can legislate against a minority who are hedonistic and unhealthy. Further, it is not possible to differentiate neatly between lung cancer caused by excessive smoking (bad life style) and lung cancer caused by polluted air. Differentiating between life style saints and sinners is then not a tenable public policy. National health insurance will be designed, therefore, to serve both the prudent and the profligate, a policy I would regard as equitable.

Another observation is that given certain policies and their implementation it is possible to alleviate some major health problems by target programs. These problems are specific enough to show measurable changes judging by programs in this country and elsewhere. Certainly, the reduction in infant mortality rates in high mortality areas can be accelerated by appropriate standard public health measures. Certainly, hypertension can be targeted, and there are others. A general national health insurance scheme, however, will affect the general health level very little. In this regard, another perversity is that in order to apply the occasional heroic measures such as open heart surgery, organ transplant, dialysis and other high medical technology procedures, it is necessary to maintain an enormously expensive critical mass of high modern technology and personnel so that marginal costs of serving less serious patients are relatively small. In individual cases, certainly, life has been lengthened and even improved, but there are not enough such incidents to be reflected in overall health indicators.

A final observation is that the problem of equity may be more than distributing services according to need, independent of social and economic characteristics. It is also tied to the dignity and relative convenience of access and the amount of money paid directly when services are sought. Enforcement of dignity is difficult to legislate, but convenience and the reduction of out-of-pocket expenses can certainly be legislated.

Appendix

Variable Definitions for Chapter Two

Distribution of Persons Within Classes of Variables

Variable classes	Unweighted N	Weighted percent of sample
1 Hospital contact		
Yes	1342	11
No	10277	89
2 Hospital volume		
Continuous ($\bar{x}$ = 12.1)	1342	11
3 Physician contact		
Yes	6662	65
No	4957	35
4 Physician volume		
Continuous ($\bar{x}$ = 5.4)	6662	65
5 Dentist contact		
Yes	3962	44
No	7358	54
NA (no answer)	199	2
6 Dentist volume		
Continuous ($\bar{x}$ = 3.1)	3962	44
7 Age		
Under 6	1283	10
6–15	2680	22
16–44	4057	38
45–64	2093	20
65–74	939	6
75 or over	567	4

continued

Variable classes	Unweighted N	Weighted percent of sample
8 Sex		
Male	5515	49
Female	6104	51
9 Marital status		
Married	4569	44
Separated/divorced	619	4
Widowed	848	6
Never married	2127	18
Under 14	3438	28
NA	18	*
10 Family size		
1	915	8
2	2116	18
3	1732	15
4	1930	19
5	1680	17
6	1105	10
7 or more	2150	14
11 Birth order		
Not child of family head	6722	59
First	1879	17
Second	1251	11
Third	796	7
Fourth	436	3
Fifth or higher	535	3
12 Past hospitalizations		
0	6710	51
1	2221	22
2	1084	10
3–5	1108	11
6–9	296	3
≥ 10	180	2
NA	20	*
13 Neighborhood tenure		
≥ 6 months	846	7
6–11 months	788	6
12–23 months	1118	9
24–59 months	1972	17
≥ 5 years	6683	60
NA	212	1

continued

Variable classes	Unweighted N	Weighted percent of sample
14 Education head		
0–6	1713	9
7–8	2139	15
9–11	2686	20
12	2896	29
≥ 13	2048	26
NA	137	1
15 Social class head		
1–19 (low)	1721	9
20–29	1414	10
30–39	2825	25
40–49	2417	25
50–79	1602	22
80–98 (high)	25	1
NA	190	*
No occupation	1425	7
16 Occupation head		
Professional, manager**	3279	32
Sales, clerical	1107	12
Craftsmen	1943	21
Operatives	2082	16
Laborers-service	2286	13
Farm	732	4
NA	190	1
17 Ethnicity		
White	7299	85
Black	3696	12
Mexican, Puerto Rican	487	3
American Indian	69	*
Oriental	68	1
18 Religion		
Catholic	1672	20
Jewish	186	3
Protestant	5548	42
Other	367	3
None	350	3
NA	58	*
Under 14	3438	28

continued

Variable classes	Unweighted N	Weighted percent of sample
19 Value of health services		
1,2 (low)	766	5
3	1964	13
4	2904	26
5	2788	28
6–7 (high)	1464	15
NA	1733	13
20 Value of MDs		
1–2 (low)	1628	15
3	3859	34
4	3642	31
5–6 (high)	710	6
NA	1642	13
21 Knowledge of disease		
0–11 (low)	1539	12
12–13	1926	14
14–15	2561	22
16–17	2420	23
18–20 (high)	1452	16
NA	1721	13
22 Response threshold		
1–6 (low)	1190	9
7–9	1444	13
10–11	1872	16
12–13	2296	23
14	1461	14
15–25 (high)	1714	12
NA	1642	13
23 Family income		
Under $2000	1021	5
$2000–3499	1519	8
$3500–4999	1352	7
$5000–7499	2338	15
$7500–9999	1890	17
$10000–14999	2230	26
$15000 or over	1269	22
24 Insurance		
Major medical only	469	6
Basic + major medical	3035	36
No insurance	4999	29
Basic only	3116	30

continued

Variable classes	Unweighted N	Weighted percent of sample
25 Enrollment		
Group	5160	59
Nongroup	1460	13
No insurance	4999	29
26 MD office coverage		
Yes	4419	50
No	7200	50
27 Dental coverage		
Yes	697	44
No	10623	54
NA dental contact	199	2
28 Regular care		
Clinic—no MD named	1787	8
Clinic—MD named	1155	10
General practitioner	4845	48
Specialist	2210	23
None	1547	11
NA	75	1
29 Group practice		
Belongs	2285	24
Does not belong	9334	76
30 Appointment time		
Same day	2142	20
1—2 days	1967	21
3—4	568	6
5—14	1176	13
15 days or more	529	6
NA, not applicable (NAP)	5237	35
31 Travel time		
< 15 minutes	4266	15
15—30	3978	33
31—60	1225	8
> 60	274	2
NAP	1823	13
NA	53	*
32 Waiting time		
1—15 minutes	1771	20
15—30	2684	28
31—60	2461	21
61—120	1567	11
121 or more	1196	6
NAP	1823	13

continued

Variable classes	Unweighted N	Weighted percent of sample
32 (continued)		
NA	117	1
33 Residence		
SMSA, central city	5350	30
SMSA, other	1560	27
Other urban	841	12
Rural nonfarm	2799	24
Rural farm	1069	7
34 Region		
Northeast	2418	27
North Central	2912	29
South	4703	29
West	1586	15
35 MD ratio		
≤ 49	1588	11
50–99	3265	29
100–124	1394	13
125–149	2768	20
150–174	1104	13
≥ 175	1500	14
36 Hospital bed ratio		
≤ 14	747	5
15–29	1316	12
30–44	6478	58
45–59	2412	19
60–74	212	2
≥ 75	454	5
37 Disability days		
0	6454	49
1–2	992	12
3–6	1300	13
7–14	1230	12
≥ 15	1202	11
Infants	250	2
NA	191	1
38 Symptoms		
0	4407	35
1	2180	21
2	1378	14
3–4	1457	13
5–20	1457	12
NA, infants	740	6

continued

Variable classes	Unweighted N	Weighted percent of sample
39 Perceived health		
Excellent	3910	38
Good	5005	43
Fair	1698	12
Poor	590	4
Deceased	77	*
Infant	250	2
NA	89	1
40 Worry about health		
Great deal	1117	8
Some	2057	18
Hardly any	2265	21
None	5824	50
Infant	250	2
NA	106	1
41 Pain frequency		
Very often	868	7
Fairly often	943	8
Occasionally	4492	43
Not at all	4893	40
Infant	280	2
NA	173	1
42 Dental symptoms		
0	9772	85
1	1323	11
2	225	1
NA dental contact	199	2
43 Diagnosis		
Elective only	2327	27
Elective and mandatory	2013	23
Mandatory	2307	22
NA	15	*
No MD visits	4957	28
44 Symptoms		
$\leqslant 1.00$	2980	29
1.01−2.00	1659	16
2.01−4.00	1178	10
$\geqslant 4.01$	545	4
No symptoms, NA, infants	5257	41

*Indicates less than 0.05 percent.
**Also includes persons with no occupation reported.

Variable Notes for Appendix

Variable Number	*Explanation*
1–4	Estimates of use of hospitals and physicians obtained by integrating information collected in the social survey with verifying information obtained from hospitals, physicians and insuring organizations.
1–6, 23–27, 37–38, 40–44	Relevant time period for these variables is calendar year 1970.
1	Overnight stay or surgery performed in hospitals classified as short term by the American Hospital Association.
2	Total number of days spent in short term hospitals.
3	Treatment or examination by a physician.
4	Total number of visits by a physician excluding inpatient visits and telephone calls.
5	Treatment or examination by a dentist.
6	Total number of visits to dentist's office or clinic.
7	As of December 31, 1970.
12	Total number of hospitalizations prior to 1970 excluding all those for pregnancy.
13	Response to question, "How long has (head and/or spouse) lived in this (neighborhood/suburb)?"
14	Number of school years completed.
15	Occupational prestige scores from Siegel (1971).
16	U.S. census occupational categories, 1970.
17	Interviewer designation of main respondent.
19–22	Response of family head, or spouse in cases with no response from head.
19	Replication of scale found in Andersen (1968:38).
20	Replication of scale found in Andersen (1968:95).
21	Replication of index based on knowledge of symptoms associated with cancer, heart disease, diabetes and tuberculosis found in Andersen (1968:97–98).

continued

Variable Number	Explanation
22	Respondent was asked how he would respond to five hypothetical medical conditions ranging from sharp chest pains to sore throat. For each condition the respondent was given the following five alternatives weighted as indicated: (1) Do nothing (treat it myself); (2) See my doctor within one month; (3) See my doctor within three days; (4) Go to hospital emergency room same day; (5) Call an ambulance at once. The total score was the sum of the weights over all five conditions. The exact conditions are listed in Aday and Andersen (1975:86).
23	Total family money income before taxes for the calendar year.
24	Person is insured if covered by any type of health insurance (including Medicare but excluding Medicaid) on the last day of the calendar year. Basic insurance provides first dollar coverage for hospital and/or inpatient surgical MD expenses. Major medical insurance includes a deductible and coinsurance and is designed to cover the large medical expenses resulting from a particular catastrophic or prolonged illness.
25	Group health insurance is carried through place of work or some other organization to which a subscriber belongs. Nongroup insurance is purchased directly by the respondent through an insurance agent. A person with both group and nongroup coverage is coded "group."
26	Pays for all or part of the cost of seeing the physician in his office for nonsurgical procedures. Major medical is considered office visit only if it includes basic benefits as well (see notes for 24).
28	Based on response to question, "Is there a particular medical person or clinic (person) usually goes to when sick or for advice about health?" If a person names a clinic, a further question is asked as to whether a particular doctor is seen at the clinic. Internists and pediatricians are considered "specialists."
29	Based on respondent's judgment as to whether the regular source is "part of a group practice."
30–32	Related to regular source of care.
30	Other than for emergency.

continued

Variable Number	Explanation
31	From home by usual means of transportation.
32	From arrival to seeing MD.
33	Urban, rural and SMSA (Standard Metropolitan Statistical Areas) are as defined by the U.S. census. "Central city" and "farm" are based on interviewer's report.
34	U.S. census regions.
35	Nonfederal active physicians per 100,000 population for SMSA or rural county of family residence (Haug et al. 1971).
36	Short term hospital beds per 10,000 population by SMSA or rural county of family residence (Haug et al. 1971).
37	Bed days (excluding days in the hospital) plus other restricted activity days resulting from illness or injury.
38	Number of symptoms from a checklist of 20 (excluding two experienced by individual). See Aday and Andersen (1975: 84) for a complete list of symptoms.
42	Whether individual experienced either or both of the following dental symptoms: toothache, bleeding gums.
43	Judgment by panel of physicians as to whether physician care for medically attended conditions of respondents was elective or mandatory (see Chapter Ten for detailed discussion of this variable).
44	Number of symptoms reported in variable 38 weighted by judgments of panel of 40 physicians as to the proportion of people in five age groups (1–5, 6–15, 16–44, 45–65 and 65 and over) who should see a doctor. This weighting is discussed in Aday and Andersen (1975:87–91).

Bibliography

Aday, Lu Ann, and Robert Eichhorn.
  1972 *The utilization of health services: indices and correlates.* DHEW pub. no. (HSM) 73–3003, Rockville, Maryland: National Center for Health Services Research and Development.
Aday, Lu Ann, and Ronald Andersen.
  1975 *Development of indices of access to medical care.* Ann Arbor: Health Administration Press.
Airth, D., and D. Newell.
  1962 *The demand for hospital beds.* Newcastle-on-Tyne: University of Durham, Kings College.
American Hospital Association.
  1971 *Hospital statistics.* Chicago: American Hospital Association.
Andersen, Ronald.
  1968 *A behavioral model of families' use of health services.* Research Series No. 25. Chicago: Center for Health Administration Studies, University of Chicago.
Andersen, Ronald, and Lee Benham.
  1970 "Factors affecting the relationship between family income and medical care consumption." In Herbert Klarman ed., *Empirical studies in health economics.* Baltimore: The Johns Hopkins Press.
Andersen, Ronald, and Odin W. Anderson.
  1967 *A decade of health services.* Chicago: University of Chicago Press.
Andersen, Ronald, Rachel McL. Greeley, Joanna Kravits, and Odin W. Anderson.
  1972 *Health service use national trends and variations, 1953–1971.* DHEW pub. no. (HSM) 73–3004 (October).
Andersen, Ronald, and Judith D. Kasper.
  1973 "The structural influence of family size on children's use of physician services." *Journal of Comparative Family Studies* 4, no. 1 (Spring): 116–130.

Andersen, Ronald, Joanna Kravits, and Odin W. Anderson.

1971 "The public's view of the crisis in medical care: an impetus for changing delivery systems?" *Economic and Business Bulletin* 24, no. 1 (Fall): 44–52.

1975 "Two decades of health services: social survey trends in use and expenditure." Ballinger Publishing Co., Cambridge, Mass., 1976.

Andersen, Ronald, Joanna Kravits, Odin W. Anderson, and Joan Daley.

1973 *Expenditures for personal health services: national trends and variation, 1953–1970.* DHEW pub. no. (HRA) 74–3105 (October).

Andersen, Ronald, and John F. Newman.

1973 "Societal and individual determinants of medical care utilization in the United States." *Milbank Memorial Fund Quarterly* 51, no. 1 (Winter): 95–124.

Andersen, Ronald, Björn Smedby, and Odin W. Anderson.

1970 *Medical care use in Sweden and the United States.* Research Series No. 27. Chicago: Center for Health Administration Studies, University of Chicago.

Anderson, Odin W.

1966 "Influence of social and economic research on public policy in the health field." *Milbank Memorial Fund Quarterly* 44, no. 3, pt. 2:11–51.

1972 *Health care: can there be equity? The United States, Sweden and England.* New York: John Wiley and Sons, Inc.

Anderson, Odin W., and Paul Sheatsley.

1967 *Hospital use—a survey of patient and physician decisions.* Research Series No. 24. Chicago: Center for Health Administration Studies, University of Chicago.

Andrews, Frank M., James N. Morgan, John A. Sonquist, and Laura Klem.

1973 *Multiple classification analysis.* 2nd ed. Ann Arbor: Institute for Social Research.

Antonovsky, Aaron.

1972 "A model to explain visits to the doctor: with specific reference to the case of Israel." *Journal of Health and Social Behavior* 13, no. 4 (December): 446–454.

Auster, Richard, Irving Leveson, and Deborah Sarachek.

1969 "The production of health: an exploratory study." *The Journal of Human Resources* 4 (Fall): 411–436.

Balint, Michael.

1966 "The drug, doctor." In W. Richard Scott and Edmund H. Volkart eds., *Medical care: readings in the sociology of medical institutions.* New York: John Wiley and Sons, Inc.

Becker, Marshall, R. H. Drachman, and J. P. Kirscht.

1974 "A new approach to explaining sick role behavior in low-income populations." *American Journal of Public Health* 64 (March): 205–216.

Berkanovic, E., and L. G. Reeder.

1974 "Can money buy the appropriate use of services? some notes on the meaning of utilization." *Journal of Health and Social Behavior* 15, no. 2 (June): 93–99.

Bice, T. W., D. L. Rabin, B. H. Starfield, and K. T. White.
1973 "Economic class and use of physician services." *Medical Care* 11 (July–August): 287–296.
Bossard, James H. S.
1945 "The law of family interaction." *American Journal of Sociology* 50: 292–294.
Bossard, James H. S., and Eleanor S. Boll.
1956 *The large family system.* Philadelphia: University of Pennsylvania Press.
1960 *The sociology of child development.* 3rd ed. Philadelphia: University of Pennsylvania Press.
Brown, J. Whitney, L. S. Robertson, John Kosa, and J. J. Alpert.
1971 "A study of general practice in Massachusetts." *Journal of the American Medical Association* 216 (April 12).
Bunker, J. P.
1970 "Surgical manpower: a comparison of operations and surgeons in the United States and in England and Wales." *New England Journal of Medicine* 282: 135–44.
Burns, J. L.
1951 "Why do some parents object to diptheria immunization?" *Health Education Journal,* 9 (April).
Cannell, Charles, and F. J. Fowler.
1963 *A study of the reporting of visits to doctors in the national health survey.* Ann Arbor: Michigan Survey Research Center, University of Michigan.
Carnegie Commission on Higher Education.
1970 *Higher education and the nation's health: policies for medical and dental education.* San Francisco: McGraw–Hill.
Cartwright, Ann.
1959 "The families and individuals who do not cooperate on a sample survey." *Milbank Memorial Fund Quarterly* 37 (October): 347–368.
Chiswick, B.
1973 "An analysis of hospital utilization: SMSA differences in hospital admission rates, occupancy rates, and bed rates." National Bureau of Economic Research. Mimeo.
Clausen, John, et al.
1954 "Parent attitudes toward participation of their children in polio vaccine trials." *American Journal of Public Health* 44 (December).
Coe, R. M., and A. F. Wessen.
1965 "Social-psychological factors influencing the use of community health resources." *American Journal of Public Health* 55 (July): 1024–1031.
Coleman, James S.
1972 *Policy research in the social sciences.* Morristown, N.J.: General Learning Press.
Davis, Karen, and Louise B. Russell.
1972 "The substitution of hospital outpatient care for inpatient care." *Review of Economics and Statistics* 54.

Donabedian, Avedis
   1972 "Models for organizing the delivery of personal health services and criteria for evaluating them." *Milbank Memorial Fund Quarterly* 50, pt. 2. (October).
Enterline, Phillip K., et al.
   1973 "The distribution of medical services before and after free medical care—the Quebec experience." *New England Journal of Medicine* 289, no. 22 (November 22): 1174–78.
Falk, I. S., et al.
   1967 "The development of standards for the audit and planning of medical care; I. Concepts, research design, and the content of primary physician's care." *American Journal of Public Health* 57 (July): 1118–1136.
Feldstein, Martin S.
   1971a "Hospital cost inflation: a study of nonprofit price dynamics." *American Economic Review* 61, no. 4.
   1971b *The rising cost of hospital care.* Washington: Information Resources Press.
Feldstein, Paul J.
   1966 "Research on the demand for health services." *Milbank Memorial Fund Quarterly* 44 (July): 128–162.
Fink, R. S., et al.
   1968 "The reluctant participant in a breast cancer screening program." *Public Health Reports,* 83 (June).
Flashner, Bruce A., et al.
   1973 "Professional standards review organizations." *JAMA* 223 (March 26).
Flook, Evelyn, and Paul J. Sanazaro eds.
   1973 *Health services research and R&D.* Ann Arbor: Health Administration Press.
Fuchs, Victor.
   1965 "Some economic aspects of mortality in the United States." National Bureau of Economic Research (July). Mimeo.
   1974 *Who shall live? Health economics and social choice.* New York: Basic Books.
Gibson, Geoffrey.
   1971 *Emergency medical services in the Chicago metropolitan area.* Chicago: Center for Health Administration Studies, University of Chicago.
Glazer, Nathan.
   1971 "Paradoxes of health care." *Public Interest* 22 (Winter): 72.
Goldberger, A.
   1964 *Econometric theory.* New York: John Wiley and Sons, Inc.
Goochman, D. S.
   1971 "Some correlates of children's health care beliefs and potential health behavior." *Journal of Health and Social Behavior* 12, no. 2 (June): 148–154.
   1972 "The organizing role of motivation in health beliefs and intentions." *Journal of Health and Social Behavior* 13, no. 3 (September): 285–293.

Gordon, Burgess L., et al.
  1971 *Current medical information and terminology.* 4th ed. Chicago: American Medical Association.
Grossman, Michael.
  1972 *The demand for health: a theoretical and empirical investigation.* New York: National Bureau of Economic Research.
  1975 "The correlation between health and education." National Bureau of Economic Research. Mimeo.
Hare, E. E., and G. K. Shaw.
  1965 "A study in family health: (1) health in relation to family size." *British Journal of Psychiatry* 111 (June): 461–466.
Hassinger, E., and D. Hobbs.
  1973 "Relation of community context to utilization of health services in rural area." *Medical Care* 11 (November–December): 509–522.
Haug, J. N., G. A. Roback, and B. C. Martin.
  1971 *Distribution of physicians in the United States, 1970.* Chicago: American Medical Association.
Hurtado, Arnold V., and Merwyn R. Greenlick.
  1971 "A disease classification system for analysis of medical care utilization, with a note on symptom classification." *Health Services Research* (Fall).
I.C.D.A.
  1957 *International classification of diseases, adapted for use in the United States.* 8th rev. 2 vols. Washington: U.S. Public Health Service.
Janis, I. L., and S. Feshbach.
  1953 "Effects of fear arousing communications." *Journal of Abnormal and Social Psychology,* vol. 48.
Kaitaranta, H., and T. Purola.
  1972 "A systems-oriented approach to the consumption of medical commodities." *Social Science and Medicine* 7: 531–540.
Kasl, S. V., and S. Cobb.
  1966 "Health behavior, illness behavior and sick role behavior." *Archives Environmental Health* 12 (February): 246–267.
Keeler, Emmett B., Joseph P. Newhouse, and Charles E. Phelps.
  1974 *Deductibles and the demand for medical services: the theory of a consumer facing a variable price schedule under uncertainty.* Report R–1514–OEO/NC. Santa Monica, California: The Rand Corporation.
Kegeles, S. S.
  1963 "Some motives for seeking preventive dental care." *Journal of the American Dental Association* 67 (July): 90–98.
  1967 "Attitudes and behavior of the public regarding cervical cytology." *Journal of Chronic Disease,* 20 (December).
Kessner, D. M., et al.
  1973 *A strategy for evaluating health services.* Washington: National Academy of Sciences.
Kish, Leslie.
  1965 *Survey sampling.* New York: John Wiley and Sons, Inc.

Klarman, Herbert.
1965 *The economics of health.* New York: Columbia University Press.
Koos, E. L.
1954 *The health of regionville.* New York: Columbia University Press.
Leventhal, H., et al.
1965 "Fear communications in the acceptance of preventive health practices." *Bulletin of the New York Academy of Medicine,* 41 (November).
May, Joel.
1973 "The impact of health planning." Graduate Program in Hospital Administration, University of Chicago. Mimeo.
Mindlen, R. L., and P. M. Densen.
1969 "Medical care of urban infants: continuity of care." *American Journal of Public Health* 59 (August): 1294–1302.
Monteiro, Lois A.
1973 "Expense is no object . . . : income and physician visits reconsidered." *Journal of Health and Social Behavior* 14, no. 2 (June): 99–115.
Mott, F. D., et al.
1973 "Prepaid group practice in Sault St. Marie, Ontario, II: evidence from the household survey." *Medical Care* 11 (May–June): 173–188.
National Center for Health Statistics (NCHS).
1962 *Hospital discharges.* Series B, no. 32.
1965 *Comparison of hospital reporting in three survey procedures.* Series 2, no. 8 (July).
1965 *Health interview responses compared with medical records.* Series 2, no. 7 (July).
1965 *Reporting of hospitalization in the health interview survey.* Series 2, no. 6 (July).
1969 *Factors related to response in a health examination survey.* Series 2, no. 36.
1969 *Family use of health services: United States—July, 1963–June, 1974.* Series 10, no. 55.
1971 *Children and youth selected health characteristics: United States—1958 and 1968.* Series 10, no. 62.
1971 *Persons hospitalized by number of hospital episodes and days in a year, United States—1968.* Series 10, no. 64 (December).
1972 *Interviewing methods in the health interview survey.* Series 2, no. 48 (April).
1972 *Current estimates from the health interview survey, United States—1970.* Series 10, no. 72 (May).
1973 *Utilization of short-stay hospitals, summary of non-medical statistics, United States—1970.* Series 13, no. 14 (August).
Newman, John F.
1971 "The utilization of dental service." Ph.D. dissertation, Atlanta, Emory University.
Newman, John F., and Odin W. Anderson.
1972 *Patterns of dental service utilization in the United States: a nationwide*

social survey. Research Series No. 30. Chicago: Center for Health Administration Studies, University of Chicago.

Newhouse, Joseph P., and Charles E. Phelps.

1974 "Price and income elasticities for medical care services." In Mark Perlman ed., *The economics of health and medical care.* London: The Macmillan Press Ltd. An updated version available as Rand Corporation Report R–1197–OEO/NC, The Rand Corporation, Santa Monica, California.

Newhouse, Joseph P., Charles E. Phelps, and William B. Schwartz.

1974 "Policy options and the impact of national health insurance." *New England Journal of Medicine* 290, no. 24 (June 13): 1345–1359.

Peterson, Osler

1973 "The importance of obtaining high quality medical care." Proceedings of the Fifteenth Annual Symposium on Hospital Affairs, Graduate Program in Hospital Administration, University of Chicago.

Phelps, Charles E., and Joseph P. Newhouse.

1972 *Coinsurance and the demand for physician services.* Report R–976–OEO. Santa Monica, California: The Rand Corporation.

1974a *Coinsurance and the demand for medical services.* Report R–964–1–OEO/NC. Santa Monica, California: The Rand Corporation.

1974b "Coinsurance, the price of time, and the demand for medical services." *Review of Economics and Statistics* 56, no. 3 (August): 334–342.

Public Law 93–641.

1975 National Health Planning and Resources Development Act of 1974. Washington, D.C.: Government Printing Office.

Rice, Dorothy P., and Douglas Wilson.

1975 "The American medical economy—problems and perspectives." Paper presented for the International Conference on Health Care Costs and Expenditures, sponsored by the Fogarty International Center, Bethesda, Maryland, Department of Health, Education and Welfare.

Richardson, William.

1971 *Ambulatory use of physicians' services in response to illness episodes in a low income neighborhood.* Research Series No. 29. Chicago: Center for Health Administration Studies, University of Chicago.

Robertson, Leon S., John Kosa, Joel J. Alpert, and Margaret Haegarty.

1967 "Family size and the use of medical resources." In William T. Liu ed., *Family and Fertility.* South Bend, Indiana: University of Notre Dame Press.

Rodgers, Elizabeth.

1973 "Financial incentives to encourage outpatient care: the Swedish experience." Duplicated.

Roemer, Milton.

1961 "Bed supply and hospital utilization: a natural experiment." *Hospitals* 35 (November 1).

Roemer, Milton, and Max Shain.

1959 *Hospital utilization under insurance.* Chicago: American Hospital Association.

Rogers, D. B.
  1973 "Shattuck lecture—the American health care scene." *New England Journal of Medicine* 288 (June 28): 1377–1383.
Roghmann, K. J., et al.
  1970 "Anticipated and actual effects of Medicaid on the care pattern of children." Rochester, New York, University of Rochester. Unpublished manuscript.
Rosenstock, Irwin M.
  1966 "Why people use health services." *Milbank Memorial Fund Quarterly* 44 (July): 94–124.
  1968 "Prevention of illness and maintenance of health." In John Kosa et al. eds., *Poverty and health: a sociological analysis.* Cambridge: Harvard University Press.
Rosett, Richard N., and Lien-Fu Huang.
  1973 "The effect of health insurance on the demand for medical care." *Journal of Political Economy,* 81, pt. 1 (March/April).
Schonfeld, H. K., et al.
  1968 "The development of standards for the audit and planning of medical care: pathways among primary physicians and specialists for diagnosis and treatment." *Medical Care* 6 (March–April): 101–114.
Schonfield, J., et al.
  1963 "Medical attitudes and practices of parents toward a mass tuberculin testing program." *American Journal of Public Health,* 53 (May).
Shortell, Stephen M.
  1972 *A model of physician referral behavior: a test of exchange theory in medical practice.* Research Series No. 31. Chicago: Center for Health Administration Studies, University of Chicago.
Siegal, Paul M.
  1971 "Prestige in the American occupational structure." Ph.D. Dissertation. University of Chicago.
Solon, J., et al.
  1967 "Delineating episodes of medical care." *American Journal of Public Health* 57 (March): 401–408.
  1969 "Episodes of medical care: nursing students' use of medical services." *American Journal of Public Health* 59 (June): 936–946.
Sonquist, John A.
  1970 *Multivariate model building.* Ann Arbor: Institute for Social Research, University of Michigan.
Sonquist, J. A., E. L. Baker, and J. N. Morgan.
  1973 *Searching for structure.* Ann Arbor: Institute for Social Research.
Sonquist, John A., and James N. Morgan.
  1964 *The detection of interaction effects.* Monograph No. 35. Ann Arbor: Institute for Social Research, University of Michigan.
Starfield, B.
  1973 "Health services research: a working model." *New England Journal of Medicine* 289 (July 19): 132–136.

Stewart, Charles T., Jr.
  1971 "Allocation of resources of health." *The Journal of Human Resources* 4, no. 1 (Winter): 103–122.
Stigler, George.
  1966 *The theory of price.* New York: Macmillan Company.
Suchman, E. A.
  1964 "Sociomedical variations among ethnic groups." *American Journal of Sociology,* 70.
  1966 "Health orientation and medical care." *American Journal of Public Health* 56 (January): 97–105.
Wan, T. T. H., and S. J. Soifer.
  1974 "Determinants of physician utilization: a causal analysis." *Journal of Health and Social Behavior* 15, no. 2 (June): 100–108.
Webster's third new international dictionary of the English language unabridged.
  1967 Springfield, Massachusetts: G. C. Merriam Company.
Wessen, A.
  1974 "Provider-patient relationships and the use of medical care." Workshop paper presented at Center for Health Administration Studies, University of Chicago (February 28).
Wicker, Allan W.
  1969 "Attitudes versus actions: the relationship of verbal and overt behavioral responses to attitude objects." *Journal of Social Issues,* 25, no. 4.
Wilder, C. S.
  1972 "Physician visits, volume and interval since last visit, United States, 1969." Vital and Health Statistics, Series 10, No. 75 (National Center for Health Statistics).
Vayda, Eugene
  1973 "A comparison of surgical rates in Canada and in England and Wales." *New England Journal of Medicine,* 289 (December 6).
Zborowski, Mark.
  1952 "Cultural components in responses to pain." *Journal of Social Issues* 8 (Fall): 16–30.
  1969 *People in pain.* San Francisco: Jossey-Bass, Inc.
Zola, I. K.
  1966 "Culture and symptoms: an analysis of patients presenting complaints." *American Sociological Review* 31 (October): 615–630.

Index

access: delivery care system and income groups in Shortell, 203; equalization, 266; family size in Kasper, 57; in May, 131; problems of, 175; and resource availability, 143; attitude, status and health care analysis in Kravits, 85

Aday, L.A. and Andersen, R., 166; and Eichhorn, R., 4, 13

age: adults, physician contact and family size, 58; attitudes, race and income, 85; elderly as category, 22; elderly and hospitalization, 29; and hospital admissions in Kravits and Schneider, 179; in Kravits, 259; as nonillness predictor, 47; and physician use in Andersen, 29; and policy in Newman, 36; and predisposing variables, 195; social survey bias, 248; as utilization predisposing variable, 13, 40

AID (automatic interaction detection), 12; identification methodology, 47; physician/dentist utilization, 39

Airth, D. and Newell, D., 132

Andersen, R., 36; contact decisionmaking, 57; discretionary services, 11; family analysis, 155; family composition, 56; influencing variables, 159; prediction scales, 40; subgroups, 21; et al, 3, 7, 36, 56; children/youth/dental utilization, 38; health status, 155; low income and blacks, 174; low income and hospital admissions, 178; source of care, 192; and Anderson, O.W., 192; and Benham, L., 98; and Kasper, J.D., 56; and Newman, 36, 155; health status, 153; model and variables, 134, 135; predisposing variables, 159

Anderson, O.W.: mandatory admissions, 179; and Sheatsley, 140

Andrews, F.M.: utilization rates, 22; et al, 12, 47, 157, 205

Antonovsky, Aaron, 156

attitude: analysis in Kravits, 73; correlation with income and race in Kravits, 78; low income blacks, 82; Pap smear screening, 75; summarized by Kravits, 261

Balint, Michael, 175

Becker, Marshall, et al: continuity of care, 202

Berkanovic, E. and Reeder, L.G., 166

Bice, T.W., et al., 192

Bossard, James H.S. and Boll, E.S., 56

Brown, J. Whitney, et al., 170; variable index, 172

Bunker, J.P., 179

Burns, J.L., 74; and Clausen, J., 74; and Schonfield, J., 75

Canada, 129

Cannell, C. and Fowler, F.J., 245

Carnegie Commission on Higher Education, 211

Cartwright, A., 243, 244

Center for Health Administration Studies, 219

children: financing, 192; and large families, 55; physician visit frequency, 67

Chiswick, B., 132

Clausen, J., et al., 74

Coe, R.M. and Wessen, A.F., 74, 75

Coleman, J.S.: on policy variables, 11

contact: defined by Andersen, 11; factors

About the Authors

Ronald Andersen is a research associate in the Center for Health Administration Studies, and associate professor in the Graduate School of Business and Department of Sociology, University of Chicago. He was study director on the nationwide social survey and verification which produced the data for this book. His major research interests include utilization of health services and international comparisons of health service systems. He has authored or co-authored: *A Decade of Health Services* (1967), *A Behavioral Model of Families' Use of Health Services* (1968), *Medical Care Use in Sweden and the United States* (1970) and *Development of Indicies of Access to Medical Care* (1975). He received his Ph.D. in Sociology from Purdue University in 1968.

Odin W. Anderson is professor of Sociology in the Graduate School of Business and the Department of Sociology, and director of the Center for Health Administration Studies, University of Chicago. He has been associated with four nationwide household surveys of health services use and expenditures, the first one conducted in 1953. His major research interests are health services systems and their finance and the evolution of public policy regarding them. He has authored or co-authored: *A Decade of Health Services* (1967), *Health Care: Can There Be Equity? The United States, Sweden, and England* (1972) and *Blue Cross Since 1929: The Public Trust and Accountability* (1974). He received his Ph.D. in Sociology from the University of Michigan in 1948.

Alexandra Benham is a writer and researcher. Her major interests in the health field concern investigation of factors influencing health status. In other areas she has co-authored "Hostile International Communication, Arms Production, and Perception of Threat: A Simulation Study" (1967) and "Nuclear Weapons and Alliance Cohesion" (1969). She holds an M.S. in Mathematics from Stanford University.

293

Lee Benham is an associate professor in the Department of Economics and the Department of Preventive Medicine, School of Medicine, and associate in Health Care Research, Washington University. His major research interest in the medical area is the effect of regulatory policy on prices, utilization and distribution of services. He has authored or co-authored "Health, Hours and Wages," in *Economic Analysis of Medical Issues in Developed Countries,* edited by Mark Perlman, and "The Effect of Advertising on the Price of Eyeglasses," *The Journal of Law and Economics* (October 1972). He received his Ph.D. in Economics from Stanford in 1971.

Judith Kasper is a research associate in the Center for Health Administration Studies, and a Ph.D. candidate in the Department of Sociology, University of Chicago. Her interests within Medical Sociology include utilization of health services, international comparisons of health systems, formulating health policy and ethical issues in clinical practice. To date, her research has focused on the health utilization of families, and children in particular.

Joanna Kravits is director of Information Services, Massachusetts Hospital Association. At the time this book was written, she was research associate in the Center for Health Administration Studies and assistant study director on the nationwide survey. Her major research interests include racial differences in the delivery of health care and comparisons of health care delivery systems. Among her publications are *Health Services in the Chicago Area—A Framework for Use of Data* (1969) and "The Public's View of the Crisis in Medical Care: An Impetus for Changing Delivery Systems?" (1971). She received her Ph.D. in Human Development from the University of Chicago in 1974.

Joel May is director of the Graduate Program in Hospital Administration at the University of Chicago and associate director of the Center for Health Administration Studies. His publications include articles and monographs in the area of health planning, regulation of the health services industry and hospital management. Major research interests are in the area of the economics of regulation and of resource allocation decisions in hospitals. He received his M.B.A. in Hospital Administration from the University of Chicago in 1963.

John F. Newman is associate professor, Department of Rehabilitation Services, Administration Studies Center, DePaul University. Previously, he was research associate, Center for Health Administration Studies, where he was study director on a nationwide social survey on dental service utilization and assisted in selected aspects on the social survey and verification which produced the data for this book. His major research interests include studies of health service utilization, the organization and delivery of health services, and the demography of health and illness. He has authored or co-authored *Patterns of Dental Service*

Utilization in the United States: A Nationwide Social Survey (1971), "Projections of Health Services Personnel and Facilities in the United States" (1974), and *Monitoring the Quality of Nursing Care* (1973). He received his Ph.D. in Sociology from Emory University in 1971.

Charles E. Phelps is a research economist at the Rand Corporation, Santa Monica, California. He was a research fellow at the Center for Health Administration Studies before joining the Rand Corporation in 1971. His major research interests include medical economics, particularly the demand for medical care and the demand for health insurance. Among his publications as author or co-author are *The Demand for Health Insurance: A Theoretical and Empirical Investigation* (1973), "Coinsurance, the Price of Time, and the Demand for Medical Services" (1974), and "Policy Options and the Impact of National Health Insurance" (1974). He received his Ph.D. in Business Economics from the University of Chicago in 1973.

John F. Schneider is the director of research in the Section of General Internal Medicine in the Department of Medicine and also an assistant professor of Medicine in the Pritzker School of Medicine, Division of Biological Sciences, University of Chicago. His research interests range from basic biochemistry through programs of health care evaluation. Among his publications are "Metabolite Interrelation of Sulfur, Thiosulfate and Cystine" (1969) and "The Role of Predischarge Conference in Promoting Quality Medical Care." He received his M.D. in 1963 and Ph.D. in Biochemistry in 1968 both from the University of Chicago.

Stephen M. Shortell is assistant professor, Department of Health Services, School of Public Health and Community Medicine, University of Washington. At the time this book was written, he was assistant professor and acting director, Graduate Program in Hospital Administration, Center for Health Administration Studies, Graduate School of Business, University of Chicago. His major research interests include the social organization of medical care, the management of health services delivery organizations and program evaluation. He is the author of *A Model of Physician Referral Behavior: A Test of Exchange Theory in Medical Practice* (1972). He received his Ph.D. in Behavioral Sciences from the Graduate School of Business, University of Chicago in 1972.